OUTSTANDING PRAISE FOR
LITTLE GIRLS IN PRETTY BOXES

"A must-read for all parents of teenage athletes."
—Lesley Visser, ABC/ESPN

"Ryan's findings are sad and devastating...as vital and troubling a work as the sports world has seen in a long time."
—*Philadelphia Inquirer*

"Joan Ryan's book moved me from disbelief to an aching sorrow for these gifted children whose dreams are turned against them. We have seen the beauty of the Games. Now Ryan reveals that beauty to be born of madness. This is an indictment of the U.S. Olympic movement so powerful it should change the way America thinks."
—Dave Kindred, *Sporting News*

"Strips away the graceful facade to expose the harsh, often destructive training regimes.... Never again, after reading Ryan's book, will one be able to watch those tiny, lithe silhouettes—either on the ice or the balance beam—without thinking of what they may have suffered to get there."
—*Kirkus Reviews*

"Should be a manifesto for change in the rules of these two sports."
—*Chicago Tribune*

LITTLE GIRLS
IN
PRETTY BOXES

ALSO BY JOAN RYAN

Molina
The Water Giver
Shooting from the Outside

◆

LITTLE GIRLS
IN
PRETTY BOXES

THE MAKING AND BREAKING
OF ELITE GYMNASTS AND
FIGURE SKATERS

JOAN RYAN

GRAND CENTRAL
PUBLISHING

NEW YORK   BOSTON

Published by arrangement with Doubleday, a division of Penguin Random House.

Grand Central Publishing
Hachette Book Group
1290 Avenue of the Americas, New York, NY 10104
grandcentralpublishing.com
twitter.com/grandcentralpub

Originally published in hardcover by Doubleday in 1995
First Grand Central Publishing trade paperback edition: May 1996
Reissued: August 2000, July 2018

Grand Central Publishing is a division of Hachette Book Group, Inc. The Grand Central Publishing name and logo is a trademark of Hachette Book Group, Inc.

The publisher is not responsible for websites (or their content) that are not owned by the publisher.

The Hachette Speakers Bureau provides a wide range of authors for speaking events. To find out more, go to www.hachettespeakersbureau.com or call (866) 376-6591.

Library of Congress Cataloging-in-Publication Data
The 2000 trade paperback edition is catalogued as follows:

Ryan, Joan
   Little girls in pretty boxes : the making and breaking of elite gymnasts and figure skaters / Joan Ryan.
      p. cm.
   ISBN 0-446-67682-9
   1. Gymnastics for girls—United States.   2. Skating—United States.
3. Women athletes—Abuse of—United States.   4. Sports—Moral and ethical aspects—United States.
   I. Title.
GV464.R93 2000
796.44'082'0973—dc21

00-031981

ISBN: 978-1-5387-4778-0 (trade paperback 2018 reissue)

Printed in the United States of America

LSC-C

10 9 8 7 6 5 4 3 2 1

To Barry and Ryan

CONTENTS

■

FOREWORD
by Jamie Dantzscher, former Olympic gymnast

■

I fell in love with gymnastics just before I turned three years old. I was watching the 1984 Olympics on television and, as young children do, immediately decided that I wanted to be an Olympic gymnast. Although my parents were both talented athletes, they thought I was too young to start learning gymnastics. Still, I kept begging for lessons. I wore the only leotard I owned—a purple one patterned with different colored bows—every day, and for years my uncle Kyle helped me make my own gymnastics apparatus out of furniture. Finally, when I was seven years old, my parents let me try lessons three days a week at a local gym. But I couldn't get enough; at home I watched the routines I had recorded on VHS over and over and tried to mimic famous gymnasts I admired. I practiced my salute until it looked just like theirs and made up floor routines with their dance moves. I slept in my leotard and even tried to sleep in the splits sometimes! I desperately wanted to be an Olympian, and I was going to do whatever it took to get there one day.

By age eleven, I was ready to start training as an elite gymnast. I was one step closer to achieving my Olympic dream, but it meant that I would have to start training at a gym with elite-level coaches an hour and a half from my home. The coaches there said that if I wanted to be my best, I would have to sacrifice going to a regular school in order to practice twice a day. The expense and commitment this would require of my parents, siblings, and myself was huge, but after much consideration, my parents granted me the opportunity to pursue my dream. I was exhilarated.

Immediately, my training became much more intense than I was used to. I trained thirty to thirty-five hours a week, went to school as much as I could, and spent three hours a day in the car either doing homework or catching up on lost sleep. I missed being home with my family, but I knew this is what it was going to take to reach my goals. Meanwhile, my workouts were becoming more difficult and my coaches much more intense. I started feeling like I was always in trouble for something. I was forever sore and tired, but I was too intimidated to say anything because my coaches made it very clear that to get to the top, I had to be tough and work through pain. They yelled at me when I made mistakes and made me feel like I was never working hard enough. I slowly grew discouraged and began to doubt myself. I had known that elite training was going to be hard, but I didn't know it would be *that* hard.

Then I made the USA junior national team when I was just twelve years old, competing with many of the girls I had seen on TV. Reenergized, I attended my first national team training camp soon after and realized that the other gymnasts I met were going through the same difficulties. It was normal to get yelled at on a daily basis. It was normal to work through pain and injuries. It was normal to feel like quitting almost every day.

Although I didn't read *Little Girls in Pretty Boxes* when it came out, I remember hearing all about it. My coaches, along with so many others in the gymnastics community, said the book was a horrible misrepresentation of gymnastics and that no one should support it. They said the regulations and changes Joan Ryan advocated for were completely unnecessary and would weaken the sport. They dismissed her and everyone she interviewed in the book as losers and whiners. For a while, it seemed like I would hear complaints about the book at every practice and competition, and Joan Ryan was soon considered a pariah in gymnastics circles.

About a year after *Little Girls in Pretty Boxes* came out, I was a stunt double for the Lifetime movie adaptation of the book. I never understood why my coaches asked me to be a part of it after bad-mouthing the book for so long. Then, when I saw the completed movie—in which a young woman ultimately quits gymnastics after suffering under a grueling training regimen—I couldn't understand the outrage toward the book. I thought, *This is nothing compared to what I'm actually going through.*

If I had read Joan Ryan's book then, I would have seen my own experiences on the page—they were just like the stories of the gymnasts I looked up to the most. My coaches weighed me every day, called me fat, and told me I needed to lose weight. At fifteen years old, I started making myself throw up after meals. When I told someone at USA Gymnastics that I was starving myself and throwing up meals, their only response was, "I don't care how you do it, just get the weight off." When I started my period at sixteen years old, my coach said it was because I had too much body fat and ordered me to lose weight so I wouldn't menstruate anymore. I remember once having the flu and throwing up for five days straight. When it came time for my weigh-in afterwards, I had lost seven pounds; my coach said I needed to figure out how to keep it off. At another point, my coaches made me take ephedrine for weight loss, before such usage was banned. And this was all part of my typical daily routine. Like elite gymnast Karen Reid (Chapter 4, "Do It for America: Pressure"), I hated my days off, because it meant my horrible life would be starting all over again the next day.

When my routine was interrupted due to an all-too-common injury, the challenges of training became even more insurmountable. In the aptly named chapter "If It Isn't Bleeding, Don't Worry About It: Injuries," former gymnast and Olympic medalist Betty Okino discusses training with a knee injury under the controversial coach Béla Károlyi: "He thought I was faking." Similarly, every time I told my coaches something on my body hurt, they didn't believe me. I took Advil twice a day to try to dull the pain and, like former Olympic gymnast Wendy Bruce, had many cortisone shots over the years just to be able to compete. I learned how to work through my injuries because I felt like I had no choice. After all, I wasn't a quitter. I was tougher than that, right? I trained and competed on stone bruises on my heels; with plantar fasciitis so painful that I couldn't even stand on carpet; with my hips going out of alignment on a daily basis; with sprained ankles, broken toes, fractures in my back, and torn cartilage in my wrist and ankle, just to name some of my many health issues. I remember practicing my round-off triple full dismount on beam one day when the pain in my wrist got so bad that my body simply wouldn't allow me to work through it anymore. Every time I did my round-off my hand would automatically make a fist on the beam instead of lying flat. I was terrified this would make me miss my footing and injure myself even more badly than I already had. I finally told my coaches, who refused to believe me. They shouted at me for what seemed like hours: I didn't want to work hard enough; I was acting like a spoiled brat; I was a quitter. A couple months later, I had surgery on my wrist to clean out the torn cartilage.

After enduring years of emotional, physical, and mental abuse, I couldn't get the main character of the *Little Girls* movie out of my head. I wanted to be happy. I wanted to be free. I quit gymnastics about a year before the Olympics. During that time, I was able to think and reflect on what I really wanted. I realized that more than anything I wanted to go to college, and a gymnastics scholarship was my best opportunity to get there. After taking only three weeks off, I returned to the gym to train for the chance at a scholarship to UCLA. If training my best meant making the Olympics, all the better. I had to accept that my coaches would yell and belittle me on a daily basis. I wouldn't be allowed to have friends at school or go to school dances because they were "distractions." I would never go on family vacations and rarely see my siblings perform in their sports. I wouldn't be allowed to talk to my teammates at the gym because that meant I wasn't focused. I couldn't feel like a person anymore if I wanted to reach my dream. I felt like a robot. This became my "normal."

I made the Olympic team in 2000. I was ecstatic when they announced my name, and in that moment I did feel as though my dream had come true. Unfortunately, that feeling was short lived. My Olympic experience was nothing like the dream I had harbored my whole life; it was just a continuation of the same nightmare. We placed fourth overall as a team but nevertheless were made to feel like complete failures. Ultimately, I was happy when the Olympics—the goal I had worked toward my entire life—was over, and I could smile freely again as I headed off to enjoy college.

My college experience in gymnastics was drastically different. For the first time in a long time, I felt like I was treated like a person instead of a robot. Knowing that my coaches and teammates actually cared about me brought back my love for the sport. After graduating from UCLA with a degree in psychology, I coached gymnastics at various summer camps and gyms. I enjoyed being a positive coach and wanted to inspire young gymnasts no matter what level they were going to achieve. I was determined to never be a coach who took their love for gymnastics away from them. I wanted them to never experience the twisted, harmful world I grew up in.

While I was finding a renewed sense of purpose through coaching young girls, I struggled in my personal life. In college, I began therapy for my eating disorders and the overwhelming abuse I suffered from my elite career. I felt lost for most of my twenties, engaged in a pattern of self-destructive behaviors. My threshold for pain and abuse had been built up so high that I would stay in relationships with men who abused me physically and emotionally. The feeling was all too familiar. Once again, I lost my personality. I felt like a robot, eager to please and ready to do whatever it took to get through each day, hoping there was light at the end of the tunnel. Once again, that became my new normal. I watched my friends and family members settle into their careers and get married and start families, and I couldn't figure out why I couldn't get my life together. I became so severely depressed that I wanted to take my own life. Thanks to good friends and family, I was able to come out of my depression and discover the determination to get my life on track and never fall back into the same self-destructive patterns. I moved to San Diego to pursue my new dream of becoming a motivational speaker, though I still coached young gymnasts. I stopped dating for years because I didn't want anyone else controlling my life. I thought I was heading in the right direction to live a normal, quiet life.

In summer 2016, I was working at a gymnastics camp in Concord, California, when my good friend and former elite gymnast Melissa Genovese asked me to have a conversation with Mike

Lynch, a coach who was working at the camp with me. For years, Melissa had been sexually abused by her personal coach, Keith Willette, but she had not yet spoken out against him. Melissa wanted me to ask Mike—who also knew Keith—if he had heard of any other allegations of sexual abuse about Keith. When I started talking to Mike that morning in July, I told him some of the things Keith had done to Melissa. As I described some of his disgusting violations out loud for the first time, I suddenly realized that these were very similar to what the USAG head team physician, Larry Nassar, had done to me while I was training for the U.S. national team. At first I couldn't fully believe he was the same as Keith Willette. As far as I knew, everyone in gymnastics loved Larry Nassar—including me. I didn't think that he could have hurt me. I trusted him. It was a privilege to work with a doctor who treated so many Olympians and national team members. Among all our screaming coaches when I was training, Larry was the only nice adult, and he was always on my side. He helped me with all of my injuries, snuck me food and candy when I was starving, and made me laugh and feel okay when every day in the gym and at training camps was so awful. No way he was abusive. He was supposed to be the good guy.

I went to the Olympic Trials that weekend in San Jose to hang out with some of my old gymnast friends, and I confided to Dominique Moceanu what Larry had done to me. Her response gave me the confidence and courage to act: she said she believed me and that I needed to report Nassar. Dominique put me in contact with former Olympic swimmer Katherine Starr. Katherine had been sexually abused by her coach and later started an advocacy and educational nonprofit organization called Safe4Athletes, a website where athletes could report instances of sexual abuse safely and anonymously. When I told her about Larry, she recommended I see an attorney she had worked with on sexual abuse cases. I was still filled with confusion and doubt; I didn't know what to feel or think about Larry's actions, and I didn't necessarily *feel* like a sexual abuse victim. But I understood that if Larry was really a child molester, then there were possibly other victims. During this time, I found out that Larry had resigned from gymnastics because of other allegations of child sexual abuse—and then saw on his Facebook page that he was running for a position on a school board, where he would be working with children again. I thought about Larry Nassar doing the same thing he did to me, but to one of my nieces or the little girls I coached.

It was time to speak up.

With my attorney, I filed a civil suit against Nassar and USA Gymnastics. Fearful of brutal blowback from the gymnastics community—I was accusing a popular, influential, trusted doctor of sex crimes—I filed as "Jane Doe." Soon I learned I wasn't alone in trying to hold Larry accountable. Weeks earlier, another former gymnast named Rachael Denhollander had filed a criminal complaint against him with Michigan State University, where Larry was also a team physician.

Together, Rachael and I did an interview with the *Indianapolis Star*, which had published a story about USAG ignoring sexual abuse allegations against at least fifty gymnastics coaches. I still insisted on anonymity in the *Star* story. But there was enough biographical information for gymnastics people to figure out it was me. Just as I feared, many didn't believe me. Some of the comments on social media were incredibly hurtful. I was accused of making the entire thing up for attention. The most disappointing part was that many of the people saying these negative things were those I had considered friends. One former gymnast outed me in a private message on Facebook, which she sent to several other gymnasts and coaches in order to collect positive Larry stories. It was sickening how quickly so many people took his side over mine. In short, I faced the same public response that many women who speak up about abuse receive: I was dismissed, discredited, and ostracized.

Then that all changed.

Every day after my article came out, my attorney would call to say another victim came forward until finally—as of January 2018—an unimaginable total of 265 women had joined the ranks, and I felt secure knowing I had done the right thing.

Even now, I still feel strangely disconnected from what happened to me. I can only comprehend the heinousness of what Larry did to me through other survivors' stories. But I finally understand that I subconsciously registered his abuse, along with the emotional abuse of my coaches, because it seeped into other areas of my life and echoed through my relationships, self-destructive behavior, anxiety, and depression.

People often ask how Larry Nassar could get away with this for so long. *Little Girls in Pretty Boxes* answered this question back in 1995. It's all here in these pages. Only in an environment in which abuse of all kinds is normalized could sexual abuse on this scale happen. It required the gymnasts' well-practiced silence and the adults' dereliction of responsibility. It required a culture that prized Olympic medals over the well-being of the young athletes striving to win them.

Rachael Denhollander delivered the last of 156 victim impact statements in Larry Nassar's sentencing hearing in early 2018. "How much is a little girl worth?" she asked. "How much is a young woman worth?"

It is the question that Joan Ryan asked two decades ago, and the question that must be answered still.

INTRODUCTION, 2018 EDITION

On a Monday morning in January 2018, a twenty-five-year-old former gymnast named Mattie Larson stepped up to the microphone inside a Lansing, Michigan, courtroom. It was day six of an eight-day sentencing hearing that was aired on live television across the country. A stream of girls and young women had stood where Larson stood now, facing the man who had molested every one of them, renowned USA Gymnastics team physician, Larry Nassar.

Larson took a deep breath and slowly let it out, closing her eyes for a moment. Then in a strong, even voice, she described the rot at the core USA Gymnastics that enabled the abuse to happen. For her, this corrosive, demeaning culture played out nowhere more brutally than at the monthly training camps she and the rest of the U.S. national team were required to attend. The camps were held at the isolated Texas ranch belonging to the famed—and famously abusive—coaches Béla and Márta Károlyi. It was a breathtakingly unsafe environment for young, compliant, driven girls: no parents allowed, limited access to food, pressure to train through injuries, and an expectation of blind obedience to coaches along with mute acceptance of their bullying and humiliation.

Furthermore, Nassar—who had been on USAG's medical staff since 1986 and its team physician since 1997—had unfettered access to the girls' cabins. He molested them in their own beds, with no other adult present, under the guise of medical treatment. Over the course of two decades, he molested gymnasts as young as nine years old at gyms, training centers, and competitions sanctioned by USA Gymnastics.

"The camp's complete detachment from the outside world on top of careless and neglectful adults made it the perfect environment for abusers and molesters to thrive," she said, her steady gaze lifting from her typed statement and locking on Nassar in the witness stand.

Then she began to tell the story about a particular day at her home in Southern California. She said she had been scheduled to fly to Texas the next day for the monthly camp. Suddenly her calm voice cracked and the tears fell. She described how she splashed water on the bathroom floor then battered the back of her head against the tub's edge again and again until she felt a lump. She told her parents she had slipped getting out of the shower. They took her to the hospital and canceled her trip to Texas. "I was willing to hurt myself," she said, crying, "to get out of the abuse I received at the ranch."

One after another, some with tears and trembling hands, some with voices nearly strangled by anger finally unleashed, some steely-eyed as prosecutors, this army of girls and young women told their stories of physical violation and emotional wreckage. Eighty-eight had been scheduled to read victim impact statements at the sentencing hearing. But seeing the proceedings on CNN, gymnasts and former gymnasts began showing up from all over the country, more every day, until finally 156 women in all had spoken by the time it was over. Most had kept the abuse a secret. Now on live television, for everyone to hear, they spoke directly and openly—not only about the perpetrator of the biggest sexual abuse scandal in sports history but also about the national federation that enabled him, USA Gymnastics.

The reckoning was a long time coming.

The alarms about abuse in elite gymnastics have sounded for years. This book was one of them. First published in 1995, *Little Girls in Pretty Boxes* described the physical and psychological damage inflicted by tunnel-vision parents, dictatorial coaches, and willfully blind federation officials. (The book included a photo of gymnast Kristie Phillips receiving treatment on her ankle from Larry Nassar [still included in this edition's insert], but I knew nothing about him at the time.) In my research I found a culture as destructive, secretive, and indifferent to the athletes' well-being as any I had seen in my years as a sports journalist. Elite gymnastics systematically strips away a girl's connection to her own body and mind as she is groomed from a young age to distrust what her body and mind are telling her. When she's in too much pain to train, her coach says she's lazy. When she's hungry, he says she's fat and eats *too* much. When she's too exhausted for one more high-risk vault, she's a loser. She comes to understand that her own feelings and perceptions not only are unreliable, they don't matter. Her pain is dismissed. Her hunger is dismissed. Her exhaustion is dismissed. To fit into elite gymnastics' reality, a gymnast has to deny her own. She becomes an expert at withstanding all manner of insult to her body. She doesn't complain or make waves. She is the perfect target for a sexual predator like Larry Nassar.

The young gymnast would therefore distrust her own feelings of alarm and discomfort when a doctor slides his fingers in her vagina and anus. If she does tell an adult, she is neither surprised nor offended when she is dismissed as a naïve girl who doesn't know the difference between a medical exam and molestation. "Because people at MSU and USAG had to be aware of what Larry was doing and had not stopped him," Rachael Denhollander said in her victim statement, "there could surely be no question about the legitimacy of his treatment. This must be medical treatment. The problem must be me."

The first edition of *Little Girls in Pretty Boxes*, which criticized elite gymnastics' brutal training and its severe emotional and physical consequences on young women, prompted widespread and scathing criticism of the federation, coaches, and parents. But the outrage didn't stick. The notion of broken bodies and psyches, eating disorders and suicide attempts, didn't square with Americans' perception of the ponytailed pixies. And whatever momentum there might have been to address the abuses was undermined by a few champion gymnasts who dismissed the accounts in my book as sour-grape exaggerations from failed gymnasts. You don't hear the *winners* telling those stories, they scoffed. USAG weathered the storm and sailed on as if all was well.

And from the outside it was. The U.S. women won the team gold at the Olympics in 1996, bronze in 2000, silver in 2004 and 2008, and back-to-back team golds in 2012 and 2016. No team since 1972 won more Olympic medals in a single Olympics than the U.S. women in Rio in 2016. Since 2004, every women's individual all-around Olympic gold medal has been won by a U.S. gymnast. The U.S. women won the world championship in 2011, 2014, and 2015.

The U.S. teams were media stars with spirited nicknames like the Magnificent Seven, the Fierce Five, and the Final Five. The shine of gold medals and the sparkle of celebrity obscured the fact that USAG was still employing the abusive Béla Károlyi, whose harmful training methods were brought to public attention in the first 1995 edition of this book. In 1996, USAG made his wife, Márta, the head coach for women's Olympic team; they made Béla the national team coordinator in 1999 and then handed it back to Márta in 2001, and she held the job through the Olympics in 2016. In 2011, USAG doubled down on their embrace of the Károlyis, eliminating any doubt that it valued winning over the health and safety of its gymnasts: The federation made the ranch the official training center for U.S. teams heading to the world championships and Olympic Games. The athletes had no choice but to train there. It was easy for Nassar to shine as the girls' ally and confidant.

A day before the Opening Ceremony for the 2016 Olympics in Rio de Janeiro, the *Indianapolis Star* published an explosive investigative story that set in motion the cascade of events that would take down both Nassar and the power structure at USAG. The newspaper's first story wasn't about Nassar at all; the reporters didn't know about him yet. The story detailed USAG's gross mishandling of sexual misconduct complaints against dozens of male coaches. The federation shared the complaints with neither police nor parents. Thus most of the accused men continued to coach young girls, and some continued to molest them. USAG did little more than shove the complaints in a file alongside complaints against fifty or so other USAG-member coaches. The federation's policy was to follow up only on complaints made by an athlete or parent; alerts from fellow coaches or support staff were not investigated. USAG did nothing, for example, about a complaint against Marvin Sharp, the 2010 Women's Coach of the Year. Four years later he was charged with abusing a twelve-year-old girl and killed himself in jail.

In Louisville, Kentucky, a thirty-two-year-old woman named Rachael Denhollander read the *Star*'s story with a pounding heart. She had been molested when she was fifteen years old at a gymnastics club affiliated with Michigan State University. She wrote a letter to the newspaper. Her abuser was not a coach, she told them, but instead a well-known Michigan State athletic department physician and faculty member named Larry Nassar. For sixteen years, she had wrestled with the decision to come forward and hold the man accountable. "It was kind of a shot in the dark," she told a reporter afterward. "It was the first chance I ever saw that somebody would believe me." The *Star* reporters did believe her and began digging around.

Three weeks later, on August 29, 2016, Denhollander filed a criminal complaint against Nassar with the MSU police department.

Twenty-two hundred miles away in California, another former gymnast, unaware of Denhollander's complaint, was also considering legal action against Nassar. Jamie Dantzscher, who competed on the 2000 Olympic team in Sydney, Australia, had been molested by the USAG doctor beginning in 1994, when she was twelve years old. Like Denhollander, she worried about the backlash. She had been sharply denounced at the Olympics by both the gymnastics community and some reporters for daring to criticize the brutal and demeaning tactics of the great Béla Károlyi, the national team coordinator at the time. But ten days after Denhollander's complaint, Dantzcher filed a civil suit against both Nassar and USAG,

LITTLE GIRLS IN PRETTY BOXES

becoming the first Olympic athlete to sound the alarm. She identified herself as "Jane Doe."

Four days later, Dantzcher—still anonymous—and Denhollander made their stories public in an explosive front-page interview with the Star. USAG released a statement that afternoon claiming it had fired Nassar a year earlier—"[i]mmediately after learning of athlete concerns about [him] in the summer of 2015."

This was news to almost everyone in gymnastics.

Yes, Nassar had left USAG. In a Facebook post in September 2015, he announced he was resigning from his post at the federation but staying on at Michigan State. Only USAG and, it turns out, the FBI knew the real reason he left. In June 2015 a coach attending a training camp at the Károlyi ranch overheard two gymnasts talking about Nassar's invasive, unorthodox medical treatment. The coach called the mother of one of the gymnasts; the mother called USAG. She wanted President Steve Penny to call the police right away, according to the *New York Times*. Instead, the *Times* reported, he told her not to tell anyone and that USAG would contact law enforcement. But he didn't until forty-one days later, contrary to USAG's claim that it immediately fired Nassar. Only after meeting in person with the FBI more than a month after the complaints did USAG officials quietly relieve Nassar of his duties. They never corrected Nassar's Facebook post. In other words, they let a sexual predator walk away with his reputation intact. They never notified Michigan State of the allegations. They stood by in silence as Nassar continued to work at MSU, Twistars USA Gymnastics Club in Michigan, and Holt High School in Lansing for another full year. And only when Nassar's crimes were exposed in the *Star* in 2016 did they even acknowledge the firing. The *Star* discovered another forty girls and women who said Nassar molested them during that time. Clearly, the FBI also did not alert MSU, Twistars, or Holt.

In November 2016, fifteen months after USAG first contacted the FBI, the agency finally filed charges: three counts of first-degree sexual assault involving at least one victim under the age of thirteen. Later Nassar also would be charged with possession of child pornography and another twenty-two sexual assaults.

The *Star*'s story with Denhollander and Dantzcher in September 2016 prompted sixteen more women to file criminal complaints in Michigan. Then twenty more came forward. Then eighteen more. By February 2017 the number of civil and criminal complaints against Nassar had reached eighty. By June it was one hundred and still climbing.

In the midst of the unfolding scandal, USAG scrambled to salvage its reputation with periodic press statements. One included this sentence: "We are focused on further developing a culture that has safe sport as a top priority throughout the organization."

My response was fury.

I had heard that same promise eighteen years ago when I wrote a new afterword for an updated edition of this book in 2000. The chapter is included, unchanged, in this edition. Five years after the original publication, USAG seemed committed to changing, and I was optimistic for one reason: a bright, determined woman named Nancy Thies Marshall, who was heading up the federation's new wellness program.

Marshall and I had talked a lot while I wrote the book's first edition and even more when I wrote the afterword of the second edition. She was the only person at USAG who didn't answer my questions in a defensive crouch. She acknowledged the problems. She had endured many of them herself. She was on the 1976 Olympic gymnastics team and four years later was one of the first athletes on the USAG board of directors.

In 1992, she pushed for and headed up a task force focused on eating disorders and other damaging health issues among female gymnasts. After delivering more than thirty recommendations to the board, USAG hired her to develop and direct a program that addressed openly, for the first time, the eating disorders, injuries, and abuse that crush so many elite gymnasts. She created a curriculum for coaches and a manual for athletes and parents. She felt strongly that in an organization in which 90 percent of its athletes are children, an understanding of child development was essential to keeping the gymnasts mentally and physically safe. (Not surprisingly, there is nothing in USAG's bylaws that acknowledges its special responsibility for training children.) Marshall created a referral network of health care providers around the country, and she started a mentoring program that connected current gymnasts to former gymnasts. Her hope was that young gymnast could share with the former gymnast the feelings and experiences no one else could understand. A couple years into the effort, USAG doubled the program's funding from $40,000 to $80,000.

"A new USA Gymnastics…emerged," I wrote in 2000, "one that had become a model to other Olympic governing bodies looking to protect and improve the health of their female athletes."

So how, eighteen years later, could more than 250 of USAG's female gymnasts have been sexually abused by the federation's own doctor? Why were so many still suffering physical, emotional, and sexual abuse in USAG-sanctioned gyms? What had happened to Marshall's program?

I tracked her down in February 2018 at Corban University in Salem, Oregon, where she is vice president for human resources. She answered the phone on the first ring. I heard a soft intake of breath when I gave her my name.

"You don't know what this call means to me," she said. "I've been nauseated to no end about what's happening. It's been like a punch to the gut." The words caught in her throat. "I can't tell you how often I just cried. I kept wondering what if I had stayed…if I had pushed…"

She said at the end of the 1990s, USAG cut her budget back to $40,000 and told her to stay away from the national team. Béla and Márta Károlyi didn't want psychologists and nutritionists interfering with their work and influencing their athletes at training camps. She said the Károlyis and other dictatorial coaches were leery of the mentoring program for the same reasons. Marshall grew increasingly frustrated and disillusioned. She pushed without success to make the wellness curriculum mandatory for coaches. With no knowledge of the psychological makeup of preadolescent and adolescent girls, how could coaches and USAG officials understand their vulnerability to abuse—particularly sexual abuse?

"I got the message that I was to be the face of USAG wellness, but I wouldn't carry any weight," she said. "I didn't want my name attached to something that wasn't going to make a difference."

She resigned in 2001.

After that, Marshall wasn't in touch with anyone from USAG until 2015, when Luan Peszek, a vice president at USAG at the time, called to ask Marshall if she would update her wellness manual. Marshall thought, *It hasn't been updated in fifteen years?* She declined. The task went to another former gymnast, Theresa Kulikowski-Gillespie. Marshall had a long phone conversation with Kulikowski-Gillespie and was pleased the manual was finding new life, but she hasn't heard anything since. Marshall doesn't know if USAG's renewed interest in the manual had anything to do with the start of the FBI's investigation of Nassar or if the timing was coincidental. Were they scrambling to produce proof that they actually put the well-being of their athletes ahead of winning?

Whatever measures USAG officials took to save their jobs, they didn't work. President Steve Penny was pressured to resign in March 2017. The board chair, vice chair, and treasurer resigned in January 2018. Under threat of decertification by the USOC, the entire board resigned. Women's national team coach John Geddert, who also operated Twistars, was suspended and soon retired. Veteran coach and women's national team coordinator Valeri Liukin resigned, as did Luan Peszek, ending her thirty-year career at USAG.

Marshall told me that her three grown children asked her the question that punctuated every conversation about the gymnastics scandal like a fist slamming a table: *How could this have happened?* Marshall answered by telling them about a day in New Haven, Connecticut, when she was fifteen years old and the youngest member of the 1972 Olympic team. On the first day of Olympic training camp in the Yale University gym, Marshall had the flu and was fading fast. Her coach wended his way through the warren of hallways in the building that housed the gym, leading Marshall to a room where she could lie down. Then he left.

An hour passed. Two hours. Three. She wondered if anyone was coming to fetch her. She had no idea where she was. She inched down the darkened hall, took an elevator to the bottom floor, and found herself facing one locked door after another. With rising panic, she ran down hallways until she burst through an open exit and onto a campus that was completely unfamiliar. "I sniffed my way back to the dorm," Marshall said. When she got to her room, her roommate was gone. She had been moved to another room. Fifteen-year-old Nancy was alone.

"That summed up my entire gymnastics experience," Marshall told her three children. "I was forgotten."

That is the paradox for elite gymnasts. They are scrutinized, analyzed, monitored, weighed, measured, primped, pushed, examined, adjusted. The gymnasts are never forgotten. Only the girls are.

In that Lansing courtroom, the girls and young women made sure they were not forgotten. The cameras brought their pained faces and voices directly into America's living rooms. It turned our pixies into human beings, people we know, our daughters and sisters. The truth of their abuse was plain. And unlike two decades earlier, when the whistle-blowers were painted as sore losers, now the winners were stepping forward, too. The biggest names—gold medalists Aly Raisman, McKayla Maroney, Simone Biles, Gabby Douglas—joined their fellow gymnasts from every level of the game and said, "Me, too." The judge sentenced Nassar to up to 175 years in prison.

"The tables have turned," Raisman famously said during the hearing. "We are here. We have our voices, and we are not going anywhere."

For the first time in twenty-three years, I have hope for real change.

A week or so after talking with Marshall, a package from her arrived in the mail. It was the athlete wellness manual from 1999. I had forgotten how thorough it was. Its one hundred pages are filled with research and resources. As I put the manual away, it fell open to a foreword praising Marshall and USAG for enhancing "our effectiveness as teachers, coaches, parents, administrators and health care providers" in keeping the federation's young athletes safe. It is written by Larry Nassar.

INTRODUCTION

The little girls marched into the Atlanta arena in single file, heads high, shoulders back, bare toes pointed. Under hair ribbons and rouged cheeks, their balletic bodies flowed past bleachers where expectant fathers craned forward with videocameras. Small and pretty in their shimmery leotards, the girls looked like trinkets from a Tiffany box. They lined up facing the crowd, and when the announcer summoned the winners of the Peachtree Classic, the gymnasts stepped forward and bowed their heads as soberly as Nobel laureates to receive their medals. Mothers with score-sheets tucked under their arms clapped until their hands hurt, shooting hopeful glances at the ESPN cameras roving among the girls. Along velvet ropes strung across the base of the bleachers, awestruck seven- and eight-year-olds stretched toward the winning gymnasts clutching programs and gym bags for them to sign.

On the opposite coast, at a skating rink in Redwood City, California, one fifteen-year-old skater—in a ponytail, braces and baby-blue sequins—stood at the edge of the rink, eyes wide, listening to her coach's last-minute instructions as her parents held hands in the bleachers, packed solid for the Pacific Coast Sectional Championships. She glided to the center of the ice. Then, as her music began, she spun like a jewel-box ballerina, executing the intricate choreography of leaps and footwork she had practiced nearly every day for as long as she could remember. On her ¼-inch skate blades rode her hopes of qualifying for the U.S. Figure Skating Championships, moving her one step closer to the Winter Olympic Games.

In gyms and rinks across the country, the air is thick with the scent of the Olympics. And the parents, coaches and young athletes chase it like hounds, impatient for the rewards of the sports that captivate American audiences as no others do. Gymnasts and figure skaters hold a unique and cherished place among American athletes. Gymnasts are the darlings of the Summer Games, figure skaters the ice princesses of the Winter Games. Every four years they keep us glued to our televisions for two weeks with their grace, agility, youth and beauty. They land on magazine covers, Wheaties boxes, the "Today" show. Television ratings for Olympic gymnastics and figure skating events rank among the highest for any sport on television. Helped by the Tonya Harding–Nancy Kerrigan saga, the women's technical program at the 1994 Winter Games drew the fourth-highest rating of any show in the history of television, placing it up there with the final episode of *M*A*S*H*. But even at the controversy-free 1992 Winter Games, women's figure skating attracted a larger television audience than either the final game of the 1992 World Series or the 1992 National Collegiate Athletic Association basketball championship game between Michigan and Duke. Americans are so enchanted by gymnasts and figure skaters that in a 1991 survey they chose gymnast Mary Lou Retton and skater Dorothy Hamill—both long retired—as their favorite athletes, beating out the likes of Chris Evert, Michael Jordan and Magic Johnson.

Yet while gymnastics and figure skating are among the most-watched sports in the country, the least is known about the lives of their athletes (with the exceptions, of course, of Harding and Kerrigan). We watch thirteen-year-old Michelle Kwan, an eighth grader, land six triple jumps to finish second at the 1994 U.S. Figure Skating Championships. We see sixteen-year-old Shannon Miller soar above the balance beam as if it were a trampoline to win a silver medal at the 1992 Olympics. But we know little about how they achieve so much at such a young age or what becomes of them when they leave their sport.

Unlike women's tennis, a sport in which teenage girls rise to the highest echelon year after year in highly televised championships, gymnastics and figure skating flutter across our screens as ephemerally as butterflies. We know about tennis burnout, about Tracy Austin, Andrea Jaeger, Mary Pierce and, more recently, about Jennifer Capriati, who turned pro with $5 million in endorsement contracts at age thirteen and ended up four years later in a Florida motel room, blank-eyed and disheveled, sharing drugs with runaways. But we hear precious little about the young female gymnasts and figure skaters who perform magnificent feats of physical strength and agility, and even less about their casualties. How do the extraordinary demands of their training shape these young girls? What price do their bodies and psyches pay?

I set out to answer some of these questions during three months of research for an article that ran in the *San Francisco Examiner,* but when I finished I couldn't close my notebook. I took a year's leave to continue my research, focusing this time on the girls who never made it, not just on the champions.

What I found was a story about legal, even celebrated, child abuse. In the dark troughs along the road to the Olympics lay the bodies of the girls who stumbled on the way, broken by the work, pressure and humiliation. I found a girl whose father left the family when she quit gymnastics at age thirteen, who scraped her arms and legs with razors to dull her emotional pain and who needed a two-hour pass from a psychiatric hospital to attend her high school graduation. Girls who broke their necks and backs. One who so desperately sought the perfect, weightless gymnastics body that she starved herself to death. Others—many—who became so obsessive about controlling their weight that they lost control of themselves instead, falling into the potentially fatal cycle of bingeing on food, then purging by vomiting or taking laxatives. One who was sexually abused by her coach and one who was sodomized for four years by the father of a teammate. I found a girl who felt such shame at not making the Olympic team that she slit her wrists. A skater who underwent plastic surgery when a judge said her nose was distracting. A father who handed custody of his daughter over to her coach so she could keep skating. A coach who fed his gymnasts so little that federation officials had to smuggle food into their hotel rooms. A mother who hid her child's chicken pox with makeup so she could compete. Coaches who motivated their athletes by calling them imbeciles, idiots, pigs, cows.

I am not suggesting that gymnastics and figure skating in and of themselves are destructive. On the contrary, both sports are potentially wonderful and enriching, providing an arena of competition in which the average child can develop a sense of mastery, self-esteem and healthy athleticism. But this book isn't about recreational sports or the average child. It's about the elite child athlete and the American obsession with winning that has produced a training environment wherein results are bought at any cost, no matter how devastating. It's about how our cultural fixation on beauty and weight and youth has shaped both sports and driven the athletes into a sphere beyond the quest for physical performance.

The well-known story of Tonya Harding and Nancy Kerrigan did not happen in a vacuum; it symbolizes perfectly the stakes now involved in elite competition—itself a reflection of our national character. We created Tonya and Nancy not only by our hunger for winning but by our criterion for winning, an exaggeration of the code that applies to ambitious young women everywhere: Talent counts, but so do beauty, class, weight, clothes and politics. The anachronistic lack of ambivalence about femininity in both sports is part of their attraction, hearkening back to a simpler time when girls were girls, when women were girls for that matter: coquettish, malleable, eager to please. In figure skating especially, we want our athletes thin, graceful, deferential and cover-girl pretty. We want eyeliner, lipstick and hair ribbons. Makeup artists are fixtures backstage at figure skating competitions, primping and polishing. In figure skating, costumes can actually affect a score. They are so important that skaters spend $1500 and up on one dress— more than they spend on their skates. Nancy Kerrigan's dresses by designer Vera Wang cost upward of $5000 each.

Indeed, the costumes fueled the national fairy tale of Tonya and Nancy. Nancy wore virginal white. She was the perfect heroine, a good girl with perfect white teeth, a 24-inch waist and a smile that suggested both pluck and vulnerability. She remained safely within skating's pristine circle of grace and femininity. Tonya, on the other hand, crossed all the lines. She wore bordello red-and-gold. She was the perfect villainess, a bad girl with truck-stop manners, a racy past and chunky thighs. When she became convinced Nancy's grace would always win out over her own explosive strength, Tonya crossed the final line, helping to eliminate Nancy from competition. The media frenzy tapped into our own inner wranglings about the good girl/bad girl paradox, about how women should behave, about how they should look and what they should say. The story touched a cultural nerve about women crossing societal boundaries—of power, achievement, violence, taste, appearance—and being ensnared by them. In the end, both skaters were trapped, Tonya by her ambition and Nancy by the good-girl image she created for the ice—an image she couldn't live up to. The public turned on Nancy when foolish comments and graceless interviews made it clear she wasn't Snow White after all.

Both sports embody the contradiction of modern womanhood. Society has allowed women to aspire higher, but to do so a woman must often reject that which makes her female, including motherhood. Similarly, gymnastics and figure skating remove the limits of a girl's body, teaching it to soar beyond what seems possible. Yet they also imprison it, binding it like the tiny Victorian waist or the Chinese woman's foot. The girls aren't allowed passage into adulthood. To survive in the sports, they beat back puberty, desperate to stay small and thin, refusing to let their bodies grow up. In this way the sports pervert the very femininity they hold so dear. The physical skills have become so demanding that only a body shaped like a missile—in other words, a body shaped like a boy's—can excel. Breasts and hips slow the spins, lower the leaps and disrupt the clean, lean body lines that judges reward. "Women's gymnastics" and "ladies' figure skating" are misnomers today. Once the athletes become women, their elite careers wither.

In the meantime, their childhoods are gone. But they trade more than their childhoods for a shot at glory. They risk serious physical and psychological problems that can linger long after the public has turned its attention to the next phenom in pigtails. The intensive training and pressure heaped on by coaches, parents and federation officials—the very people who should be protecting the children—often result in eating disorders, weakened bones, stunted growth, debilitating injuries and damaged psyches. In the last six years two U.S. Olympic hopefuls have died as a result of their participation in elite gymnastics.

Because they excel at such a young age, girls in these sports are unlike other elite athletes. They are world champions before they can drive. They are the Michael Jordans and Joe Montanas of their sports before they learn algebra. Unlike male athletes their age, who are playing quarterback in high school or running track for the local club, these girls are competing on a worldwide stage. If an elite gymnast or figure skater fails, she fails globally. She sees her mistake replayed in slow motion on TV and captured in bold headlines in the newspaper. Adult reporters crowd around, asking what she has to say to a country that had hung its hopes on her thin shoulders. Tiffany Chin was seventeen when she entered the 1985 U.S. Figure Skating Championships as the favorite. She was asked at the time how she would feel if she didn't win. She paused, as if trying not to consider the possibility. "Devastated," she said quietly. "I don't know. I'd probably die."

Chin recalled recently that when she did win, "I didn't feel happiness. I felt relief. Which was disappointing." Three months before the 1988 Olympics, Chin retired when her legs began to break down. Some, however, say she left because she could no longer tolerate the pressure and unrelenting drive of her stern mother. "I feel I'm lucky to have gotten through it," she said of skating. "I don't think many people are that lucky. There's a tremendous strain on people who don't make it. The money, the sacrifices, the time. I know people emotionally damaged by it. I've seen nervous breakdowns, psychological imbalances."

An elite gymnast or figure skater knows she takes more than her own ambitions into a competition. Her parents have invested tens of thousands of dollars in her training, sometimes hundreds of thousands. Her coach's reputation rides on her performance. And she knows she might have only one shot. By the next Olympics she might be too old. By the next *year* she might be too old. Girls in these sports are under pressure not only to win but to win quickly. They're running against a clock that eventually marks the lives of all women, warning them they'd better hurry up and get married and have children before it's too late. These girls hear the clock early. They're racing against puberty.

Boys, on the other hand, welcome the changes that puberty brings. They reach their athletic peak after puberty when their bodies grow and their muscles strengthen. In recent years Michael Chang and Boris Becker won the French Open and Wimbledon tennis titles, respectively, before age eighteen, but in virtually every male sport the top athletes are men, not boys. Male gymnastics and figure skating champions are usually in their early to mid twenties; female champions are usually fourteen to seventeen years old in gymnastics and sixteen to early twenties in figure skating.

In staving off puberty to maintain the "ideal" body shape, girls risk their health in ways their male counterparts never do. They starve themselves, for one, often in response to their coaches' belittling insults about their bodies. Starving shuts down the menstrual cycle—the starving body knows it cannot support a fetus—and thus blocks the onset of puberty. It's a dangerous strategy to save a career. If a girl isn't menstruating, she isn't producing estrogen. Without estrogen, her bones weaken. She risks stunting her growth. She risks premature osteoporosis. She risks fractures in all bones, including her vertebrae, and she risks curvature of the spine. In several studies over the last decade, young female athletes who didn't menstruate were found to have the bone densities of postmenopausal women in their fifties, sixties and seventies. Most elite gymnasts don't begin to menstruate until they retire. Kathy Johnson, a medalist in the 1984 Olympics, didn't begin until she quit the sport at age twenty-five.

Our national obsession with weight, our glorification of thinness, have gone completely unchecked in gymnastics and figure skating. The cultural forces that have produced extravagantly bony fashion models have taken their toll on gymnasts and skaters already insecure about their bodies. Not surprisingly, eating disorders are common in both sports, and in gymnastics they're rampant. Studies of female college gymnasts show that most practice some kind of disordered eating. In a 1994 University of Utah study of elite gymnasts—those training for the Olympics—59 percent admitted to some form of disordered eating. And in interviewing elites for this book, I found only a handful who had not tried starving, throwing up or taking laxatives or diuretics to control their weight. Several left the sport because of eating disorders. One died. Eating disorders among male athletes, as in the general male population, are virtually unknown.

"Everyone goes through it, but nobody talks about it, because they're embarrassed," gymnast Kristie Phillips told me. "But I don't put the fault on us. It's the pressures that are put on us to be so skinny. It's mental cruelty. It's not fair that all these pressures are put on us at such a young age and we don't realize it until we get older and we suffer from it."

Phillips took laxatives, thyroid pills and diuretics to lose weight. She had been the hottest gymnast in the mid-1980s, the heir apparent to 1984 Olympic superstar Mary Lou Retton. But she not only didn't win a medal at the 1988 Summer Games, she didn't even make the U.S. team. She left the sport feeling like a failure. She gained weight, then became bulimic, caught in a cycle of bingeing and vomiting. Distraught, she took scissors to her wrists in a botched attempt to kill herself. "I weighed ninety-eight pounds and I was being called [by her coach] an overstuffed Christmas turkey," Phillips said in our interview. "I was told I was never going to make it in life because I was going to be fat. I mean, in *life*. Things I'll never forget."

Much of the direct blame for the young athletes' problems falls on the coaches and parents. Obviously, no parent wakes up in the morning and plots how to ruin his or her child's life. But the money, the fame and the promise of great achievement can turn a parent's head. Ambition gets perverted. The boundaries of parents and coaches bloat and mutate, with the parent becoming the ruthless coach and coach becoming the controlling parent. One father put gymnastics equipment in his living room and for every mistake his daughter made at the gym she had to repeat the skill hundreds of times at home. He moved the girl to three gyms around the country, pushing her in the sport she came to loathe. He said he did it because he wanted the best for her.

Coaches push because they are paid to produce great gymnasts. They are relentless about weight because physically round gymnasts and skaters don't win. Coaches are intolerant of injuries because in the race against puberty, time off is death. Their job is not to turn out happy, well-adjusted young women; it is to turn out champions. If they scream, belittle or ignore, if they prod an injured girl to forget her pain, if they push her to drop out of school, they are only doing what the parents have paid them to do. So, sorting out the blame when a girl falls apart is a messy proposition; everyone claims he was just doing his job.

The sports' national governing bodies, for their part, are mostly impotent. They try to do well by the athletes, but they, too, often lose their way in a tangle of ambition and politics. They're like small-town governments: personal, despotic, paternalistic and absolutely without teeth. The federations do not have the power that the commissioners' offices in professional baseball, football and basketball do. They cannot revoke a coach's or an athlete's membership for anything less than criminal activity. (Tonya Harding was charged and sentenced by the courts before the United States Figure Skating Association expelled her.) They cannot fine or suspend a coach whose athletes regularly leave the sport on stretchers.

There simply is no safety net protecting these children. Not the parents, the coaches or the federations.

Child labor laws prohibit a thirteen-year-old from punching a cash register for forty hours a week, but that same child can labor for forty hours or more inside a gym or an ice skating rink without drawing the slightest glance from the government. The U.S. government requires the licensing of plumbers. It demands that even the tiniest coffee shop adhere to a fastidious health code. It scrutinizes the advertising claims on packages of low-fat snack food. But it never asks a coach, who holds the lives of his young pupils in his hands, to pass a minimum safety and skills test. Coaches in this country need no license to train children, even in a high-injury sport like elite gymnastics. The government that forbids a child from buying a pack of cigarettes because of health concerns never checks on the child athlete who trains until her hands bleed or her knees buckle, who stops eating to achieve the perfect body, who takes eight Advils a day and offers herself up for another shot of cortisone to dull the pain, who drinks a bottle of Ex-Lax because her coach is going to weigh her in the morning. The government never takes a look inside the gym or the rink to make sure these children are not being exploited or abused or worked too hard. Even college athletes—virtually all of whom are adults—are restricted by the NCAA to just twenty hours per week of formal training. But no laws, no agencies, put limits on the number of hours a child can train or the methods a coach can use.

Some argue that extraordinary children should be allowed to follow extraordinary paths to realize their potential. They argue that a child's wants are no less important than an adult's and thus she should not be denied her dreams just because she is still a child. If pursuing her dream means training eight hours a day in a gym, withstanding abusive language and tolerating great pain, and if the child wants to do it and the parents believe it will build character, why not let her? Who are we to tell a child what she can and cannot do with her life?

In fact, we tell children all the time what they can and cannot do with their lives. Restricting children from certain activities is hardly a revolutionary concept. Laws prohibit children from driving before sixteen and drinking before twenty-one. They prohibit children from dropping out of school before fifteen and working full-time before sixteen. In our society we put great value on protecting our children from physical harm and exploitation, and sometimes that means protecting them from their own poor judgment and their parents' poor judgment. No one questions the wisdom of the government in forbidding a child to work full-time, so why is it all right for her to train full-time with no rules to ensure her well-being? Child labor laws should address all labor, even that which is technically nonpaid, though top gymnasts and figure skaters *do* labor for money.

In recent years the federations have begun to pay their top athletes a stipend based on their competition results. The girls can earn bonuses by representing the United States in certain designated events. Skaters who compete in the World Figure Skating Championships and the Olympic Games, for example, receive $15,000. They earn lesser amounts for international competitions such as Skate America. They also earn money from corporate sponsors and exhibitions. The money might not cover much more than their training expenses, which can run $75,000 for a top skater and $20,000 to $30,000 per year for a top gymnast, but it's money—money that is paid specifically for the work the athletes do in the gym and the skating rink.

The real payoff for their hard work, however, waits at the end of the road. That's what the parents and athletes hope anyway. When Mary Lou Retton made millions on Madison Avenue after winning the gold medal at the 1984 Olympics, she changed gymnastics forever. "Kids have agents now before they even make it into their teens," Retton says. Now the dream is no longer just about medals but about Wheaties boxes and appearance fees, about paying off mom and dad's home equity loans and trading in the Toyota for a Mercedes. It doesn't seem to matter that only six girls every four years reach the Olympics and that winning the gold once they get there is the longest of long shots. Even world champion Shannon Miller didn't win the all-around Olympic gold in 1992.

Figure skating, even more than gymnastics, blinds parents and athletes with the glittering possibilities, and for good reason. Peggy Fleming and Dorothy Hamill are still living off gold medals won decades ago. Nancy Kerrigan landed endorsements with Reebok,

Evian, Seiko and Campbell's soup with only a bronze medal in 1992. With glamorous and feminine stars like Kerrigan and Kristi Yamaguchi to lead the way, the United States Figure Skating Association has seen the influx of corporate sponsorship climb 2000 percent in just five years. Money that used to go to tennis is now being shifted to figure skating and gymnastics as their popularity grows. The payoff in money and fame now looms large enough to be seen from a distance, sparkling like the Emerald City, driving parents and children to extremes to reach its doors.

I'm not suggesting that all elite gymnasts and figure skaters emerge from their sports unhealthy and poorly adjusted. Many prove that they can thrive under intense pressure and physical demands and thus are stronger for the experience. But too many can't. There are no studies that establish what percentage of elite gymnasts and figure skaters are damaged by their sports and in what ways. So the evidence I've gathered for this book is anecdotal, the result of nearly a hundred interviews and more than a decade of covering both sports as a journalist.

The bottom line is clear. There have been enough suicide attempts, enough eating disorders, enough broken bodies, enough regretful parents and enough bitter young women to warrant a serious reevaluation of what we're doing in this country to produce Olympic champions. Those who work in these sports know this. They know the tragedies all too well. If the federations and coaches truly care about the athletes and not simply about the fame and prestige that come from trotting tough little champions up to the medal stand, they know it is past time to lay the problems on the table, examine them and figure out a way to keep their sports from damaging so many young lives. But since those charged with protecting young athletes so often fail in their responsibility, it is time the government drops the fantasy that certain sports are merely games and takes a hard look at legislation aimed at protecting elite child athletes.

Summer 2000

It was my hope when I wrote *Little Girls in Pretty Boxes* that by dramatizing the particularly intense subculture of gymnastics and figure skating that could better understand something of our nature as a country bent on adulating, and in some cases sacrificing, girls and young women in a quest to fit them into our pretty little boxes.

In the five years since the book came out, gymnastics and figure skating are still popular, but they no longer dominate women's sports as they once did. Basketball and soccer have elbowed their way onto the stage. Two professional women's basketball leagues attracted thousands of fans in arenas around the country and on television, allowing our best college players to play professionally in America instead of leaving for pro leagues in Europe and Asia. The American Basketball League folded after three seasons, but the other—the Women's National Basketball League—continues to thrive behind the marketing power of the men's NBA.

Then in the summer of 1999, another group of female athletes captivated America. The Women's World Cup culminated in a thrilling final between the United States and China in a sold-out Rose Bowl, catapulting the U.S. players to national stardom. The U.S. team's exuberance and grit pulled in fans who had never watched a soccer game in their lives. The players landed on magazine covers and talk shows. They were mobbed for autographs wherever they went.

The basketball leagues and the women's soccer team not only

have given young girls new role models, but by showcasing large, strong athletes, they went a long way in helping to reshape America's perceptions of femininity. Little girls who pasted Shannon Miller's poster over their beds now are adding basketball star Lisa Leslie and soccer star Mia Hamm.

Still, among females athletes at the 1996 Olympics in Atlanta, the gymnasts captured the most attention, as they have done for the past thirty years. As we watched the young girls and women, there was cause for hope. The women were older and bigger than they'd been since the 1970s. And in the four years since the Olympics, there has been real progress. The gymnastics community, after so many years of refusing to acknowledge the depth of its problems, has taken bold steps toward transforming itself. The changes in gymnastics have been so encouraging that I've added a new chapter to the book to bring readers up to date.

I've also included in the new chapter the setbacks that make clear there is still much work left to be done. I hope this book continues to be something of a thorn in the side of those who are charged with guiding and protecting young girls striving for Olympic glory. I hope it serves as a reminder of what can, and does, happen when the purpose of sports becomes the color of the child's medal rather than the content of her character.

1

IF IT ISN'T BLEEDING, DON'T WORRY ABOUT IT

INJURIES

.

It was two o'clock in the morning when the phone rang in Otilia Gomez's Houston apartment. She wasn't alarmed. Her fifteen-year-old daughter, Julissa, was in Japan competing in a gymnastics meet and, ignoring the time difference, had been calling her mother in the middle of the night for a week. Otilia didn't mind. She loved talking to Julissa. Otilia was close to both her daughters, but she and Julissa shared a special bond. Her younger daughter, thirteen-year-old Kristy, was like most teenagers, vaguely embarrassed to be seen in public with her parents and prickly to their affections. But Julissa had always remained a little girl with her mother, never tiring of her hugs and kisses. Even as a teenager, Julissa didn't go a day without telling her mother she loved her. As a fifth grader, she still believed in Santa Claus. When Otilia broke the news to both her daughters, concerned that classmates would tease them, Kristy shrugged it off with "I had a feeling." Julissa cried.

Physically and socially, Julissa was Kool-Aid and fingerpaint, as tiny and shy as a grade-schooler. She looked ten years old even at fifteen. She stood 4 feet 10 inches and weighed 72 pounds. No breasts, no hips. She knew few girls outside the gym because she didn't know how to talk to them. Like most elite gymnasts, Julissa grew up too slowly and too quickly at once—in some ways she was already a grown woman. She put in more hours at the gym than many adults at their full-time jobs. During the week, she moved from the gym to school and back to the gym, thirteen hours a day between the two. On Saturdays she worked out again, and on Sundays she rested, marshaling her energy to begin it all again. She rarely took in a movie or walked the mall or sat in an ice-cream parlor with her friends. She had no time, plus she had to watch every calorie.

Julissa wanted to do well in gymnastics for herself, but she also knew how much money and hope her parents had invested. The children of migrant farmers from the dusty Texas border town of Laredo, Otilia and Ramiro had grown up working in the fields alongside their parents in the summer, thinning sugar beet crops in Colorado, picking carrots and peppers in Minnesota. In Laredo from fall to spring, they spoke English only to their teachers, their sole contacts with the non-Hispanic world. Otilia always loved school and dreamed of becoming a teacher, though her family had no money for college. After high school she worked as a teacher's aide at the migrant school in Laredo, where she caught the eye of administrators. They paid her way through Texas Women's University to earn her teaching credentials.

After college she married Ramiro, who like most children of migrant farmers had never graduated from high school. He delivered eggs, hauled produce, worked the fields, then, during a two-year stint in the Army, learned welding. By the time Otilia finished college, Ramiro had earned his welder's license, and the couple left Laredo for jobs in San Antonio, where their daughters were born.

Julissa knew what her gymnastics meant to her parents. Nothing pleased Otilia more than watching her gifted daughter soar with such elegance and grace alongside the daughters of lawyers and oilmen. And nothing meant more to Julissa than pleasing her mother. She wanted to repay her mother's love with ribbons and trophies and, if she worked hard, harder than any other gymnast, an Olympic medal.

When at age ten Julissa had outgrown the gymnastics programs in San Antonio, the family packed up and rented an apartment in Houston, America's hotbed of gymnastics. For them, it was unthinkable to send Julissa to Houston alone and let some other family raise her. They had promised themselves they wouldn't let gymnastics break up their family, as they had seen it break up others. Ramiro lost his job as welder the first month in Houston and considered moving the family back to San Antonio, but Julissa was blossoming at the gym of world-famous coach Béla Károlyi. So Ramiro found work as a cook. But after five years in Houston, Károlyi's charm had worn thin. Julissa could no longer tolerate his abusive training methods. Ranked thirteenth in the country and with the 1988 U.S. Olympic Trials six months away, Julissa needed to find a new coach quickly. She settled on Al Fong, who was training world-class gymnast Christy Henrich at his gym in

Blue Springs, Missouri. This time Otilia and Ramiro saw no other alternative than to break up the family, at least for a few months.

Ramiro moved to Blue Springs with Julissa in February 1988, transferring to a TGI Friday's restaurant in nearby Kansas City. Otilia and Kristy would move up at the end of May when school let out. Kristy protested the move, upset that her life would be uprooted. "I didn't want to move either," Otilia recalls. "But we had invested so much money and it was what Julissa wanted. We were so close to the end that we just couldn't say no."

When the phone rang in Otilia Gomez's apartment on the night of May 5, boxes bound with packing tape stood against the walls. In two weeks Otilia and Kristy planned to load the car and drive up to Missouri. The family, Otilia thought, would soon be together again.

"Hello!" she answered cheerfully. Julissa had told her the night before how well she had performed on the first day of the competition in Tokyo, and Otilia was eager to find out how she had fared on the second day.

"Mrs. Gomez?"

It was Al Fong's voice. To this day Otilia can't remember what Fong told her. But she knows his words registered because she turned on all the lights, got dressed, called her husband in Missouri, packed her bags and, when it was light, boarded a plane for Japan.

■   ■   ■

For many young gymnasts, the road to the Olympics winds through a steamy metal-roofed gym in suburban North Houston, down the road from Hi-Lo Auto Parts. It is the home of famed coach Béla Károlyi, who trained Olympic gold medalists Nadia Comaneci and Mary Lou Retton. When ten-year-old Julissa Gomez visited Károlyi to see if she wanted to train at his gym, Károlyi asked her to start that day. Julissa had just finished second in the state meet for her level. Károlyi wanted her. He wanted every promising gymnast. He ran what came to be known as The Factory, gathering to his gym as many flexible young girls as he could find, then winnowing out the weak, the rebellious and the unappealing until he found those he could mold into champions.

Though Julissa didn't fit Károlyi's idea of a star—she was timid and frail-looking—she was talented, worked hard and never complained. Even if she wasn't going to be another Mary Lou, she could be valuable in pushing the star gymnasts to greater heights, plus her parents were willing to pay. Károlyi placed her on the "Hopes" team, a group of talented youngsters who were groomed by coach Rick Newman as candidates for Károlyi's special elite team: six girls whom Károlyi handpicked to train for the Olympics. Károlyi's six gymnasts were the queens of the gym. They paid for their status with a grueling schedule. Forty-six hours a week. Sundays off. Three days off at Christmas, another on the Fourth of July. Despite the sacrifices, they held the spots every girl wanted—and every parent too. From those six could emerge the next Mary Lou. Parents paid hundreds of dollars to Károlyi every month, often sacrificing piano lessons or a new bike for their other children in service to that dream. And to protect their investments, they quickly learned to keep their mouths shut when Newman or Károlyi called their daughters bloody imbeciles or fat cows or kicked them out of the gym for crying in pain. Parents knew that if they complained, Károlyi would invite them and their daughters to leave. Where would they go? Károlyi's was the best.

"Because you've given your children all your support, you don't think people can come and destroy all of that," Otilia Gomez reflects, talking of gymnastics in a flat voice, as if the words were sea pebbles worn down by pain and anger. "You really think that they're sheltered against that, that they can hear somebody being abused or they can be verbally abused and that it's not going to affect them, because you've built them up so much. Now, looking back at Julissa and what she went through, I know all she heard and all she went through took its toll.

"But as a parent, you become so involved in it you just really can't see the whole picture. You're only seeing what you want to see."

The competition in Károlyi's gym was intense by design. The day after each meet, Károlyi's wife, Márta, also a coach, would stretch the girls in the order in which they placed in the competition, carefully pulling and pushing on their muscles and joints like clay in a sculptor's hands. Kristie Phillips and Phoebe Mills, the two hotshots, almost always finished first and second, so Márta stretched them in that order—a subtle but clear privilege in a place where privileges were doled out by the teaspoon. The message: You're worth only as much as your latest ranking. Károlyi wanted the girls to battle each other every day in the gym. "These girls are like little scorpions," he once said. "You put them all in a bottle, and one scorpion will come out alive. That scorpion will be champion." If one girl didn't perform a routine to his liking, he often made one of her teammates do extra work, building a climate of resentment among them where only the strongest would survive.

Julissa's body thrived at Károlyi's; she was learning new skills, moving up from Class 1 to junior elite to elite and finally to Károlyi's special team of six. But along the way she closed something down inside herself, as if her hardening muscles became a fortress around her soul. She barely smiled anymore. She hoarded pain and anger like a miser, stashing them in dark nooks no one else could see, not even her mother. "Julissa had always been extremely positive until she started working with Béla," Otilia remembers. "She had always said, if you asked how her workout went, 'Oh, it was great. I had a little problem on beam today, but I'll do better tomorrow and I did really wonderfully on bars.' She was always real positive. Then when she started working with Béla, we stopped hearing those kinds of things. It got so that she didn't even want to talk about it at all."

And after Julissa joined Károlyi's, she was always in pain, first from a stress fracture in her ankle, then shinsplints, then hamstring pulls and finally a sprained knee that would eventually drive her from Károlyi's for good. Károlyi, like a lion circling hobbled prey, picked on her, testing her survival instincts. Either she would grow stronger from his abuse or she would quit. Károlyi needed to know which it would be. In or out. Black or white. Yes or no. He had no time for doubts, hesitations or fears.

"Béla was mean to her. He would call her names, say mean things," says Carrol Stack, mother of 1988 Olympian Chelle Stack. "She had a lot of talent. But she was quiet and shy. Didn't have much personality. You've got to have personality with him."

"He called [Julissa] stupid all the time," says Chelle. "Then he didn't really pay much attention to her at all. She didn't get the hard-core coaching."

No matter what ugly words the coaches threw at her, Julissa didn't fight back. Few do. A gymnast on the elite level learns to stand still—mouth closed, eyes blank—and weather her coach's storms. A gymnast is seen and not heard. Even when she's in pain, she says nothing until she can no longer work. Nadia Comaneci once cut her hand on the plastic-and-foam hand guards the gymnasts wear to perform on the uneven bars, and by the time she told anyone, she had blood poisoning up her arm. Even when she's scared, the gymnast says nothing. *Especially* when she's scared. "Chickening out" before a trick is the unforgivable sin.

Elena Moukina could have told Julissa how dangerous this code of silence can be. The Soviet gymnast won the World Gymnastics Championships in 1978, and at the age of twenty on the eve of the 1980 Olympics in Moscow, she attempted a tumbling trick—a 1¾ salto with 1½ twists—during training. Plagued by injuries, she knew she wasn't prepared for it, but she never questioned whether she should do it. She crashed to the mat. The fall broke her neck and left her a paraplegic.

"I was let down by my own inability to say no," Moukina said in an interview with *International Gymnast* magazine in 1987. The coaches' demand for complete subservience, she said, is one reason they prefer their gymnasts young. "It is far easier to work with small, mute creatures who look at a coach as an idol and perform everything without ever talking back."

Julissa never voiced her fears about anything. She was flexible and graceful, making her a beautiful performer on the beam, but her frail body lacked the power for the explosive moves demanded in the vault. Julissa's coaches had her doing the most technically difficult vault at the time, the Yurchenko. It didn't take as much power to perform as the Tsukahara, for example, but it required precise positioning and timing. The vault was introduced by the Soviet Union's Natalia Yurchenko in 1983, when she used it to win the World Championships. In the individual finals a day later, however, she cracked both ankles. Yurchenko had trained for years to perfect the vault, but young American girls had to learn it almost overnight to keep pace with the Soviets.

"Everybody felt like they had to do it," says 1984 Olympian Kathy Johnson, now a television commentator, "and they rushed it. It's not that hard to do, but if something goes wrong, it's a disaster.

That was the problem. You need to be so confident with it and so competent that a mistake on it would only mean you'd land short and jam an ankle or whatever...Now I'm totally relaxed watching the vault. It doesn't worry me at all as long as the gymnast has mastered the technique. But back then I wouldn't watch them. I just didn't think we had it down pat. Too much could go wrong."

In the Yurchenko the gymnast sprints down the runway and does a roundoff onto a springboard positioned about four feet from the horse. She lands both feet on the springboard with her back to the horse. She then leaps, back arched, as if doing a backward dive into a pool. Her hands land on the horse for a split second. She pushes off, twists in the air and lands on her feet.

The vault scared many gymnasts because they couldn't see where their feet were landing on the springboard, opening the possibility of overshooting the board and slipping their feet off the back. And because they leapt off the springboard backward, blindly, they could miss the horse altogether.

Julissa's teammates at Károlyi's knew she never felt confident with the vault. It required a consistency Julissa could never find. A gymnast's feet should land on the springboard in the same place every time, and the feet should never land closer than 4 inches to the back edge of the board. Julissa was all over the place. Gymnasts remembered Károlyi warning Julissa she was going to miss the springboard someday. "You could tell it was not a safe vault for her to be doing," says Chelle Stack, who watched Julissa every day in practice. "Someone along the way should have stopped her."

But no one did. The easiest way for a weak vaulter to earn high scores was to perform the Yurchenko because the roundoff entry gave her the explosive power she couldn't generate on her own. Some said that, despite the risks, the Yurchenko was safer for someone like Julissa because she didn't have the strength to propel herself safely through the more traditional vaults. And Julissa performed the vault well enough in competitions to drive her vault scores from the low 9's to the mid to high 9's (on a scale of 10). That was what she needed if she was going to reach the Olympics.

For Julissa, as for most of the elite gymnasts, the Olympics loomed in the distance like some dreamy, magical place that would make the long journey worthwhile. At training camp for the national gymnastics team one year, the coaches showed the girls *16 Days of Glory,* filmmaker Bud Greenspan's stirring documentary on the 1984 Olympics. Julissa cried. "That's going to be us," she whispered to a teammate. "We're going to do it, right?"

* * *

One day Károlyi announced he was adding a midday practice to the morning and evening workouts. When Julissa asked about school, Károlyi shrugged. If she wanted to be the best, she had to make sacrifices. "This isn't golf," Károlyi liked to say. Julissa dropped out of ninth grade and signed up for correspondence courses, as her five teammates had already done.

With the Olympics just a year away, Károlyi grew more intense. The days in the gym piled on Julissa like bricks until she finally told Károlyi how miserable she was.

"Who said you had to be happy?" Károlyi replied.

A short time later, in the spring of 1987, Julissa sprained her knee. Though her doctor told her to stay off it for a month, Julissa still went to the gym every day—fevers, chicken pox, broken bones and sprains were unacceptable excuses for missing practice. She worked only on the uneven bars, where she would put no strain on the ankle (she did no dismount). Károlyi alternately ignored and harangued her. In his mind, perhaps, he was trying to motivate

Julissa to rise above the injuries. The Gomezes were paying him to produce the best gymnast he could, and Julissa could become a great gymnast only by pushing herself through the pain. Like a boot-camp sergeant producing hardened soldiers through humiliation, extraordinary work and blind obedience, Károlyi had turned a handful of gymnasts into champions. But because twelve-year-old girls aren't soldiers, most of Károlyi's elite gymnasts didn't become champions. Most became entries on a hospital log.

"I drank beer with Béla on many occasions and he's an entertaining man, but he's a miserable SOB when he's coaching those kids," says Jack Rockwell, former trainer for the United States Gymnastics Federation (USGF) and other athletic organizations. "He forced kids to do things when they were hurt. His philosophy was the Eastern Bloc philosophy: If it isn't bleeding, don't worry about it." At a 1983 exhibition against China at UCLA, for example, Mary Lou Retton broke a small bone in her wrist. Rockwell told her to give the training a rest, but within the hour he saw her working again. At least keep ice on the wrist to help with the pain, Rockwell told her. She agreed. Moments later Béla Károlyi came by and kicked the ice bag off Retton's arm.

"It tears you up after a while to see how these girls are treated," says Rockwell, now retired.

One early summer evening, at the end of the day's training, Béla Károlyi finally let loose on Julissa. He was tired of her babying her sprained knee and delivered an ultimatum. She could either work out like the rest of the girls or leave. Otilia, who had just arrived from work to pick her daughter up, saw Károlyi yell at Julissa but couldn't hear what he was saying. Parents watched workouts from a small, sparse room separated from the gym by a thick pane of soundproof glass. They became adept at reading Károlyi's face and their daughters' faces, divining from the clues who was in favor and who was out in the complicated and ever-changing caste system Károlyi had created.

"What happened out there?" Otilia asked in the car.

"Nothing."

Otilia persisted. "What was that all about?"

Julissa started to cry. "I hate him. I don't want to go back."

The Gomezes had just paid Károlyi $1000 for a month of basic tuition, and extra for private lessons in uneven bars, private lessons in ballet and private stretching. "It was getting completely out of hand," recalls Otilia, who taught in a year-round school to earn two months' extra pay to foot Károlyi's bill.

The 1987 U.S. Gymnastics Championships were a week away. How the athletes fared there would go far in handicapping the field for the following year's Olympics. Julissa's options in coaches when she left Károlyi's were slim. Only one other coach in Houston had elites in his gym, so Julissa signed on with him. But seven months later, in January 1988, Julissa knew she was getting nowhere, and time was running out. During that month, her last in Houston, Julissa had a disturbing and prophetic dream—that the reigning world champion from the Soviet Union had died. When she related the dream to her mother the next morning, she was still upset. "It seemed to me like part of her wanted to say, 'I don't want to do this anymore.' I think part of her wanted to give it up," Otilia says. "I know she didn't like to compete, but she loved everything that went with it: going on trips, signing autographs, going to good restaurants, staying in hotels. That was exciting for her. We kept asking if she wanted to quit, and she kept saying no. I think she sort of felt the same way we did, that she had come this far..."

One thing was clear: Julissa needed to find a new coach. Otilia called Al Fong in Blue Springs, Missouri, where world-class gymnast Christy Henrich trained. Julissa had befriended Christy at an international meet, and they had become pen pals. Julissa moved up to Blue Springs in February and was so homesick that she once asked her mother to put her toy poodle, Snowball, up to the phone so she could talk to him. She talked to her mother every day, always asking when Otilia was coming to visit again.

Days after Julissa arrived, Fong hosted a meet at his gym that was shown on local television. "It's sort of a coup for us to have Julissa," one commentator said as the camera focused on the new gymnast.

■ ■ ■

Al Fong had opened the Great American Gymnastics Express in Blue Springs in November 1979 against all odds. He had just been fired from his coaching job at a Kansas City club because he refused to sign an agreement not to open a competing gym. Having his own gym had been his ambition almost since he first competed as a child at the YMCA in Seattle and then at Louisiana State University. With financial backing from two Blue Springs businessmen, the ambitious young man opened his gym. "My team is going to be a national team," he told the local newspaper five months after opening the doors. "I think I'll have kids on the national team in two years."

It took him seven. Fong talked big—he had also predicted having "the top gym in the United States by the year 2000"—and drove his gymnasts hard. A coach becomes a star only by producing stars, and Fong's best shot at stardom in the winter of 1988 was fifteen-year-old Christy Henrich.

Henrich's quick climb through the national ranks earned Fong the USGF's Coach of the Year award in 1987. Henrich was Fong's first gymnast with a shot at the Olympics. Then Julissa came on board in February and—bingo!—Fong doubled his Olympic chances. And right behind Henrich and Gomez waited rising star Karen Tierney, a junior elite who was too young to qualify for the Olympics in 1988. (Gymnasts must turn fifteen during the year of the Summer Games: after 1996 they will have to be sixteen.) "I think she will be the number one girl in America in two years and one of the top athletes in the world," Fong said of Tierney at the time.

The three gymnasts formed the foundation Fong needed to create his dynasty. He was going to train them as no other coach had trained gymnasts. Fong detailed to reporters how he would create world champions in a family setting, how he wanted to let his "girls be girls" and go to dances and eat pizza and go out on dates. "I don't want to be responsible someday for any young woman coming up to me and saying, 'You robbed me of my childhood.'"

He railed against coaches who were like animal trainers. He was set on proving those coaches wrong by beating them. "Check me in ten years," he challenged in 1983, "and see if it works."

By 1993 not one of the three was competing in gymnastics. None had made it to the Olympics.

Unbeknownst to Fong, Karen Tierney's Olympic aspirations died at the U.S. Olympic Festival in the summer of 1987. She missed her hands on the horse performing a Yurchenko vault and landed on her head. When she rose, she held her neck, then saluted the judges as gymnasts are supposed to. Suddenly she felt light-headed and lay down on the mat. Ten minutes later, however, pumped up on adrenaline, she took her second vault and nailed it. It would have earned a 9.6 of a possible 10, but because she took too much time between vaults, the score was knocked to 9.1.

Tierney continued to compete that day despite the pain. She hadn't heard anything pop, so she figured she was okay. But on the uneven bars her head suddenly felt so heavy she couldn't hold it up. The room began to spin. Doctors strapped her to a stretcher and rushed her to the hospital. She still couldn't lift her head. For the first time she was scared. X rays showed she had cracked the C-1 vertebra in her neck. Had she cracked the C-2 or C-3, she could have been paralyzed. She spent three months in a neck brace.

When she returned to the gym, she couldn't make herself do the Yurchenko, even though in practice the springboard is nestled inside a thick U-shaped mat to protect gymnasts if they miss the board. The top of the mat is flush with the top of the board. So if a gymnast's foot misses the board, the foot won't plunge to the floor; instead, it lands on the mat, giving the gymnast something to push off of and propel her over the horse. But the mats were not allowed in competitions until late 1988.

Tierney never again performed a Yurchenko at Fong's gym. Every time she sprinted down the runway, she stopped before reaching the horse, frozen with fear. Her father finally told Fong that she was through with the Yurchenko. It wasn't worth the risk. But the next day, according to Tierney, Fong urged her to try it again, infuriating Karen's father. Fong further angered the family, Tierney said, when he failed to show at a meeting with Karen's psychologist, who was helping the girl tame her fears of the vault. After another heated meeting with Tierney's father, Fong stopped pushing Karen to perform the vault. Fong insists he never pushed Karen to continue with the Yurchenko, but a year after the accident the Tierneys moved their daughter to a gym in Arizona. "Boom, she was gone," Fong recalls, still mystified. "The parents were the ones that instigated that whole thing. The Tierneys, they think strange."

Tierney never became America's number one gymnast, as Fong had predicted. "After I hurt my neck, I gave up my dream," she says. "The Olympics no longer seemed important." Battling her own fears, Tierney also cringed when she watched Julissa do the Yurchenko. "She had her own way of doing it. She was always real close to the end of the board. And she had a weird approach. I remember once or twice she missed the end of the board."

Fong saw Julissa's flaws too, later testifying that he had noticed her poor technique at competitions when she was still with Károlyi. She wasn't landing within the "safety zone" of the springboard, 4 to 5 inches from the edge. So Fong tinkered with her approach and her roundoff and felt so confident of her progress he accepted an invitation for her to compete at the World Sports Fair in Japan just three months after she arrived in Missouri. Fong knew that a gymnast's performance in international meets carried weight with the USGF, so he wanted to get Christy and Julissa as much international exposure as he could before the U.S. Olympic Trials. Christy represented the U.S. team at the International Invitational in March in Budapest. And Julissa was headed for Japan in May. But first there was a meet in South Dakota the weekend before she left for Tokyo. Julissa begged her mother to come.

"I'm going to be seeing you in two weeks," Otilia said, referring to her and Kristy's imminent move. "By the time you get back from Japan, I'll be in Missouri."

"But I want you to come," Julissa pleaded.

At such a late date Otilia couldn't get decent airfare. She didn't have money to throw away like that. But she hadn't seen her daughter since Easter, nearly a month before. ("I wanted to see her," Otilia says. "I always wanted to see her.") She caved in. She flew to Kansas City, then she and Ramiro drove eight hours to South Dakota. They arrived when Julissa was already in the arena doing warm-ups. Though Julissa's bar and beam routines were still a little weak, she did well in her floor routine and especially in the vault. She performed a Yurchenko with a tucked full—a somersault in the air—for the first time in a year, scoring a 9.7. She scored the same as Christy Henrich, who did an even more complicated version of the Yurchenko, one with a full twisting layout—a rotation in the air with the body straight.

"When I do a layout, I'm going to score even higher!" Julissa said to her parents later.

That night Julissa stayed in her parents' hotel room. As she often did at home, she got into bed with her mother, leaving her father to sleep alone in the second bed. Otilia and Julissa flipped through magazines, looking at clothes and hairstyles, laughing and talking. The family spent part of the next day together, then Otilia and Ramiro took their daughter back to the team's hotel late that afternoon. They had to start driving back to Missouri. Julissa said good-bye to her parents four times.

On the drive back, Otilia smiled. "I feel so good having seen her," she said to Ramiro. She felt unusually happy.

The week after she returned to Houston, Otilia Gomez took communion for the first time since her marriage. For several weeks before, she had a gnawing compulsion to pray. But she felt she couldn't just start praying to a God she had neglected for so many years. So when her niece made her first communion, she took the opportunity to return to the Catholic Church. "I had this feeling that God was calling me, asking me to pray," Otilia recalls. "I felt like He was preparing me for something that was about to come."

■ ■ ■

Of the two hundred or so gymnasts who compete on the elite level every year, only twenty make the national team. Only six compete in the Olympics. A gymnast's elite career usually lasts five or six years, generally from age twelve to age eighteen. Some go on to college gymnastics, a more forgiving environment. Others walk out of the gym and never return. How many leave because of injuries or eating disorders? No one keeps a tally. But at the highest level few quit simply because they have lost interest, as a child might quit violin lessons. "Gymnasts don't so much retire as expire," says one coach.

Because the athletes' careers are so short, an elite gym moves to a single beat: the ticking clock. The gymnasts race against time to transform themselves into perfect little machines before their bodies turn against them, swelling and rounding into a woman's or simply giving out. To rest an injury is to kill precious time. One might miss a meet, and every meet is another block in a gymnast's career; in a short span of time, a few years at most, she must build a strong enough foundation to lift her into the Olympics. So the gymnast, and the gymnast's coach, will do anything to keep the girl competing, uninterrupted, no matter what.

Betty Okino was carefully climbing toward the 1992 Olympics as one of Károlyi's stars when her body began to break down like an old car, part by part. Before the 1991 World Championships she was diagnosed with a stress fracture in her right elbow and was told by doctors to stop training. "But that wasn't really an option," she recalls. "It was just like, either you are paralyzed and you can't move, or you train."

When the arm predictably broke, she refused to let the doctor put it in a cast, though she agreed to rest it for two weeks. She still went to the gym to work her legs. "No matter what," she says, "you went to the gym."

Less than a year later Okino heard a sickening pop as she sprinted down the runway for a vault. Her right leg buckled and she crashed to the floor, the tendon having ripped away from the bone below her knee. After doctors reattached it with screws, Okino returned to the gym, where Károlyi yelled at her for slacking off. "He thought I was faking," she says. "He'd tell me he thought I was overreacting. I'd go to the gym and I couldn't really walk or run on it yet. I'd ride the bike and try to bend it and straighten it. All my teammates were training and improving and he'd sort of ignore me. And that's hard, going from getting so much of the attention to getting just like nothing."

Three months later she won a silver medal in uneven bars at the 1992 World Championships in Paris. "What Béla did worked," Okino says. "He motivated me by getting me mad."

No sooner had Okino returned from Paris than she began feeling sharp pains in her back. Her doctor found stress fractures in her vertebrae and gave her a brace to wear when she wasn't training. Still, two weeks later, on a dismount off the uneven bars, pain exploded through her back. She had fractured the L3 and L4 vertebrae in her lower back. She had a 2 percent chance of paralysis if she continued gymnastics. Her mother urged her to quit, but Okino said no.

"Ever since I was nine, my goal had always been to go to the Olympics and win a medal," she says. "And I had gotten this far. There was just six weeks until the Olympics. So what that I had fractured my back? I could still walk. And I figured as long as I'm capable of moving my body and I'm not paralyzed and I could deal with the pain, I could keep trying."

She popped anti-inflammatory drugs and eight Advils every day. She wore a brace in training. Still, pain shot down the backs of both legs. It hurt to breathe. "I was able to block out a lot of the pain by thinking about the Olympics," Okino remembers.

She was too injured to compete in either the U.S. Gymnastics Championships or the U.S. Olympic Trials, the meets designated to determine the 1992 Olympic team. But in a remarkable move the USGF put her on the team anyway after a quickly assembled second "trial." Under extraordinary circumstances and controlling enormous amounts of pain, she helped the United States win a team bronze medal at the Olympics, contributing more points toward the team score than anyone except Shannon Miller.

The elbow has never fully healed. Today Okino can't write without pain. She can't completely straighten her arm. She needs surgery to clean out pieces of bone that have chipped off, but she's still touring in gymnastics shows and claims she can't afford to take the time off.

Most gymnasts begin the sport so young, as toddlers, that the plague of injuries seems normal. No one tells them their bodies belong to them and not to their coaches or parents. No one tells them they are disposable heroes. No one needs to. They know. They've seen the endless stream of girls skip through the gym's front door and hobble out the back. They know when their bodies give out, there's someone else ready to take their places. So they hide their sprained ankles, deny their broken toes, downplay their pulled muscles.

After making the 1988 Olympic team at the ancient age of twenty-one, Kelly Garrison knew her body couldn't withstand the eight hours of daily workouts that were routine for her teen-age teammates. She was nursing an eight-month-old stress fracture in her left ankle and was dogged by pain in her lower back and one of her hips from a sciatic nerve problem. Garrison downplayed her ailments, fearful that she might lose her spot on the team if Olympic coach Béla Károlyi thought she wasn't in top shape. Neither Garrison nor her regular coach, Becky Buwick, wanted to give Károlyi or USGF officials any reason to replace her with an alternate. "It can be very political," Buwick says.

During the weeks-long Olympic training camp at Károlyi's gym in Houston, Garrison participated in almost every practice session, though Buwick made sure she didn't wear herself out. Even so, Garrison hurt her hand. Blessed with a high threshold for pain, she kept it to herself and continued training until she and Buwick went to the hospital a few days later to have her troublesome hip examined. At the same time, the doctor gave Garrison a shot in the hand to numb the pain. But it was in X-raying the back and hips that the doctor made a startling discovery: Garrison had twenty-two old stress fractures in her back caused by years of gymnastics training. All had healed, and Garrison believed that whatever ailments she was now suffering would pass too. She put them out of her mind, and she asked her Olympic roommate not to mention them to anyone. She was too close to competing in the Olympics to let anything get in her way now.

So when the pain from the stress fracture in her ankle flared one day at the Olympics in Seoul, she kept quiet. She didn't want it known that her body was less than 100 percent, and there was nothing a doctor could do anyway. What the ankle needed was rest, the one thing Garrison couldn't give it. Instead, she devised her own treatment. Warming up before the competition, Garrison jumped repeatedly until the pounding numbed the pain. Then she competed.

Garrison suffered in silence because she was not America's number one gymnast. There is a different set of rules for the gymnast who happens to be the star at that moment. The coaches and federation officials allow her to compete no matter what the injury. Indeed, they sometimes insist on it. By showcasing their best athletes, the coaches and federation showcase themselves. When his gymnasts compete, Károlyi—an unabashed publicity hound—can bound across America's television screens, scooping up his tiny girls in bear hugs. Steve Nunno, coach of two-time world champion Shannon Miller, can swagger around the gym, clapping other coaches on the back, smiling for the cameras, showing off the 4-foot-10-inch, 79-pound champion he created inside his Oklahoma City gym. Nunno was once quoted as saying, "You can talk a kid into being healthy for as long as you need her. Once the meet is over, then you can let her be hurt."

Brandy Johnson, a 1988 Olympian, was the top U.S. gymnast going into the 1989 World Championships in Stuttgart, Germany. The day before she left for Europe, she landed between the mats on a tumbling trick and hurt her foot. She iced it on the plane, but by the time she arrived, the foot was swollen and painful. USGF officials and coaches watched practice in the days before the meet to decide the order in which the gymnasts would compete: the gymnast who looked best in practice would compete last, giving her the best chance for high scores. (Judges generally score early competitors lower to leave room for better performances by subsequent gymnasts.) Johnson pushed herself to do well in practice so she wouldn't lose her coveted last spot.

She pushed so hard that the pain in her foot worsened. USGF officials, who noticed her wincing, took her and her coach into a room. According to Brandy, the officials told her she had to perform. She was the top athlete—they needed her. Brandy was stunned. "I don't think I would have competed if it were up to me. The amount of pain I was in, I could have hurt myself worse."

Brandy trained and competed, crying in pain every night when she returned to her room. Despite the injury, she won a silver in the vault, thrilling the federation. When she returned home, doctors diagnosed a fracture. Her foot stayed in a cast for a month.

Every elite gymnast understands the basic rule of injuries: Deal with them. A gymnast without a high pain threshold is a gymnast without a career. "Their body is a machine and they are a person," says Sandy Henrich, mother of gymnast Christy Henrich. "The two are separate." Christy once competed in the World Cup with a broken foot. "If they're in pain, they don't feel it. They don't acknowledge it," her mother says.

Gymnasts take care of the pain as routinely as they take care of their teeth and their hair. Olympian Wendy Bruce had fifteen cortisone shots in her feet over the course of her career. Before the last one her doctor made her sign a paper saying he had advised against it. "I didn't think twice about it," Bruce says. "I wouldn't have been able to compete otherwise."

Before and during training, gymnasts pop handfuls of painkillers. Every day. According to Brandy Johnson, "You never come into the gym and not have something wrong with you. That would be amazing." Kathy Johnson took aspirin every day with a Maalox chaser. Erica Stokes, who trained with Károlyi and then with Steve Nunno, took five to seven Advils every day. "It was kind of a group thing," she says. "We'd all have these huge bottles in our gym bags." Elizabeth Traylor, another Károlyi gymnast, took six to eight Advils daily during workouts and sprayed her knees with an anesthetic to further dull the pain of Schlatter's disease. She was eleven years old. During one stretch while Kristie Phillips was training with a broken wrist, she took twelve Advils and six anti-inflammatory Naprosyns daily. "It was pill after pill after pill," she remembers.

Such high doses of Advil can cause bleeding in the lining of the stomach and lead to kidney disease. Kenny Easley, a former safety for the Seattle Seahawks football team, sued the manufacturer of Advil and team doctors when he contended his kidney failure was caused in part by taking Advil to relieve the pain of an ankle injury. Easley underwent a kidney transplant in 1990. He settled out of court with Whitehall Laboratories and the doctors in 1991.

■ ■ ■

If Béla Károlyi is the high priest of insensitivity, he's not alone at the altar. The adults around elite gymnasts become so accustomed to the braces and splints and cries of pain that they're dulled to the damage the sport can inflict. Kathy Kelly, the director of women's gymnastics for USA Gymnastics (formerly the United States Gymnastics Federation), answered cheerfully when asked about the problems of the sport, particularly injuries. Kelly had just returned from the funeral of an anorexic gymnast who died at the age of twenty-two. On top of that, a recent article in *Sports Illustrated* had blasted women's gymnastics as a breeding ground for eating disorders. But Kelly has become accustomed to defending the sport, one in which she has catapulted from a federation secretary to a director in just ten years, without ever having competed in or coached gymnastics herself.

She talks enthusiastically of the federation's new health programs, of how she had recently hired a female sports psychologist and installed a hotline for the athletes and coaches to call her. She mentions the safety certification program and voluntary training courses for coaches. She describes in meticulous detail the thorough examinations the federation's battery of doctors, scientists and nutritionists put the gymnasts through during the annual national training camps.

"Our nutritionist has a machine that you can put the kids through now and it does all their bone density, their whole body," Kelly says, leaning forward, her eyes wide. "Then he asks the kids for their injury history. If they're prone to stress fractures and their bone density is low, they're missing some nutrients in their diet."

She talks about muscle mass ratios and fortified orange juice and sleeping patterns. She mentions a study by a Utah exercise physiologist on menstruation.

"We have a healthier group of kids out here now," she concludes.

The fallacy of the federation's safety and health programs is that the federation has no teeth. It can dispense the best advice in the world to the coaches and athletes, but it can't make them follow it. The federation can't ban a coach unless he has been charged with a crime. Repeated injuries to his gymnasts, abusive language, ignorance of eating disorders—none of these are grounds for expulsion from the federation. Kathy Kelly can talk informally to a coach who has aroused safety concerns. But the federation can't put limits on the hours a coach can train a girl or the number of repetitions he can demand. It can't require medical care on-site at the gyms. It can't order coaches to throw out their scales.

So where is the safety net if the coach is damaging the gymnast and the parents have neither the confidence nor the brains to stop him? "There is none," concedes education and safety director Steve Whitlock.

Yet the federation actually adds to the problems in several ways.

In recent years USA Gymnastics began awarding stipends to gymnasts based on their national rankings, which are calculated every six months. The money helps the girls offset training costs, which run into the tens of thousands every year. But by basing the stipends on competition results, the federation has unwittingly created a system whereby the girls feel enormous pressure to keep their rankings up at all costs. "Kids want to lift the financial burden from their parents, so they want to compete even if they're injured," says Nancy Marshall, the federation's vice chairwoman for women's gymnastics.

And the federation's own mandate, which is to field the best national teams it can and to develop the sport's popularity, sometimes means pushing a tired and sore Shannon Miller to appear at meets and exhibitions to ensure a decent crowd. It means angling to make sure a talented gymnast competes even if she isn't healthy, as the federation did for the 1992 Olympics when it held its makeshift "trial" after the official Olympic Trials—to allow injured Betty Okino to qualify for the team because she had a strong reputation among the international judges.

Okino wasn't the only injured Olympian. Shannon Miller had a screw in her elbow to hold down a bone chip. Kim Zmeskal, the favorite going into the competition, had a stress fracture above her ankle and a bad wrist. Michelle Campi, with a fractured hip, couldn't compete at all. Dominique Dawes hurt her back during pre-Olympic training in Europe and had to sit out for two days. And Wendy Bruce tore her thumb muscle away from the bone shortly before the Olympics and had it shot up with cortisone so she could compete.

"We are commodities," former Olympian Kelly Garrison says of the sport's hierarchy. "We make their living, really."

. . .

Gymnasts get hurt so often because the sport demands ever-increasing training hours and ever-diminishing bodies. Dr. Lyle Micheli, a pediatric orthopedist at Harvard Medical School and former president of the American College of Sports Medicine, says gymnasts who train more than sixteen hours a week are at high risk for repetitive stress fractures, most dangerously in the back. Most elite gymnasts train between thirty and forty-five hours a week, and nearly all complain of back pain. A 1990 study of Swedish male gymnasts found they had as many degenerated discs in their spines as the average sixty-five-year-old man, leading the researchers to suspect that the spinal damage had occurred during the young athletes' growth spurts. The muscles of children can develop and strengthen like those of adults, allowing them to perform difficult maneuvers, but their bones do not keep pace.

These findings are more dire when applied to female gymnasts. Unlike their male counterparts, most female gymnasts reach their peak when they are still children, so the pounding on their still-forming skeletal structures can have long-term consequences. Some permanently damage their joints and backs. Some don't grow to full height. Researchers have seen growth plates in gymnasts' arms close up early because of repeated pounding.

An elite gymnast's intense training sets off a domino effect of physical problems. Strenuous exercise coupled with poor eating habits delays the onset of puberty for years. A 1992 Oregon State University study of college gymnasts found they began menstruating significantly later than the general population—at sixteen compared with thirteen. The gymnasts reached puberty two years later than even competitive runners. A 1994 study at the University of Utah by former gymnast Michelle Elbogen compared the onset of menstruation between elite gymnasts and their mothers and sisters to see if there was a genetic explanation rather than an athletic one. She found no family link: on average the mothers reached puberty at age 12.9, the sisters at 13.4 and the gymnasts at 15.5. Many gymnasts don't start menstruating until they retire from the sport. Olympian Kathy Johnson, for example, began menstruating only when she quit gymnastics at age twenty-five.

This can have a profound effect on a girl's skeletal development: between 48 and 70 percent of bone mass and 15 percent of height are achieved during adolescent years. If a girl isn't menstruating, she isn't producing estrogen. If she isn't producing estrogen, her bones cannot develop properly. The problem is widespread. As many as 66 percent of all female college athletes have irregular or nonexistent menstrual periods, a condition called amenorrhea. It is so prevalent among elite athletes that when California endocrinologist Robert Marcus began his 1984 study comparing the bone densities of amenorrheic and normally menstruating athletes on the Stanford women's track team, he had to go outside the team to find a control group. Every athlete on the team was amenorrheic.

The consequences are serious.

Four separate studies over the last ten years have concluded that girls and women who lose menstrual function lose bone density— about 5 percent a year, a rate similar to that of postmenopausal women. Athletes in their twenties have been found with bone densities of fifty-year-old women. In a 1984 study by Seattle research physiologist Barbara Drinkwater, a twenty-one-year-old ballet dancer who had been amenorrheic for six years had the spinal bone density of a ninety-year-old woman. Amenorrheic athletes thus are more susceptible to stress fractures, premature osteoporosis and curvature of the spine.

This accounts, at least in part, for the high rate of injury among female gymnasts. A 1992 study by the National Collegiate Athletic Association found that they sustained more injuries in training than any college athletes except spring football players. Male gymnasts ranked eighth. Autumn football players—who have shaped up since spring—ranked tenth.

Because studies of young female athletes began only in recent years, researchers can only guess at the long-term impact of such intensive training. But based on his study of the Stanford team, Robert Marcus predicted a two- to threefold increase in osteo-porosis for amenorrheic athletes. Doctors used to think athletes could regain the bone mass once they retired and resumed normal menstruation. But a 1986 study of ballet dancers by Drinkwater showed that bone density remained well below average for their age group four years after they began menstruating again. "We may have found only the tip of the iceberg," Marcus says.

Part of the problem in gymnastics, of course, is simply that the sport grows riskier and more demanding each year. "It scares the hell out of me what kind of skills these girls are doing," says Jack Rockwell, the longtime trainer. "I've talked to coaches and offi-cials and they say we're not surpassing the physical capability of the body, but my God, they've got to be awful close."

Ten years ago routines on the uneven bars included just one release—an athlete leaving the apparatus to perform a move, then regrasping it. Today gymnasts perform two or three releases in a single routine. Similarly, a spectacular dismount from the bars used to be a double tuck—two airborne somersaults. Now dou-ble tucks are not considered especially daring, and the gymnasts have had to find new tricks to impress the judges. Thus, dismounts today are mind-boggling blurs of intricate twisting and flipping.

When Olga Korbut performed a back flip—one full rotation in the air without using her arms—on the balance beam in the 1972 Olympics, the move was so revolutionary it wasn't included in the International Gymnastics Federation's code of points. Today gym-nasts perform three back flips in a row on the beam.

Dr. Aurelia Nattiv, the team physician for Pepperdine Uni-versity and a leading researcher on bone density and menstrual patterns among gymnasts, argues that if the way gymnastics is judged were to change, injuries would drop. Nattiv would like to see dismounts, responsible for so many injuries, eliminated or at least downgraded. "Certain things are clear about gymnastics: We know dismounts lead to injuries. We know that is a significant part of the judging. And yet nothing's been done about it yet." Most in gymnastics consider Nattiv's proposal absurd. Dismounts are the exclamation points to performances. And, these boosters say, the gymnasts enjoy doing them.

But more than that, dismounts are here to stay because they are spectacular. They encapsulate part of the sport's appeal—the idea of pushing the human body past its limits, of watching the human form distilled to its essence, lean and muscled, powerful and graceful, beautifully proportioned. Yet gymnastics, particularly the soaring, twisting dismounts, also attracts us for less aesthetic reasons, the same reasons we thrill to the circus performer lunging for the swinging trapeze—the wonderful and terrible possibilities of each death-defying moment.

■ ■ ■

Julissa read *Catcher in the Rye* on the plane to Tokyo. She and the U.S. team arrived on Monday, four days before the competition. This meet was important to Julissa. She wanted to show Al Fong she was as good as Christy Henrich. Then, she thought, he would pay as much attention to her as he did to Christy.

Sunya Knapp, a teammate, noticed during training on Tuesday that Julissa was struggling with her Yurchenko vault. She was rebounding too high off the springboard, barely brushing her fingertips on the horse. Fong had been working with Julissa on her vault since she arrived at his gym three months earlier. He had noticed her tendency to "jump" onto her hands as she launched into her roundoff onto the springboard. He reminded her to keep one foot in contact with the floor before touching her hands down. The foot acted like a rudder, controlling the direction of her body. She needed to launch her body into the air at such an angle that she would land upright on the springboard with her feet together and her back parallel to the horse. Never, Fong later claimed, had Julissa missed her feet off the back of the springboard, though she had come close. Fong had seen Karen Tierney do it once, and she managed to slide across the horse, flip over and land on her feet. At the World Championships one year, Fong saw a Soviet gymnast miss her feet and hit the horse so hard with her upper back that she moved the horse, despite chains lashing it to the floor.

While he worked with her in Japan, Fong was not alarmed by Julissa's trouble with the vault. It wasn't unusual for a gymnast to take time adjusting to a new environment and foreign equipment. And on the first day of competition, Fong's instincts proved right. Julissa finished higher in the vault than any other American and qualified for the individual finals the next day.

She called her mother about midnight Houston time with the good news. She said she would call again the following day.

That night Julissa couldn't get Elena Moukina out of her head. She had begun thinking about her when someone had pointed across the floor of the Tokyo arena to the Soviet coach. "Do you know who that is? Elena Moukina's old coach." Elegant and powerful, Moukina had been world champion when Julissa started in gymnastics and immediately became her favorite gymnast. Julissa mentioned Elena at dinner later that night, then again back at the hotel, where she and Sunya stayed up talking in Sunya's room. Julissa told Sunya all about Moukina, how at the age of twenty she landed on her head during a tumbling trick and became paralyzed from her neck down. "I can't believe that was her coach," Julissa said.

At ten-thirty Julissa returned to her own room but soon called Sunya. "Can I sleep in your room tonight?" Julissa asked. "I don't want to be by myself." As Julissa slid in next to Sunya, she mentioned Elena yet again. "It's such a shame what happened to her."

The next morning, on the second day of competition at the World Sports Fair, Julissa lined up at the vault for the individual finals. When it was her turn to take a second practice vault, she stood straight and still, as if rooted, staring at the horse at the end of the runway. Her face darkened with concentration, her chin tilted forward. The muscles in her legs looked like ropes. Across the chest of her red leotard, she wore the three letters she hoped to wear in the Olympics four months later: USA. A red bow gathered her curly hair in a bun.

Behind her, gymnasts flipped through the air and landed with thuds as they practiced their floor routines. Coaches delivered last-minute rebukes and encouragements. Julissa stood transfixed as if in a glass box, sealed off from the hum of the arena. Her gaze traveled 82 feet down the long strip of green carpeting, past the springboard, to the vaulting horse. Was she beating back thoughts of Elena Moukina? Did she have doubts about the vault? And if she did, how could she tell her coach? She wanted to prove she was Olympic material—tough, unflappable, fearless. Despite Julissa's chronic troubles with the vault, Fong watched her from yards away rather than right next to the horse, where he might have given her the security of knowing that if anything went wrong, he could catch her.

With a deep breath Julissa took off. She ran, legs and arms pumping. She whipped into a roundoff in front of the springboard. When she popped upright out of her roundoff with her back to the horse, she was slightly out of control, so slightly that the untrained eye wouldn't have noticed. Her left foot landed on the springboard, but her right foot slipped off the back and plunged to the floor. Her body jerked as if she had stepped off a curb unexpectedly.

Every instinct told her not to pull out of the trick. Keep going, her coaches always told her, because she could hurt herself worse by balking. So she arched her back as if doing a backward dive, with her neck stretched and her head upside down. But she had no lift. Her head didn't clear the top of the horse. She crashed full speed, forehead first, into the side of the horse. Her neck snapped. The force of the vault carried her body over the horse. She flopped to the mat like a shot bird.

People began shouting and running as Fong stood rooted, stunned. A trainer performed mouth-to-mouth resuscitation. Julissa slipped in and out of consciousness on the way to the hospital. She didn't feel pain until doctors snaked a tube down her throat for the respirator. She couldn't talk. She couldn't understand what people were saying around her. They kept draping more wires and tubes on her and she didn't know what they were for. She couldn't remember what had brought her to this white bed, her body laid out as if in a coffin, her head in a steel grip. Elena Moukina could have told her. Like Julissa, Moukina had allowed her body to be transformed into a machine that acknowledged neither fear nor pain, a machine that didn't know any better than to keep working until it broke.

■ ■ ■

Julissa was conscious and alert when the Gomezes arrived in Japan. The first thing Otilia did was devise a way for Julissa to communicate beyond blinking once for "yes" and twice for "no." Otilia bought letters and a board. She arranged the letters in rows. When Julissa wanted to say something, Otilia pointed to a row until Julissa blinked "yes," then Otilia would point to each letter in the row until Julissa blinked "yes" again. Julissa would spell out every word this way. She never brought up the accident or the injury, though Otilia suspected she knew what they knew: a Houston doctor who flew to Tokyo within a day of the accident had told the Gomezes he was 99 percent certain her paralysis from the neck down was permanent.

A week passed as the Gomezes waited for word from the Japanese doctor that Julissa was stable enough to be flown back to the States. She had had a tracheotomy, and every day she was breathing more on her own. Upon receiving the doctor's approval late the second week, the Gomezes went directly to the U.S. Embassy to arrange the final details for using the American military's medical transport plane. When they arrived at the hospital in the early afternoon, their spirits were high. Finally they could give Julissa some good news. They were going home. Their translator, who had gotten to know the family well, brought Julissa a going-away gift: a pearl choker to hide the scar from the tracheotomy. The three waited in the hospital lobby to be called into intensive care.

They waited. And waited. Finally the receptionist summoned them.

The doctor spoke in Japanese, but Otilia and Ramiro knew what he was saying. They saw him mimic the motion of the tracheal tube coming out. During the night Julissa had become disconnected from her oxygen supply. She was in a coma.

When Otilia and Ramiro went in to see her, Julissa's eyelids were fluttering and her mouth was twitching. She had wires taped to her skull. The two Houston doctors who had flown to Tokyo to accompany Julissa home arrived not knowing what had happened. They examined her and delivered the grim news: Julissa had considerable brain damage. She was having seizures, and each seizure was killing more brain cells. Even if she came out of the coma, she would spend the rest of her life in a vegetative state.

The Gomezes flew home that night on the military plane, their daughter strapped to a stretcher behind them, tubes and wires forming a grotesque web around her.

Otilia never returned to her old apartment. She had all her furniture put into storage. While Julissa was in intensive care at Methodist Hospital in downtown Houston, the family stayed with Otilia's sister, then in the Ronald McDonald House, for families of hospitalized children, then in a rented house near the hospital. Otilia was in her own kind of coma. She wasn't accepting calls. She refused to let people visit.

"I think I was trying to take myself to a place that wasn't real, where I didn't really have to accept what happened," Otilia recalls. "In Japan it wasn't real because it was a place we had never been. A language we didn't understand. It was so strange that it didn't seem real. It was like living a nightmare. Coming home, if I had gone back to the apartment, and back to the people I knew, then it would have to be real."

In September, four months after the accident, doctors told the Gomezes there was nothing more they could do. They said Julissa could live five years or fifty years and recommended placing her in a long-term-care facility. The Gomezes decided to care for her at home and spent three months at the Institute for Rehabilitation and Research learning how. They learned how to work the ventilator, suction fluids from the trachea, inject Julissa's food from a large syringe into her feeding tube every three hours, use the catheter and change her diapers, clean the tubing connected to the equipment, bathe her, change her sheets. Otilia and Ramiro moved their daughter into the master bedroom of their house, the only room large enough to accommodate her machines.

For the first year, the Gomezes had round-the-clock nurses to help them. But the second year, the school district in which Otilia worked changed to an insurance company that did not cover at-home nurses. The USGF's insurance would pay nurses for only forty hours a week. So Otilia and Ramiro began a grueling schedule to care for their daughter. A nurse worked from 7 A.M. to 3 P.M., when Ramiro returned home from the restaurant. When Otilia got home from school at 6 P.M., she went to bed and slept until midnight. Then she took over and Ramiro slept until seven, when the nurse arrived again and the Gomezes left for work. They shared duty on the weekends, and Kristy eventually learned how to wash the tubing, sterilize the syringes and monitor the machines, though she would sometimes go weeks without stepping inside her sister's room. She told few friends at her new school about Julissa and rarely invited them to her house, which softly echoed with the rhythmic whirr of the ventilator.

Julissa was no longer in a coma and so would open her eyes, wince as if in pain and even cry at times. But she usually slept or stared into space. She doubled her weight to 140 pounds, making her virtually unrecognizable as the Julissa they once knew.

In August 1991, three years after going home, Julissa contracted an infection and had to be rushed to the hospital. A doctor encouraged the Gomezes to let the illness take its course, but they insisted he treat the infection so they could take her home again. But as her condition worsened and she needed to be hooked up to yet another machine to clear her lungs, Otilia and Ramiro decided to let Julissa go. She had been through enough. For three days they stayed at her bedside. When the doctor told them it was time, Otilia took Julissa in her arms, something she hadn't done in three years because of the ventilator tubes. She felt her daughter's last faint breath on her cheek.

. . .

The USGF barely mentioned Julissa's accident and death in its official magazine. There was no tribute at any gymnastics meet. It was as if her years of training and competing had been wiped away like chalk on a blackboard. "It was the Olympic year and that was what was important," says Libby Wells, mother of one of Fong's other gymnasts. "Nothing was said about her at all. Nothing."

But the accident had sent shivers through every gym in America. No young gymnast could say she didn't think about Julissa as she stood at the end of the runway facing the vault. Some spent months tortured by fear. But, as always, the fears went unspoken. For some, Julissa's accident would change forever the way they looked at gymnastics. But for most, the fear eventually disappeared, muscled out by ambition and a powerful drive to please.

Inside a bedroom in Independence, Missouri, a thousand miles from Julissa's grave, Christy Henrich hung a picture of her good friend. Christy knew what had killed Julissa, but she never made the connection to herself. Gymnastics could never break Christy's body. She was too tough.

So it went after her soul.

2

THEY STOLE HER SOUL
AND THEY STILL HAVE IT

EATING DISORDERS

∎

Fifteen-year-old Christy Henrich could think of little except her weight on the long flight from her gymnastics meet in Budapest. When she spotted her mother waving by the boarding gate at the Kansas City airport, she didn't say hello.

"I've got to lose weight," she announced.

Sandy Henrich looked at her daughter. Christy weighed 90 pounds and stood 4 feet 11 inches. Lose weight?

"A judge told me I'd never make the Olympic team if I don't lose weight," Christy explained.

Sandy rolled her eyes. "You have got to be kidding," she said. "You're fine."

Christy had never mentioned weight before. But now she held on to the judge's words like a key that would unlock a magic door. *Lose weight and make the Olympics.*

That night Christy virtually stopped eating.

Christy didn't know how to do anything halfway. Once she wrapped her mind around a notion, it was there to stay. She began gymnastics before kindergarten and by the time she was seven, her coach, Al Fong, had her training four to five hours a day, four days a week. Her drive and courage were a marvel in one so young, earning her the nickname ET, for Extra Tough. "What she lacked in talent she was able to gain just from sheer work ethic," Fong recalls. "She was her own worst enemy. If anything, I was constantly pulling on the reins to keep her from hurting herself. She had blinders on. She knew exactly what she wanted and she was going to get there no matter what. But she crossed the line. And that's a touchy one. Who can prevent a person from crossing the line?"

Christy made the junior national team in her first try at age twelve. By thirteen she was rising at 5 A.M. to reach the gym by 6, training until 9, going to school until 2 P.M., then returning to the gym from 2:30 to 9—more than nine hours of training a day. Sometimes she returned home so tired she could barely drag herself up the stairs to her bedroom. Her hands bled from the uneven bars. Her legs throbbed. With both ankles soaking in ice buckets and her wrists wrapped in Ace bandages, she sat at her desk and studied until midnight. She was also a straight-A student. She was either in school or at the gym all day, so no one noticed she was eating just an apple, sometimes just a slice of apple, each day.

Sandy Henrich's stomach sometimes tightened as she watched her daughter. Sandy and Paul Henrich were not people who dreamed big dreams. Paul operated a Phillips 66 filling station for fifteen years before working as a mechanic at Barr's Auto Service near their home in Independence, Missouri, a suburb of Kansas City. Sandy is a nurse's aide for St. Mary's Hospital in nearby Blue Springs. Their daughter's ambition awed them. Though Sandy worried that Christy pushed herself too hard, she knew gymnastics meant everything to her—the vanity plates on Christy's bright red Toyota read GMNAST—so Sandy let her go on.

As a junior at Fort Osage High School, Christy began dating Bo Moreno, a wrestler on the high school team. Soon they talked about getting married. Christy had mapped out her life as if it were a floor routine. After she married Bo, they would move to Florida and she would work as a nurse until their son and daughter were born. She and Bo had even picked out the children's names: Jesse Joseph and Maya Maria. But all that would come later, after she competed in Barcelona at the 1992 Olympics. Every day brought her closer to Barcelona and closer to the perfect gymnast's body. In her mind the two goals were flip sides of the same shining medal. She once asked Moreno how wrestlers lost weight, and he told her about taking Ex-Lax, running in a steaming shower, wearing plastic while working out. Bo didn't know that Christy tried all three.

If Christy was unhappy, she kept it to herself. She learned, as elite gymnasts do, to seal her emotions in little boxes and store them somewhere dark and deep. The coaches could scream, throw tantrums, stamp in frustration, but the girls had to hold their tongues. To her acquaintances, Christy seemed a happy, energetic girl whose muscular, compact body looked more like a soccer player's than a gymnast's. But inside, Christy churned with feelings of failure. Al Fong, like most gymnastics coaches, dwelled on mistakes, relentlessly demanding the sport's elusive ideal: perfection. No matter how well Christy performed, she could have been higher on her dismount or steadier on her landing. She was always slow to pick up new skills—a sort of physical dyslexia, as Fong put it. If he said right, she'd go left.

"What I do feel guilty about is not recognizing that Christy was a child growing up in a world where she was always told, 'You're never going to be good enough,'" Sandy Henrich says.

"He was absolutely insane," recalls athletic trainer Jack Rockwell, who watched Fong push Christy through one routine after another during training for a meet in China, even though Christy was hobbled by an ankle injury. "Christy idolized Al. He's not a bad person, he just had a bad attitude. She'd do anything for him. She was the girl who was going to take him to the top."

Christy knew she shouldered not only her own expectations but those of her coach. Plus, after Julissa Gomez broke her neck three months before the 1988 U.S. Olympic Trials, all of Fong's hopes fell on Christy. She was his ticket to the Summer Games. When in early 1988 she finished tenth in the all-around competition at the U.S. Gymnastics Championships, her hopes of making the Olympic team soared. But at the Trials, recovering from both mononucleosis and a fractured vertebra in her neck, she missed making the team by 0.118 of a point. When the final standings flashed on the board inside the arena, Sandy Henrich watched her daughter's face. "Totally devastated," she recalls. "It was like her whole world was crushed. Like everything had ended."

Christy returned to the gym in Blue Springs, determined to push herself harder, her eyes fixed on the 1992 Summer Games. When a year later a judge told her to lose weight, a light went on in her head. The words resounded as if from a loudspeaker, drowning out reason, drowning out her mother's worried questions. *Lose weight and make the Olympics.* Every day when Christy looked in the mirror, she saw a loser. A fat loser. The medals hanging from the walls of her home, the newspaper clippings, the national rankings, the fourth-place finish at the 1989 World Championships—they were no match for her own certainty that she was a failure. She carried the failure in the curve of her thighs, the soft skin under her chin, anywhere she couldn't see bone.

"I remember a top American official saying to Mary Lou Retton a year after the [1984] Olympics, 'You know, if I could, I'd take half a point off just because of that fat hanging off your butt,' " Jack Rockwell recalls. "Mary Lou laughed it off. Unfortunately, Christy couldn't. She got all screwed up. It's just a tragedy."

Food became the enemy. When forced to eat, she threw up afterward. At training camps for the national team, the coaches measured her body fat and recorded her weight. They told her what to say and what not to say in interviews. She learned to shut down her brain and her body. She taught herself to feel no pain. She trained with a broken vertebra in her neck, ripping off the neck brace her doctor had told her to wear. She never felt hunger pangs. "I numbed myself," Christy later explained. "That's why the eating disorder got so bad. I didn't feel any pain."

Christy was a prime candidate for anorexia—self-imposed starvation—and bulimia, the potentially fatal cycle of bingeing and purging. Anorexics and bulimics usually are adolescent girls who tend to be perfectionists, who conform and please, who gauge their worth on other people's judgments. They also are girls who have been belittled and humiliated, who believe they are as worthless as the authority figures in their lives say they are. Gymnasts, in general, fit the bill. The girls make few decisions on their own, transforming themselves into whatever their coaches, parents and judges want them to be. *Put your hair in a bow. Don't talk back. Forget the pain. Lose weight. Be tough. Be quiet. Smile pretty.*

"Eating disorders are not just about weight but about self-esteem," Sandy Henrich says. She has read the books, talked to the psychologists, listened to her daughter. She has learned about eating disorders the way a soldier learns about war, reluctantly and too well. "These girls never feel they measure up."

Christy's weight dropped to 85 pounds. Then to 80. Her coach had been telling her to suck in her gut. According to Christy, he once remarked that she looked like the Pillsbury Doughboy, and frequently reminded her how wonderfully thin the Russian gymnasts were. Then when Christy began losing weight, he told her she looked great, reinforcing her obsession with being thin.

Fong's memories are different. He insists he never talked about weight. "No, no, no, no!" he says. "I don't know where this is coming from."

Other girls at his gym, however, say that he did. And if he never talked about weight, he must have been the only elite gymnastics coach in America who didn't. Nearly every coach weighs his or her athletes, preaching to them the religion of weight. During one international meet, then national coach Don Peters told trainer Jack Rockwell to weigh in the gymnasts every day to discourage them from eating too much. One day the West German team asked Rockwell if he could weigh them in too. They feared their own coach and didn't want to hear his tirades if they were overweight. Rockwell agreed. A few minutes later Rockwell heard the American gymnasts gasp. The entire West German team was walking toward him stark naked. They weren't taking any chances that the weight of their clothes would put them over their limit.

As Christy's weight dropped, her strength waned. When she

fell on her head twice at the 1989 World Championships Trials, a United States Gymnastics Federation official confronted Fong about training the girl too hard. But Fong dismissed her concerns, later blaming the falls on Christy's infuriating inconsistency—"I could never count on her, never"—and her weakened body. After the trials, Fong says, he confronted Christy about his suspicions of an eating disorder and says he called the USGF to get help. But he claims that Christy resisted help from a nutritionist and psychologist and that her parents denied there was a problem.

By the fall of 1990, Christy was so weak that she was pulled from the USA-USSR Challenge meet in Oregon. According to Fong, he became so alarmed about her deterioration that he finally kicked her out of the gym and told her not to return until she gained weight. Again, Christy had different memories: Fong simply gave up on her. "It got to the point where I was so weak he didn't want to fool with me anymore," Christy recalled four years later, anger spiking her weak voice. "He could care less about me. He's just worried about his reputation. That's how he is."

Fong claims he had no clue about the Henrichs' bitterness until he read a deposition they had given to the lawyers suing him on behalf of Julissa Gomez's parents. "A sizzling deposition that just nailed me," Fong remembers. "They were saying I called her a fat kid when she was little and things like this, that I worked her too hard. I was sitting there and my mouth was open. I couldn't believe it." Memories of the deposition stuck with him as Christy's condition worsened. "I think if Christy should ever die," he said in June 1994, "and I think she will some day, early, before her time, I think they'll prepare a lawsuit against me...They don't have much evidence, but they're simple enough to try to imagine they do."

Christy knew her dreams of the Olympics were disappearing along with her body. But she couldn't stop herself. Her mind had latched on to some perverse logic. She was simply demanding of herself what her sport had always demanded of her: perfection. A perfect body, a body with no disfiguring fat, a body lighter than those of the Russians, lighter than air.

In early 1991, about eighteen months before her second shot at the Olympics, Christy announced her retirement from the sport. She could no longer push herself through a routine, but she denied she was leaving because of her physical condition. She still wouldn't admit to a problem. "I thought, 'What the hell am I doing? Why should I let them control the way I wear my hair, what colors I wear on my leotard, what patterns I wear. Why am I letting them control my life?'" Christy said in explaining her retirement. "I couldn't take it anymore."

She was eighteen years old and weighed less than 80 pounds. The worst was yet to come.

■ ■ ■

When Christy retired, many suspected an eating disorder, but they whispered the words. "There's a paranoia," said one USGF official. "The USGF doesn't want to be connected with the problem." Even Christy and her parents would not publicly acknowledge the depths of the problem until 1993. Only in recent years—nearly a decade after 1972 Olympian Cathy Rigby was hospitalized twice during a twelve-year bout with bulimia—has the gymnastics federation stopped pretending that eating disorders don't exist. The federation has organized seminars for coaches; printed articles in its two official magazines; created an advisory board to address the issue; made plans to produce a video of testimonials from gymnasts who have survived eating disorders; and offered psychiatric counseling to any senior or junior national team member who wants it.

Yet despite their efforts to combat the problem, gymnastics officials still bristle at the mention of it. The sport—how it is judged and how it is taught—does not cause eating disorders, they continue to insist. They point instead to parents, a few uneducated coaches and, more than anything, the mass media's glorification of thinness. "It's a female thing. If it was just an athlete issue, then it would just be athletes that suffer from it," says Kathy Kelly of USA Gymnastics. "I said to one reporter, 'Do you know any woman under thirty-five who likes her body?' She said, 'I don't know any woman *over* thirty-five'...I know kids that are fourteen, little girls that aren't athletes who are on diet pills, taking Ultra Slim-Fast, force-vomiting, so that they can be appealing to some boy."

Yet the incidence of eating disorders is disproportionately high among gymnasts, even when they are compared to other young female athletes. "I don't know about that," Kelly says when this is pointed out to her. "I haven't looked."

The research is there, and its conclusions are clear. In a 1992 University of Washington study of 182 female college athletes, 32 percent practiced at least one form of disordered eating (vomiting or the use of laxatives, diuretics or diet pills). Among college gymnasts the percentage nearly doubled—to 62 percent. By contrast, 18 percent of the general female population suffer from eating disorders. And in a 1992 survey by the NCAA, 51 percent of college gymnastics programs reported eating disorders among team members, higher than in any other sport. Both the NCAA and the United States Olympic Committee were concerned enough with the problem to begin distributing posters, literature and videos to their athletes and coaches five years ago.

USA Gymnastics officials are correct in claiming that the sport, by itself, does not cause eating disorders. Anorexia and bulimia are not diseases whose source can be excised and examined under

lissa Gomez was sixteen when she broke her neck on a vault. She died three
ars later. (Nancy Raymond/*International Gymnast*)

above: Brandy Johnson says the United States Gymnastics Federation pressured her to compete in the 1989 World Gymnastics Championships despite a fractured bone in her foot. (© Steve Lange 1995)

above right: Karen Tierney cracked vertebrae in her neck on the same vault that paralyzed Julissa Gomez. (© Steve Lange 1995)

right: Betty Okino competed in the 1992 Olympics with stress fractures in her back and elbow and a screw clamping the tendon to her shin. (© Steve Lange 1995)

above: Christy Henrich missed making the 1988 Olympic team by .118 of a point. (AP/Wide World Photos)

above right: American Olympian Cathy Rigby was hospitalized twice during a twelve-year battle with bulimia. (AP/Wide World Photos)

right: In 1993, a year before her death, an anorexic Christy Henrich weighed less than 70 pounds when she joined her boyfriend at a lunch to raise money for her medical expenses. (AP/Wide World Photos)

right: When 85-pound Olga Korbut captivated the 1972 Olympic audience, she transformed gymnastics from a women's to a girls' sport. (From the historic archives of the International Gymnastics Hall of Fame & Museum)

below: Four years after Olga Korbut's triumph, fourteen-year-old Nadia Comaneci sealed the sport's trend toward young, tiny and light bodies. (From the historic archives of the International Gymnastics Hall of Fame & Museum)

above: The 1976 U.S. Olympic gymnasts were on average seventeen and a half years old, stood 5 feet 3½ inches and weighed 106 pounds. (AP/Wide World Photos)

below: By 1992 the average U.S. Olympic gymnast was 16 years old, stood 4 feet 9 inches and weighed 83 pounds. (AP/Wide World Photos)

above left: By age ten Erica Stokes had already moved away from home to train for the Olympics with Béla Károlyi in Houston. (Courtesy of Erica Stokes)

above right: Battling bulimia, Erica Stokes quit gymnastics at age sixteen, nine months before the 1992 Olympics. (© Steve Lange 1995)

right: Kathy Johnson starved to keep her twenty-four-year-old body looking like a fourteen-year-old's in order to make the 1984 Olympic team. (©1994 Dave Black)

above left: Two years after *Sports Illustrated* touted her as America's best bet for the 1988 Olympics, a burned-out Kristie Phillips failed to make the Olympic team. (SI/Time Inc.)

above right: Terri Phillips moved her daughter, Kristie, to four gyms within five years in pursuit of their Olympic dream. (SI/Time-Life)

left: With one bobble on the balance beam, world champion Kim Zmeskal's hopes for a gold medal in the 1992 Olympics were gone. (AP/Wide World Photos)

above left: Thirteen-year-old Michelle Kwan, the silver medalist at the 1994 U.S. Figure Skating Championships, signaled skating's transformation into a children's sport. (©1994 Dave Black)

above center: The grace and femininity of 1968 Olympic gold medalist Peggy Fleming defined the image of the Ice Princess. (SI/John G. Zimmerman)

above right: After winning the World Figure Skating Championships in 1981 at age fifteen, Elaine Zayak battled her weight, her parents and her coaches and never won another major tiile. (AP/Wide World Photos)

left: Olympic gold medalist Oksana Baiul, flanked by silver medalist Nancy Kerrigan and bronze medalist Chen Lu, embodied the characteristics of the 1994 Ice Princess: light, young and pretty. (AP/Wide World Photos)

far left: Tonya Harding and Nancy Kerrigan posed side by side with the 1994 U.S. Olympic team just days after the attack on Kerrigan. (AP/Wide World Photos)

below: The tense showdown between Tonya Harding and Nancy Kerrigan at the 1994 Olympics drew television ratings that rivaled the final episodes of "M*A*S*H" and of the *Roots* miniseries. (AP/Wide World Photos)

above: When Kristi Yamaguchi won the 1992 Olympic gold medal, agents said the title was worth about $10 million in endorsements and appearances. (*San Francisco Chronicle*)

above right: Kristi Yamaguchi, Nancy Kerrigan and Oksana Baiul helped CBS cash in on skating's booming popularity by announcing their participation in a made-for-TV competition called "Ice Wars" in the fall of 1994. (Stephanie Berger, © 1994)

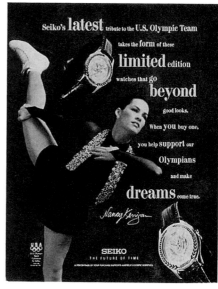

above: Nancy Kerrigan's carefully packaged princess image made her one of the most marketable female athletes in the country. (Courtesy of ProServ)

below: A year after the 1991 World Figure Skating Championships, where Americans Tonya Harding, Kristi Yamaguchi, and Nancy Kerrigan swept the medals, Kerrigan improved her marketability by having her teeth capped. (SI/Heinz Kluetmeer)

right: Bill Bragg turned guardianship of his seven-year-old daughter, Holly, over to her skating coach because he felt skating could give her a better life than he could. (Courtesy of Tracy Prussack)

below: Competing against each other strained the relationship between twin skaters Amy and Karen Grossman, whose parents had become consumed with winning. (Courtesy of Wendie Grossman)

above: By the time Amy Jackson was six years old, her father, Bill, was convinced she would compete in the Olympics and moved her around the country to find the right coaching. (Courtesy of Amy Jackson)

right: Amy Jackson overdosed on aspirin as a high school senior and needed a pass from a psychiatric hospital to attend graduation. (Courtesy of Amy Jackson)

above: Chelle Stack still doesn't talk about the 1988 Olympics, where she fell during her uneven bar routine, prompting her mother's tearful lament, "We went through everything and this was it?" (© Steve Lange 1995)

left: U.S. champion Debi Thomas called her 1988 Olympics experience, in which she won the bronze medal, "like one of the tortures in Dante's Inferno." (© 1994 Dave Black)

above: Laying the political groundwork for the 1996 Olympics, Steve Nunno touted twelve-year-old Jennie Thompson as Shannon Miller and Kim Zmeskal wrapped up into one; she later left to train with Béla Károlyi. (© Steve Lange 1995)

above right: Kim Kelly had called her mother to tell her she had made the 1992 Olympic team, only to discover hours later that U.S. coaches had voted her off the team. (Courtesy of Stephanie Kelly)

right: Steve Nunno considered Shannon Miller's victories his own. He saw his gymnasts as empty vessels to fill with his expertise and energy. (AP/ Wide World Photos)

above left: Béla Károlyi's former assistant Rick Newman said he had no idea he might be damaging his young pupils by calling them idiots and imbeciles. (Nancy Raymond/ *International Gymnast*)

above right: When Olympian Michelle Campi sustained her third significant injury under Rick Newman's coaching, Newman was fired from Geza Pozsar's gym. (© Steve Lange 1995)

above: Béla and Márta Károlyi changed American gymnastics forever when they imported their controversial training methods from Romania, producing the first American to win an Olympic all-around gold medal and the first to win the World Championships. (© Steve Lange 1995)

above right: Mary Lou Retton's gold medal in the 1984 Olympics solidified Béla Károlyi's reputation and seemed to validate his abusive coaching methods. (© 1994 Dave Black)

above: With the 1996 Olympics looming, Béla Károlyi emerged from retirement and into the spotlight once again to coach veterans Kim Zmeskal and Svetlana Boginskaya and rising stars Dominique Moceanu and Jennie Thompson. (NYT Pictures)

right: Skating's newest phenom, Tara Lipinski, moved away from home with her mother to train and won the 1994 U.S. Olympic Festival three weeks after her twelfth birthday. (NYT Pictures)

a microscope. But when one combines the high-achiever personality type of the elite gymnast, the abusive methods of coaches, the unforgiving aesthetic standards of judges and the spoken or unspoken pressure from parents, the sport is a petri dish of disaster. "It's like a germ," according to Nancy Marshall, 1972 Olympian and the federation's vice chair for women's gymnastics, who battled an eating disorder as a gymnast. "If you put the germ in a certain culture, it's going to grow. If you have trusting parents, an ambitious coach and a gymnast like Christy, who is a textbook perfectionist, highly intense, driven—you have a time bomb."

Women's gymnastics, more than figure skating, more than any other sport except perhaps horse racing, demands that its best athletes be not only small but unnaturally small. At the 1992 Olympics in Barcelona, Russian gymnast Svetlana Boginskaya was nineteen years old, stood 5 feet 4 inches and weighed 95 pounds. She had won two golds, a silver and a bronze four years earlier, but now she was too tall and womanly. Her grace couldn't make up for her inability to explode as high or flip as fast as her 4-foot-6-inch, 70-pound competitors—for whom the balance beam seemed as wide as a sidewalk. She finished fifth in the quest for the all-around gold. "Four years have passed," she said afterward, shrugging. "The smaller girls, the younger ones, they can do more complicated elements."

In 1956 the top two Olympic female gymnasts were thirty-five and twenty-one years old. In 1968 gold medalist Vera Caslavska of Czechoslovakia was twenty-six years old, stood 5 feet 3 inches and weighed 121 pounds. Back then, gymnastics was truly a woman's sport. It was transformed in 1972 when Olga Korbut—seventeen years old, 4 feet 11 inches, 85 pounds—enchanted the world with her pigtails and rubber-band body. Four years later fourteen-year-old Nadia Comaneci clutched a baby doll after scoring the first perfect 10.0 in Olympic history. She was 5 feet tall and weighed 85 pounds.

The decline in age and size among American gymnasts since Comaneci's victory is startling. In 1976 the six U.S. Olympic gymnasts were, on average, seventeen and a half years old, stood 5 feet 3½ inches and weighed 106 pounds. By the 1992 Olympics in Barcelona, the average U.S. Olympic gymnast was sixteen years old, stood 4 feet 9 inches and weighed 83 pounds—a year younger, 6½ inches shorter and 23 pounds lighter than her counterpart of sixteen years before.

Is gymnastics simply attracting tiny girls? Or does the intensive training required of today's gymnastics stunt their growth? The answer to both questions is yes. American gyms have imported the mindset and methods of the old Eastern Bloc. Béla Károlyi used to scour the kindergarten classes of Romania in search of small, flexible girls he could mold into Olympic champions. Though American coaches don't stake out playgrounds, they pay special attention to the youngest children who walk through their doors. They assess a girl's body type when she's five or six years old. They inquire about the parents' height and body type. If a girl seems destined to be small, the coaches want her. She has a chance.

But recent research has shown that the gymnasts' tiny bodies are not entirely the work of nature. A study published in 1993 in *The Journal of Pediatrics* found that a prepubescent gymnast who trains more than eighteen hours a week and continues that level of training throughout puberty can experience such an altered growth rate that she doesn't reach full adult height. (A typical elite gymnast trains between twenty-five and forty-five hours a week.) A girl's final growth spurt generally occurs with the onset of menstruation. But intense training coupled with low food intake often delays menarche, perhaps because the body senses inadequate energy stores to support a fetus. If a girl doesn't begin menstruating until she's older, her final growth spurt may never occur, or it may occur to a lesser degree. Olympic medalist Kathy Johnson, who didn't begin menstruating until she retired at age twenty-five, grew an inch when she was twenty-eight.

An elite female gymnast's career is a race against time and nature. The window of opportunity is so narrow: from about thirteen to the onset of puberty. Then the window slams shut. Not so for men. On the 1994 U.S. national team, for example, the oldest female gymnast was still two years younger than the youngest male gymnast. And at a prestigious international competition called the American Cup, held in 1994 in Orlando, Florida, the youngest male competitor was eighteen; the youngest female, twelve. Only one female competitor was older than seventeen.

Because a female gymnast's career is so short, the year she is born has as much bearing on her success as talent. Kristie Phillips, primed to be the next Mary Lou Retton, peaked a year too early. By the time of the 1988 Olympics her body had changed and she was finished. She didn't even make the team. Even 1991 world champion Kim Zmeskal was a year off for the Olympics. At the 1992 Summer Games she wasn't the gymnast of the year before.

Since 1968 no female gymnast has won all-around gold medals in successive Olympics. Few have won back-to-back World Gymnastics Championships. Shannon Miller did it in 1993 and 1994, despite physical ailments. She is the rare gymnast who has stayed on top for more than a year.

Gymnasts, coaches and parents grab at any stick that will keep the window open. A trainer for the USGF once asked the mother of a 1992 Olympian if her seventeen-year-old daughter had begun menstruating yet. The mother said no. He suggested she take the girl to a doctor, citing the potential growth and bone-density problems. The mother shook her head. "No, we want to keep her this way so she can compete in the 1996 Olympics."

Some might argue that many sports require specific, even freakish, body types for participants to excel. One must be tall to play professional basketball, bulky to play certain positions in professional football, obese to compete in sumo wrestling, light and tiny to race horses. However, unlike athletes in those other sports, the world's best female gymnasts are children. The showdown for the gold medal at the 1992 Olympics pitted two fifteen-year-olds—both 4 feet 6 inches tall, one 70 pounds, the other 69 pounds—against each other. The sport has evolved to the point where only children can excel. The difficult tricks require a child's small, lean, limber body. One physician says today's gymnastics puts bodies under "unusual biomechanical stresses that are more designed for monkeys." There is no place anymore in elite women's gymnastics for women.

If horse racing, for example, required children as jockeys in order to survive as a sport, and if those children were training eight hours a day at the track under the supervision of screaming trainers, and if the children were already used up by the sport before they turned twenty, their malnourished bodies a mess of broken bones and torn muscles—wouldn't there be an outcry? Wouldn't somebody suggest this was a violation of child labor laws, if not outright child abuse?

But there is little outcry about gymnastics, perhaps because the sport's amateur status suggests that the athletes are competing for fun. And perhaps because the girls seem so *cute*. We want to believe they are what they seem to be, extraordinarily gifted girls who happen to be small. They spring onto our TV screens—their size makes them the perfect television athletes—free of the sticky issues of power, sexual orientation and aggression that encumber most other female athletes. Gymnasts, like figure skaters, are "acceptable" female athletes who are brave but not macho, muscled but not bulky, competitive but still vulnerable. Most parents looking for sporting role models for their daughters find few from which to choose, as there still are no successful professional baseball, softball, soccer or basketball leagues for women. Among available role models, Shannon Miller is a more comfortable choice for many parents than large and powerful women like Martina Navratilova and Jackie Joyner-Kersee, because gymnasts play into a parent's fantasy about their daughters. They are pink satin sashes and Maryjanes. Daddy's girls. In a modern sports world grappling with the changing roles of women, from the front offices to the playing fields, gymnasts are beacons of feminine simplicity and innocence.

We as a culture often look to sports for a purity we can't find elsewhere. They show us what is best in ourselves—how high we can jump, how bravely we can battle, how graciously we can face defeat. If sports are our national fairy tales, gymnasts, along with figure skaters, are the storybook princesses. So we don't look too closely. We'd rather not know the price Cinderella paid for her night at the ball.

■ ■ ■

After Christy Henrich left gymnastics, her weight continued to fall. She dropped to 75 pounds. Then 70. Then 65. Her parents were frantic. What was happening? Christy told them she was simply losing muscle because she wasn't training anymore. When her weight dropped to 60 in early 1992, her parents checked her into St. Joseph Health Center in Independence despite Christy's angry objections. She gained weight there, mostly from the fluids pumped into her, but promptly lost it again when she returned home. Her parents put her back into the hospital. She gained weight, left and lost the weight again. She checked in and out of hospitals ten times in eighteen months.

Christy was in between hospital stays during the 1992 Olympics in Barcelona—what should have been her Olympics. As she watched on television, part of her longed to be there and part of her ached for the girls who were. "I knew what they were going through," Christy said. Sandy Henrich had no mixed feelings. She felt only repulsion. She recoiled at the sight of the gymnasts' bony backs and sunken cheeks. She studied their faces. She wanted to see joy, satisfaction, any flicker of emotion that would tell her gymnastics had not stolen the souls of those girls too. She saw nothing. Gymnastics, she realized, perverted the lessons of sports. Sports should empower, yet she saw it dismantle and strip. She saw it reduce a strong young woman's self-esteem to a thin soup of inadequacy, shame and imperfection. She was afraid for the girls on her TV screen.

She wasn't alone.

The hollow-eyed look of the gymnasts in Barcelona prompted some sports columnists to denounce the sport as child abuse. Dave Anderson, the Pulitzer Prize–winning columnist for the *New York Times*, called for the sport to be banned from the Olympics. The USGF received dozens of letters from people disturbed by what they saw. But the gymnastics community has remained unfazed by the attacks.

"It's not child abuse," says 1992 Olympian Betty Okino, one of Béla Károlyi's protégées. "Because if it were child abuse, they would have to be tying us down and holding us in the gym and not letting us leave and forcing us to do gymnastics and not eat. And when we were [living] in Houston, we lived in our own homes. We could have eaten whatever we wanted, although they did weigh us in [every other day], so you had to watch what you ate."

Okino admits, however, that Béla Károlyi fed them little when they traveled to competitions. They couldn't order from room service if they were hungry, because Károlyi and his wife stayed across the hall and monitored everyone who went in and out of their gymnasts' rooms. Any time a gymnast's door would open, even if it was just to return a borrowed shirt to a teammate in the next room, Károlyi's own door would fly open.

So the gymnasts concocted complicated plots to secure food. A friend—a trainer, a sympathetic USGF employee, a male gymnast—would drop off a small bag of PowerBars, fruit, bagels and other healthful food at a prearranged spot—a hotel hallway, a stairwell. The gymnasts would hide it under their coats and stash it in their rooms. One trainer said he was so bothered by the gymnasts' diets that he took it upon himself to feed them behind Károlyi's back. He said he would get the hotel keys from the girls and, while they were at the arena competing or training, would leave food in their closets. A former employee for the USGF also admits to having fed the girls secretly, saying, "If Károlyi found out even now, he'd go ballistic."

Scoring food was like a game to the gymnasts. They would empty the hotel vending machines in clandestine raids, competing to see who could get the most. Brandy Johnson, the 1989 national champion, says her coaches used to search under the mattresses, under the beds and in the trash for signs of food. She hid it in her suitcase, where they never seemed to look. At the 1988 Olympics in Seoul, all the American athletes received official "care packages" from the States, but coaches for the female gymnasts forbid the girls' accepting them. Scott Johnson, on the U.S. men's team, stuffed food from the packages in the girls' gym bags, which the girls then smuggled into their rooms like contraband. But some gymnasts still lost weight in Seoul. Carrol Stack says her daughter Chelle dropped from 74 pounds to 66 pounds during her month there. Weak, she fell during her uneven bars routine in the competition. Károlyi called her an idiot. Chelle Stack still doesn't talk about her experience at the Olympics. When anyone asks, she says, "The shopping was good." She kept a diary while she was there but, six years later, still can't bring herself to read it.

Károlyi got manic again about his gymnasts' weight as the 1992 Olympics drew near. During a week of training in France before the Summer Games in Barcelona, Károlyi's girls ate an apple for breakfast, and for lunch, a salad and half a portion of whatever the hotel served as a main course. They were also allowed raw carrots. "We were eating very little," Okino recalls. She says Károlyi was purposely trying to get his gymnasts to lose weight before the Olympics. "We were eating much less than we normally eat. I don't think it was even a thousand calories a day."

Those thousand calories had to fuel their bodies through eight hours of training.

Okino says the starvation diet made her weary in France, but adrenaline took over once the team arrived in Barcelona. Some, however, say it was weight loss rather than a bad ankle that doomed world champion Kim Zmeskal. A favorite going into the Olympics, Zmeskal fell from the balance beam for the first time in a major competition.

In the Olympic Village, Károlyi's three gymnasts lived like soldiers in the brig. Márta Károlyi never let Okino, Zmeskal and Kerri Strug out of her sight. Márta slept in a room by the front door. No gymnast could get in or out without Márta's knowing. She accompanied them to every meal in the athletes' dining room and monitored what they ate. The Olympic Village was on the beach and teeming with athletes from all over the world. But the American gymnasts did nothing but eat their light meals, sleep, train and ride the bus to the gym. They watched the Opening Ceremonies on television. Their competition began the next day and the coaches wanted to make sure they weren't tired. "We'd count the days until it was over," Okino lamented to a reporter later.

Károlyi draws the most criticism of any gymnastics coach for mistreating his athletes. Perhaps it's because he's the most famous coach and thus the easiest target. Or perhaps it's because his track record for producing gymnasts with eating disorders is stunning. Being painfully thin at Károlyi's gym is so accepted—and the physical consequences of such thinness taken so lightly—that one reportedly anorexic gymnast, Tricia Fortsen, actually dressed up as a starving Ethiopian for Halloween one year. Nearly everyone, including Fortsen's mother, thought the get-up—a halter top, diaper, black shoe polish and a bowl of gruel—was amusing.

Another gymnast, Michelle Hilse, ended up in the emergency room with malfunctioning bowels from years of eating nothing but quick-burning carbohydrates like bread. Her obsession with weight, begun at Károlyi's, then reinforced at the University of Utah, drove her to take diuretics when she gained weight after gymnastics. "The weight issue is something I deal with every day," says Hilse, now a bank executive in North Carolina. "We've been conditioned to believe that whatever type of person I am depends on what the scale says." She says she has never had a boyfriend. "I think it's attributable to how I feel about myself."

Chelle Stack drank twelve-ounce bottles of laxatives—"The liquid works better than the tablets," she says—two or three times a week for six months to keep her weight down when she left Károlyi's. She threw up every day after school. "I'd go three or four weeks trying to lose weight by eating healthy, then I'd go out and do laxatives," she says.

Kristie Phillips, convinced from her years at Károlyi's that her weight determined her worth, became bulimic when she gained weight after retiring from the sport at age seventeen. She was still bulimic four years later as a sophomore at Louisiana State University.

And then there was Erica Stokes, another Károlyi gymnast. The 1992 Olympics in Barcelona were supposed to be Erica's Olympics, but like Christy Henrich, she never made it.

■ ■ ■

While Christy lay in a hospital bed in Kansas City in the summer of 1991, Erica Stokes slipped away from the dinner table in her Houston home to throw up. She had become an expert at vomiting, simply contorting her abdominal muscles to force her meals out. No finger down the throat. No spoon. She had begun throwing up two years before, when she was fourteen and Béla Károlyi was calling her a pregnant goat. He called everyone names: her teammate Betty Okino was a pregnant spider, Kim Zmeskal was a pumpkin or a butterball, Hilary Grivich was a tank. Erica tried not to take it personally, but the words burrowed into her brain like parasites. She began to see herself as if in a fun house mirror—squat, bloated, grotesque. She tried giving up food altogether, but she enjoyed eating. So she threw up.

She rarely ate in front of people, a behavior instilled by Károlyi. During the summers, she and the other members of Károlyi's elite team lived at the coach's 53-acre ranch north of Houston. Károlyi ran gymnastics camps for youngsters from across the country while also training his elites. After practicing from 7 A.M. until late morning, the girls would hit the kitchen in the cabin where they stayed under the supervision of an adult. None ate breakfast before working out, so they were starving. They grabbed cereal or fruit, then plopped down in the living room to watch *The Price Is Right*, listening for the tires of Károlyi's four-wheel drive. The coach stopped by every day to announce the rest of the day's schedule. Whenever they heard him approaching, they stashed the food. Károlyi equated eating with sloth and weakness.

One day, arriving on foot, he was almost to the door before anyone spotted him. "Oh my God, here he is!" The girls lunged toward the kitchen, slamming the cereal boxes behind cabinets. They shoved their bowls under the couch. But Erica sat calmly eating her peach. How could Károlyi mind her eating a peach?

Károlyi took one look at the peach and exploded. "You're so lazy!" he bellowed. "You're so fat! You just come in and pig out after workouts. All you think about is food."

That night, Károlyi made the team train an extra two hours for Erica's transgression.

Throwing up became Erica's solution to satisfying both herself and Károlyi. She didn't know it was dangerous, that the gastric acids in the vomit could corrode the enamel on her teeth and tear her esophagus, or that electrolyte imbalances could disrupt her heart rate. She didn't even know it had a name: bulimia. Like stress fractures and torn muscles, vomiting was simply another unavoidable insult her body would have to tolerate if she was going to survive in elite gymnastics.

The strategy worked at first and Erica lost weight. But then she began bingeing, using food as reward, refuge, painkiller, weapon. Whenever she found herself alone in her house, she'd dash to the kitchen, grabbing whatever food was quick and easy to eat, stuffing herself until someone came home. If she knew her mother would be out for ten minutes, she'd grab whatever she could eat in that time—toast with butter and jelly, cereal, chips. Bingeing on food was a way of seizing control over one small part of her life, which increasingly seemed like some *thing* separate from herself, like a marionette tied to the fingers of her coaches and parents. But her attempts at control inevitably spun out of control.

During workouts, pain stabbed her abdomen. Once the room turned gray and Erica collapsed. After eating crackers and resting in Károlyi's office, she resumed her workout. At other times her muscles quivered. She fell on dismounts and struggled to push herself up into handstands on the uneven bars.

One day at the ranch Erica and the rest of the team were strengthening their legs by doing squat jumps—explosive frog leaps. Károlyi hovered over Erica. "Not high enough! Move!" Erica was recovering from heel and shoulder problems, but Károlyi had no patience with injuries. He made her do the squats over and over until her legs burned.

"If you're going to keep doing them this way," he finally hollered, "you can just go pack your bags and leave!"

It was an invitation he frequently offered to his gymnasts. This time Erica, furiously cursing him in her head, accepted. She left the gym, called her parents and packed her bags. The drive from the Stokeses' home in Houston to the ranch took ninety minutes, so Erica was still waiting for her mother when her teammates returned to the cabin after the workout.

"Whose bags are those?" someone asked.

The other girls couldn't believe Erica was leaving, with the Olympics less than a year away. Erica had always been one of Károlyi's hotshots. She had recently appeared in a commercial for Minute Maid orange juice that featured Olympic hopefuls. The

Stokeses were so certain of their daughter's success that they had accepted money from Minute Maid and a $12,000-a-year stipend from the USGF, knowing the money would render Erica ineligible to compete in college gymnastics. They couldn't worry about college when the Olympics shimmered on the horizon. "She was guaranteed a spot on the '92 Olympics team as much as anyone can be guaranteed a spot a year ahead of time," Erica's mother, Susan, recalls.

Erica had seemed destined for gymnastics greatness from her first moment of life. When Susan Stokes made one final push during Erica's birth, the baby shot out as if from the vault. The doctor caught her like a football, breaking her collar bone in the process. Erica took up gymnastics at age three in her hometown of Kansas City, and by the time she was seven, people were telling Susan she had an Olympic champion on her hands.

Erica spent three summers at Károlyi's camps as a youngster, returning home one year at age nine to announce that Károlyi wanted her to move to Houston and train year-round with him. Her parents protested at first but relented. "My ego kind of got in the way," Susan admits. "I thought, 'This is pretty neat that Béla wants her.'"

With help from a wealthy friend in Los Angeles, the family came up with $1000 a month for Erica's expenses in Houston. When Erica's parents and younger brother Marc moved to Houston the following year, Susan's mother-in-law thought they had lost their minds.

"If your child's handicapped, you'd go anywhere to help them so they can live as fully as possible," Susan told her. "This is the same situation, but this child is exceptional. We're trying to do the best for her."

If Erica wanted to reach the Olympics, Károlyi's was the place. Yet now, five years later, Erica was leaving. "I'm not dealing with this anymore," she told her stunned teammates.

Erica and her mother cried all the way home. When Erica spotted a Burger King, she asked her mother to stop. She hadn't had a hamburger since she was ten. Afterward, for the first time in months, she didn't throw up her meal. When they arrived home that afternoon, Susan called Steve Nunno, who coached rising star Shannon Miller at his Oklahoma City gym. Get her up here right now, Nunno warned. If she steps out of the gym, she'll see what she's missing and you might never get her back. Susan put Erica on a plane the next day.

Nunno couldn't know Erica was bulimic, so he couldn't know he was exacerbating the problem by weighing her every day and encouraging her to lose 10 pounds from her 110-pound frame. He gave her a strict but healthful diet, and Erica dropped to 100 pounds. Though she was still vomiting after meals, she was in better shape than she had been in months as she entered the World Championships Trials; the top six would compete for the United States. When Erica finished sixth, she was ecstatic. Making the World Championships team would strengthen her position going into the 1992 U.S. Olympic Trials. But the USGF decided to choose the World team by combining the gymnasts' scores from the Trials and the national championships, which had taken place several months earlier. Erica had missed the Nationals because of a shoulder injury. She dropped to ninth in the standings and didn't make the team.

That was it. She had lost weight, trained hard, performed well—and she still hadn't made the World team. She wondered if the USGF would do the same thing to her when it came time to choose the Olympic team. She descended into a dark funk.

Depressed and weary from bingeing and vomiting, she came down with the flu and wouldn't leave her bed. "The Olympics had been my dream my whole life, but it just kind of faded away. It wasn't important anymore," she recalls. "It just kind of slowly faded away."

Her weight climbed to 113. She kept missing workouts, saying she was sick. Her mother, who had moved to Oklahoma with her eleven-year-old son to be with Erica, suspected something more serious than the flu. Susan had seen signs in the sink that someone had gotten sick, but she never followed up. Perhaps she didn't want to know. She had invested so much of herself in Erica's career. She was chauffeur, masseuse, dietician. "Our hearts," Susan says, "were set on grabbing the gold." In the past she had sent Erica to the gym with fevers, stomachaches, colds, flu, because she feared Károlyi would kick Erica off the team if she didn't show up. "We had come too far," Susan goes on, trying to explain her own obsession. "It was to the point where if one girl quit the gym, you wouldn't let your daughter spend time with her. You didn't want her to find out there was more to life."

Then late one night in November, less than three months after moving to Oklahoma, Susan heard a noise in the living room. She found Erica on the couch holding a glass filled with what looked like chocolate milk. The next morning Susan couldn't find the box of chocolates Erica claimed to have bought for a friend. She finally confronted her daughter.

"I'm not doing gymnastics for myself," Erica said, crying. "I'm doing it for everybody else."

"I always told you if you want to quit, you can quit," Susan countered.

"I do want to quit."

Susan wanted Erica to see a psychologist first, and he confirmed

Erica's instincts. If she removed herself from the environment that created the bulimia, she would go a long way toward healing herself. So after twelve years of training, Erica quit gymnastics, nine months shy of the Olympics.

Susan cried for eight straight hours while her children were in school the next day. She pounded on the walls in anger and grief. Her own dream had died with Erica's. She wouldn't be the mother of an Olympian, riding the buses through the streets of Barcelona with other mothers of Olympians, sitting together in the arena in their red, white and blue clothing, waving American flags, bathed in both the camera lights and the reflected glory of their children. Susan wanted to kill something.

"I was grieving the loss of everything we put into this," she says. "I knew she could have walked away with medals at the Olympics. I'll tell you what it's like. It's like a death. All the steps you go through when someone close to you dies. It was the same thing. Overnight a door slammed shut."

Susan Stokes was so bitter that when she and her children moved back to Houston at the end of the school semester, she filed for divorce from her husband of twenty-five years. "This sport really tears families apart," she says. "I remember thinking, 'Why can't we be a normal family?' I don't know if we could ever be a normal family again. I don't know if we know how to be normal anymore."

She and her husband eventually reconciled. "We're *trying* to be normal."

Erica went back to high school in Houston and became a cheerleader. As a senior, two years after quitting gymnastics, she weighed 135 pounds and looked beautiful. She didn't watch the 1992 Olympics; her mother watched every minute.

Through the doorway of the kitchen, trophies and medals

adorn the living-room wall unit. Three thick scrapbooks lie on the bottom shelf, spilling out photographs, newspaper clippings, plane ticket stubs, programs and loose-leaf paper with names and scores from long-ago meets recorded in pencil. "I feel really good about myself now," Erica says. "I slowly stopped throwing up. Not right after I quit gymnastics. I was thinking, 'Okay, what about when summer comes and I have to wear a swimsuit, how am I going to look?' So I continued it a bit, though not as much. My appearance was the number one thing I was concerned about. If I didn't look the way somebody wanted me to look, then I must not be that great."

She speaks softly, almost hesitantly, as if on guard, unlike her mother, who recounts their gymnastics days like a preacher under a tent, confessing her sins. But for all her self-flagellation, Susan also points fingers: at the USGF for not warning parents about bulimia and for not choosing Erica for the World Championships team, and at Béla Károlyi for stripping Erica of her self-esteem.

But one wonders if she still doesn't understand what happened to her daughter and why. When Susan received a flyer in the mail about the Miss Teen Texas Pageant, she bubbled, "Erica, you don't have to do this, but wouldn't it be fun?"

Earlier that year, in an essay for English class entitled "A Disastrous Period in Time," Erica wrote, "To live your life trying to make someone else happy when you are not, or when you are struggling, is not living your life." Erica entered the pageant nonetheless. She and her mother shopped together for a pretty dress and experimented with Erica's hair and makeup. They traveled together to Dallas for the competition, staying in a hotel with the other young contestants and their mothers. It felt like old times. Erica looked stunning in her gown and sparkling jewelry, a perfect little princess parading across the stage for everyone to see.

Once again, just as in gymnastics, a panel of judges decided Erica's worth. She came in second.

．．．

In early 1993, with her weight at 63 pounds, Christy Henrich spent six weeks in the eating disorder ward of the Menninger Clinic in Topeka, Kansas. Before she checked in, her parents discovered she had lined the bottom of her suitcase with laxatives. Christy hated the clinic and rebelled, throwing up whenever she could, dumping her vitamin supplements, refusing to eat. She was rushed to the hospital when her blood pressure plummeted and her heart began beating irregularly. She returned home to Independence instead of going back to Menninger's. The treatment didn't seem to be helping. And the Henrichs' insurance had run out.

Christy's weight dropped again.

By June 1993 she weighed 52 pounds. Her body lay on the white hospital sheets of St. Joseph's like a delicate web of bone and skin, IV needles snaking from her neck and arms, a feeding tube protruding from her stomach. Her skin was stretched tight across her bones like plastic wrap, as if to seal her horrors inside. Her potassium level had dropped to 2.4; normal range is 3.5 to 4. Her mother says she should have been dead. Such a low potassium level can trigger cardiac arrest, one of the two common causes of death among anorexics. The other is suicide.

"My life is a horrifying nightmare," Christy said in an interview at the time. "It feels like there's a beast inside of me, like a monster. It feels evil."

Christy moved from St. Joseph into Cedar Ridge Hospital in Shawnee Mission, Kansas, despite no insurance. If Cedar Ridge, a psychiatric hospital, had not taken her, Christy's only option would have been the state mental hospital. Her parents promised Cedar Ridge they would come up with the $1000 a day it cost for Christy's treatment. A Houston organization called the Association for Young Athletes, created by a gymnastics fan named Keith McCaffety who grew to loathe USA Gymnastics because of the abuses he saw, collected money for her. The federation did not contribute money toward the Henrichs' bills, but it helped organize a fund-raising lunch that drew Nadia Comaneci, Bart Conner and Kim Zmeskal.

Nancy Marshall of USA Gymnastics spoke at the lunch to assure the Henrich family that Christy's struggle would not be in vain. Marshall had been pressing the federation's executive committee to do something about eating disorders in the sport. "I sort of would get this nod, like, well, okay. Then nothing would happen," she remembers. "Christy's situation forced the USGF's hand. It gave me a platform to say, 'We can't ignore this anymore.'"

With Christy in Cedar Ridge, her mother spit out her words when she talked about gymnastics. "We all get so caught up in the whole thing that we don't ever stop to think, 'This is a human being.' They're mature but underneath it all is a child. They're supposed to be so tough, never show emotion, yet the coach can. He can yell and scream and they can't say anything back. A lot of the coaches are in it for the recognition at the cost of the kids. We put too much faith in coaches. She looked up to [Fong] like a god figure.

"Now that I look back, I see that it's okay to train world-class athletes, but not at the cost of our children. Somehow change has got to come. Gold medals are good, but we're talking about people's lives. The change has got to come in the whole system: judges, officials, coaches, everybody."

Her voice flattened.

"All the strength and determination Christy put into gymnastics, she now has turned against herself. Athletes are very stubborn, very determined, and they can turn all that against themselves. This is a very, very, very hard disease to reverse. She thinks she's not good enough. She thinks she's never been good enough. She's never learned to love herself."

■ ■ ■

A decade before Christy Henrich watched her fervor for gymnastics slide into obsession, Kathy Johnson had started down a similar path. She began gymnastics late, at age twelve, and discovered she was a natural. The skills that drove others to tears came easily to Kathy. She loved the work and the discipline it demanded. She was small, even by gymnastics standards, but she was older than everyone else in the gym. By age seventeen she heard the clock ticking. "I couldn't be as young as my teammates, but I thought I could look like them if I watched what I ate," she says.

She trained in Louisiana under then Olympic coach Vannie Edwards, who remarked to her one day that she looked like a balloon. He threatened to keep her out of the prestigious American Cup competition if she didn't lose 4 pounds. Johnson had always been thin. In junior high she weighed just 50 pounds. Now, living in the dormitory at Edwards's training camp on a diet of cheese, crackers, peanut butter and slice-and-bake cookies, she was up to 96 pounds. The coach's remark devastated her.

"It hurt something deep inside me," Johnson remembers. "He might as well have said, 'You are a horrible person.' I can't tell you what happened. It's too hard to describe in words. I just cried inside. But not on the outside."

During a six-week visit with her parents in Florida, she decided to fast. She stopped eating for two days. She didn't even drink. On the third day, she ate one egg and dry toast for breakfast and went to the beach. On the two-block walk home, she began hallucinating. Black dots swirled in front of her. Suddenly her towel became too heavy to carry. The dots converged into a single black circle. She fell to the sidewalk. She remembers pulling herself up and slowly walking home, concentrating on each step. She pushed a kitchen chair in front of the refrigerator. Sick with hunger, with shelves of food within reach, Johnson made herself a salad. Even then her mind counted calories.

By day's end she felt fine. She ate lightly the rest of her stay, and when she returned to Louisiana, she had transformed her body from sturdy and muscular to thin and balletic.

"Johnson, you look great!" her coach gushed. "Man, you're skinny! Look at you! How's your strength?"

"Great," Johnson lied, beaming at his compliments. ("If you think this is great," she thought, "I could be even thinner!")

A week later Edwards wanted to see her do a double back flip, a tumbling skill for her floor routine she had learned before she went home for the summer. Not many gymnasts in the mid-1970s could perform the difficult trick—a handspring into two flips in the air. Weak from eating so little and not training in Florida, she could barely launch high enough to complete one flip. She went for the second flip anyway and landed on her head. She didn't move, paralyzed with the fear that she had broken her neck. When the X rays showed no break, her doctors gave her a neck brace and muscle relaxers and told her to take it easy. But she had to compete in a meet against Romania in a week. So two days later, still weak from dieting and now woozy from the drugs, she got up on the beam.

She practiced part of her routine without incident. In fact, she felt she was lighter than usual. Then she launched into an aerial cartwheel/back handspring. Her feet were slightly off center when she landed the cartwheel, but she continued into the back handspring. With her reflexes slowed by the muscle relaxants, she missed her hands and couldn't break her fall. Her elbow smashed into the floor, shattering the joint. Johnson screamed.

"I wasn't just screaming because of the pain," she recalls. "I was screaming because I was losing everything. What used to be so easy, what used to be something I loved more than anything, was turning into something horrible, and I couldn't stop it."

Her arm was twisted into such grotesque shape that one gymnast fled the gym in tears. Johnson herself turned away from the arm on the way to the doctor's office and during the X rays. The doctor gave Johnson a shot of Valium, then, with the help of two assistants, wrenched the joint back in place. She had broken off a piece of bone. She needed surgery. She might never compete again. Her father, standing in his Florida carport when his wife got the phone call, smashed the windshield of his Volkswagen. "What was she doing on a beam?" he hollered. The neck injury had rattled them. Their daughter's weight had been worrying them. Now this. What the hell was going on? Johnson's mother hopped on an airplane.

Kathy stayed a week in the hospital and cried when she had to leave. Inside the hospital she didn't have to think about what she had lost. She felt as if a part of her were dying. Her doctor said her only chance of making the arm strong enough to compete again was to exercise it for fifteen minutes every hour around the clock, so for weeks Kathy's mother awoke every hour through the night to exercise her daughter's arm.

During her rehabilitation Kathy weighed herself every morning. Worried that she would gain weight while she wasn't training, she began cutting her portions in half.

Six months later, after torturous workouts to regain her strength, she won the 1978 U.S. Championships in one of the best meets of her life. She had just turned nineteen. A few months later at the World Championships in Strasbourg, France, she won a bronze medal for her floor routine—a great victory at a time when American gymnasts rarely won medals on the international level. But she lost more weight in Europe. When she returned home, she was tired. She had probably pushed herself too hard after her injury. She was battling with her coach, who was quoting Scripture to her one minute, then berating her the next. All she wanted to do was rest in Florida, but Edwards had committed her to shooting an instructional gymnastics video for two days in Louisiana. Over her parents' objections, she flew back to Louisiana.

It was too much. During the shoot she broke down. Exhausted from the European competitions, weakened from losing weight, feeling a kind of postpartum blues after her great international victory, Johnson huddled in the bathroom, unable to stop crying. When Edwards announced to the crew that she was mentally unstable, Johnson was mortified. She forced herself through the video. As soon as she finished, she flew to Atlanta, where she had trained as a youngster. Friends who picked her up at the airport found a young woman they didn't know. She was withdrawn and lifeless. She lay down in a bedroom and waited to have a nervous breakdown, even though she didn't know what a nervous breakdown was. But she was sure she was going to have one. She couldn't remember winning her medal at the World Championships. "It was just weeks ago," she told her friend. "I got the medal. I see the medal. It's there. But I can't feel it. You should be able to feel that joy, that wonderful moment. There's no feeling left."

After a phone call from one of Kathy's worried friends, her mother flew to Atlanta. She took one look at her daughter, who was even thinner than she had last seen her, and threatened to pull her from gymnastics if she didn't gain weight.

"No!" Johnson protested. "I don't want to quit!" She had thought about quitting, but when her mother threatened to take her home, she held on even more tenaciously. She trained in Atlanta for two weeks, then flew to Brazil to compete in the World Cup. A strict vegetarian, she refused to eat the red meat that was served to her at every meal in South America. Her weight dropped below 90 pounds. Then she caught the flu. When she returned to the States, she was nauseous for much of the next two months. She could barely eat. Edwards decided she was anorexic, and for good reason. She was a shadow of the girl he had compared to a balloon just two years earlier. Even now, Johnson won't say she was anorexic. She knows she was compulsive about her weight and felt she was never thin enough, but she blames her severe weight loss strictly on getting sick. "I can't tell you I didn't enjoy losing the weight, though," she says.

Johnson left Edwards in 1979 when she heard he was telling people she was a basket case. She returned to Atlanta briefly, then went to train with a coach named Bill Sands in Chicago. There, Johnson began to unravel. All the control she had used to battle Edwards's mind games, all the energy she had gathered to keep training, now were slipping through her fingers like sand. She became paralyzed with anxiety. She was scared of tricks she had been performing for years. Once, a local TV crew came to the gym to do a story on her. She was fine in the interview, but when they wanted footage of her training, she froze. They left with nothing.

She still isn't certain why she fell apart in Chicago. Perhaps she felt her career was coming to an end and she couldn't accept it. Sands pushed his gymnasts hard, and at age twenty Johnson couldn't keep up. Perhaps, too, she was trying so hard to keep herself from growing up that her body and mind were rebelling. She wasn't a normal twenty-year-old. She spent all day with the twelve- and thirteen-year-olds with whom she trained. She had never had a romantic relationship. She had no life outside the gym.

"I felt like I was dying from the inside out, because I hadn't healed emotionally [from her experiences with Vannie Edwards], and here I was piling all this physical work on top of the emotional baggage," Johnson says. "And my worst nightmare was coming true. I started putting on weight."

Eating became her substitute for a social life. Food became the friends she lacked, the boyfriend she feared. She now ate as compulsively as she had once starved. It was as if she wanted to force herself out of gymnastics, yet her heart kept telling her, "Not yet." She weighed 92 pounds when she arrived in Chicago and 114 when she left seven months later. She returned to Atlanta to train, though no one in gymnastics believed she would stay. She was crazy and fat and old—that was the talk. Atlanta was just the transition place between Chicago and Florida. They said Kathy Johnson was finished.

"I think part of me maybe wanted to force myself to quit," she says today. "But fortunately the other part of me was stronger. It was, like, 'No, you're not going out this way. You might be going out, but not this way.'" Her mother and brother moved to Atlanta to lend their support, and it helped. Slowly Kathy lost weight and gained strength. The intense training inspired her. The harder the work, the greater the stress, the better Kathy seemed to perform.

In six months, at 102 pounds and stronger than she had been in a long time, she arrived at the 1980 Olympic Trials with new routines and new tricks. "I just kicked ass at the Trials," she recalls. Against the odds, she came back just as she had from her broken elbow. "That was a turning point. Of course, I had a lot of them. I felt like somebody who was nailed down by one foot and I just kept going around and around."

But the United States boycotted the Olympics. Kathy wasn't going anywhere. She was back to square one. Could she possibly last another four years? She would be one month shy of twenty-five, for God's sake. By the 1980s no gymnast went to the Olympics at twenty-five. She stayed in Atlanta for three years, living in her own apartment, coaching a team of youngsters, training almost every day. She had also begun throwing up to control her weight. Not all the time. She knew if she became a full-blown bulimic she'd run herself out of the sport. But she lived with it every day, like an alcoholic eyeing the door of the booze cabinet. "It was always an option, every day," she says. "The fear of it was always with me."

About eighteen months before the 1984 Olympics, another alarm rang in her head. She realized that with her comfortable life in Atlanta she was sliding into retirement. If she wanted to be serious about the Olympics, she would have to go someplace where a coach would push her. "I needed a place where they cared more about my gymnastics than about me," Johnson recalls. "[My coaches in Atlanta] just loved me too much, and we were too close for them to just keep pushing me."

Johnson moved to Southern California to train with U.S. national team coach Don Peters. She had not trained hard in nine months because of stress fractures in her toe and the ball of her foot. Peters was wary but, having seen Johnson rise from the dead so many times, was willing to take a chance. At the World Championships months later, she finished eleventh—the top American. When she returned home, she fell ill, just as she had after the last World Championships. She sank into another funk. Every day for two weeks she got out of bed, dressed for the gym, closed the shutters, then sat in the darkened living room and watched TV.

Finally Peters knocked on her door. "What's wrong? You did so great and we can build on that. You can do great things at the Olympics," he said.

Johnson cried. "Do you know how hard I worked to get people to believe in me, that I can still do this?" she said to Peters. "And now I finally have someone believing in me and I don't believe in myself."

Her career was a marathon and they kept moving the finish line. She pushed so hard and yet there was always another mile to go. Once again she gathered her strength and threw herself into training. She made it to the Olympics in Los Angeles and realized her dream: a medal. She won a bronze on the balance beam and retired a short time later.

She found herself adrift. She was twenty-five years old and knew nothing but gymnastics. She still hadn't had a romantic relationship. She hadn't even begun to menstruate until a few months into retirement. She had the emotional maturity of a teenager. It was as if she had grown up in a little box and now she had stumbled out, disoriented and frightened. For three years she slid into a fierce battle with bulimia, not only to control her weight but to dull her insecurities.

"If we could have just let nature take over, I would have been fine," Johnson says. "My metabolism was shot to shit, basically. We in gymnastics totally destroy our metabolism by not eating. You go into a starvation mode and your body shuts down, just slows everything down to accommodate so few calories. Finally I'm back to the way I should have always been. I'm more muscular now than when I was a gymnast." True to her obsessive nature, at age thirty-four she exercises maniacally. She takes two dance classes a day. She looks like a model, with long blond hair and a balletic body.

She still keeps in touch with the gymnasts with whom she trained in Louisiana. "We all have scars," Johnson says. "I am so much better off than a lot of them. They've all come a long way and they're all happily married and have kids. But there's this question mark that they don't totally understand, and it could still get to them...It was damaging. [Edwards] damaged them. He did. Not to the point where they're not okay and they're not happy. But I know sometimes they have to remind themselves that it's okay to eat. It's okay to look the way they do."

Johnson now earns a living talking about gymnastics for ESPN and ABC. She is articulate and smart and seems confident. She watches the girls sit silently between events and launch grimly into their tricks. She wants to take the coaches aside and show them what they're doing to these girls. But it's not her place. Sometimes she'll talk privately to a gymnast who appears to have an eating problem. The coaches are a different story. Most wouldn't listen anyway. Their gymnasts are winning, aren't they?

"The closer I watch today's gymnasts, the more my career looks better and better. I've had my spirit sapped, but not to the point where I couldn't get it back. I see today's gymnasts winning meets with no heart. There's no life there."

■ ■ ■

Christy Henrich stayed at Cedar Ridge Hospital for five months. When she returned home in the fall of 1993, she threw her scale away. Forcing herself to eat, she watched her weight slowly climb past 70 pounds.

Then she panicked when she couldn't see bone anymore. She stopped eating again. She also stopped seeing her psychologist. "Doesn't do any good," she said. "It's up to me."

In the spring of 1994, at twenty-one years old, she dropped below 65 pounds but refused to return to the hospital. In an interview in May 1994, her voice as mumbly as a ninety-year-old woman's, she talked of licking the disease before summer. "This time I want to gain weight," she said. "I want my body back. I want a nice summer. It'll be a struggle, I know that. I still have a fear of calories. So I know it's going to take a lot of time. But this time when I gain weight, I'll be happy."

She admitted, however, she hadn't eaten for a few days. Solid food pained her stomach, so she sipped on Carnation Instant Breakfast and soup throughout the day while caring for her infant nephew and, ironically, preparing the family meals. "Basically," she said, "I'm the maid."

Even if her stomach would accept food, there was nothing she wanted to eat. There was not a single food she enjoyed. "I still have a hard time with food," she said. "In gymnastics, they're always telling you, 'Don't eat that, don't eat that.' Pretty soon you become so paranoid that everyone is watching what you eat, and you feel everything is bad. You felt like you were really, really doing something wrong if you ate."

She hoped she could change the sport, that her pain would count for something. She wanted the federation and coaches to stop weighing and measuring the gymnasts. She wanted them to let the gymnasts be who they are. "Quit telling us how we feel. We know how we feel. They get you so confused. You're smiling on the outside and a mess on the inside. You don't know what to feel after a while."

In her mind, gymnastics alone was to blame for her anorexia and bulimia. The sport was trying to take her life just as it had taken her friend Julissa's. "If I wasn't in gymnastics," she said, "this wouldn't have happened to me. It's the constant putdowns, the constant criticisms, the constant mental and physical abuse. It pushes you over the edge."

Though she talked of a happier summer, she acknowledged darker possibilities. Her first realization that she might die came at Cedar Ridge when her weight dropped to 52 pounds. She stopped fighting her therapists and tried to gain weight. Her boyfriend wrote a song for her while she was there, calling it "I Believe in You." One stanza goes:

> America's sweetheart
> Brought to her knees
> Willing to do anything to please
> A product of our country
> Pushed too far
> You've got to be Extra-Tough, little lady...

Christy was trying. She wanted to get well, marry Bo, move to Florida, work as a nurse and have children.

"I know I need to eat. I know I need the nutrition. I know I need it to live. But food is like a poison to me."

A month later her weight dropped below 50 pounds and she returned to St. Joseph Health Center. She was released July 4 but within a week was rushed to the Research Medical Center in Kansas City. After nearly five years of starving, her body was giving out. It had cannibalized her muscles, her bones and her organs for fuel to keep functioning. There was nothing left.

Five days after her birthday Christy slipped into a coma. On July 26, 1994, she died of multiple organ failure.

A year earlier Sandy Henrich was asked if she would let her daughter compete in gymnastics if she could make the decision again. "You've got to be kidding. Never. Seeing my daughter lying there in her bed, her bones showing in her face, my beautiful daughter who gave all of herself—never. Never. If you ask was it worth it? No. If Christy can't look at those medals and be happy, then what is there?

"They stole her soul," Sandy Henrich said of the coaches and judges and officials who she thought were supposed to protect her child, "and they still have it."

Sandy and Paul Henrich buried their daughter in a pale pink casket at St. Mary's Cemetery in Independence. For them, the past four years had been like watching night fall, with their lovely daughter transforming into a grotesque skeleton in the darkening shadows. But morning never dawned to turn her back. They brushed their fingers along the casket one last time and headed home, where Christy's medals lay in a drawer, scattered like coins in a fountain.

3

BE THIN
AND WIN

IMAGE

■

Though Nancy Kerrigan was twenty-four when she won the silver medal at the 1994 Olympics—old by skating standards—she had the slight body of a teenage fashion model. Her coach Evy Scotvold told Kerrigan she could succeed only if she prevented nature from taking its course. "As soon as it's a woman's body, it's over," he says. "When they have lovely figures like the girl on the street, they're probably too heavy [for skating]. The older you get trying to do children's athletics, the thinner you must be."

Scotvold weighed his skaters at least once a week and forgave neither puberty nor body type for a skater's being anything but rail thin. When Kerrigan put on a few pounds in 1993 at age twenty-three, for example, she told Scotvold her body was going through its natural maturing process. Nonsense, Scotvold said. Rigorous self-discipline can beat back nature. Keep the weight down and your body won't change. "You can make Twiggies out of anybody," he says.

In truth, the perfect skater is a combination of Twiggy and Barbie, thin enough to perform the difficult jumps and desirable enough to fit skating's cover-girl image. Dating back to Sonja Henie in the 1920s, when she introduced dazzling fur-trimmed costumes, skaters have fed the cultural fantasy of the ideal female: young, beautiful, refined, glamorous, wholesomely sexy and, of course, thin. Creating a skating star, like creating a movie star, is as much an exercise in politics and public relations as it is in coaching and training. "It's a packaging process, very much so," Scotvold says. "You're trying to create a princess of the ice…You try to make sure they know they have to behave, have good manners and be well-dressed. They know they will be watched on and off the ice."

"Image," as another coach bluntly puts it, "is everything." Four-time U.S. champion Linda Fratianne once hired a special coach to teach her how to smile while she skated. Off-ice training often includes "mirror time," when skaters practice the facial expressions they'll use in their programs. In skating no aesthetic detail goes unnoticed, on or off the ice. "The judges would see you in the hotel lobby and you had to look perfect," recalls one Olympian. "Everything counts. You do your hair and makeup even in practice during Nationals. If you had a hole in your tights—oh my God!"

"Hair and weight are everything in this sport," says ice dancer Susie Wynne, only slightly exaggerating.

One Olympic skater, who has requested anonymity, recalls

days on end when she ate one can of asparagus and a frozen diet dinner and drank a dozen cups of coffee and diet Coke in a quest to fit her coach's image of the perfect skating body. She had seen what happened when her sister gained weight. The coach pulled the scale into the lobby of the rink, where girls were putting on their skates. The coach summoned the Olympian's sister and made the mortified young girl stand on the scale and announce her weight. "If you were skating better at a hundred and five pounds but looked better at a hundred, your coach wanted you to be a hundred," the Olympian says. For weeks before a competition, skaters would starve themselves, holding on to the thought of bingeing when they finished competing. "We lived for food," says one. "It's so funny to watch a group of skaters after they finish a competition. As soon as we got off the ice, we headed right for Mrs. Fields [cookie stand]. We'd eat until we felt sick. You'd be disgusted if you saw it."

Skaters who didn't throw up regularly understand why others, like Susie Wynne, did. "Even if you know something's not good for you," says one skater, "you don't think long-term. You think *now*: 'I need to lose five pounds.'" Wynne began vomiting at age nineteen when she gained weight during the off-season. To appease her angry coach, Wynne began throwing up before his daily 7 A.M. weigh-in. Then she threw up after every meal. Once, when Wynne's weight was still too high for her coach's liking, he told her to lose 10 pounds by week's end or he wasn't taking her to the national championships. Wynne stopped eating, threw up, took laxatives, tried everything. She lost the weight, and her coach was happy. He never asked how she did it.

By then Wynne knew she had a problem. She was losing control. Food became the focus of her life off the ice. She had stopped eating in front of people but binged in private. She would eat an entire pizza in a sitting, then vomit. She hated what she was doing, but she couldn't tell anyone. Her parents would have pulled her out of the sport. Her coach, she felt, didn't want to know. Oblivious to her turmoil, he kept weighing her every day. "It became over-whelming," Wynne recalls.

She found herself in church one day, listening to a priest's sermon about turning one's burdens over to God. "Take it away," Wynne prayed. "Here, God. I can't deal with it."

Soon afterward she found a support group for bulimics, hired a nutritionist and began running every day. Most important, she left her coach. "Nobody," she told her new coach, "is weighing me in. If anybody talks to me about weight, I'm leaving."

Twenty-nine, married and still competing in 1994, she wants to shake every young skater she hears fretting about her weight. Today's skaters, she says, are no smarter than she was. The same dramas keep playing out over and over again. "Now I don't weigh myself. Why should I let that thing control my life? Why should I let that little number tell me if I'm going to have a good day or a bad day?"

But the message in skating is clear: Be thin and win. When thirteen-year-old Michelle Kwan stood on the podium to accept her silver medal at the 1994 U.S. Figure Skating Championships, one skating observer cracked, "Sure she can do it now, but wait till she gets older and her body changes."

One of Michelle's coaches, Evelyn Kramer, overheard the remark and seethed, nearly spitting her words, "It's a whole image sport. It's bullshit."

Kramer is a maverick among skating's coaches. She's loud, earthy, irreverent—the anti-princess. She once told quiet and feminine Caryn Kadavy she ought to give her coach a nice "fuck you" every now and then. "I've been told," Kramer says in her unfiltered Brooklyn accent, "I'm vulgar." She holds a master's degree in psychology—earning her the nickname Rink Shrink—so she knows something about the complicated interplay between weight and self-esteem. She says every female skater she's ever known, with the exception of Kadavy, has had eating disorders. She knows a Russian ice dancer who had her teeth capped because they had been eroded by the acid in her vomit. She knows of an Olympic medalist who began pulling her hair out as she battled bulimia.

Kramer herself, now in her fifties, says she still can't shake her own preoccupation with weight and food, which she developed as a young skater. She ate herself out of the sport as a teenager, secretly consuming whole boxes of candy because her coach and her parents harangued her so incessantly about weight. Her mother put a lock on the kitchen door. "I still talk about my body all the time. My weight is up and down. I'm obsessed with food. I think about it all the time. If I hadn't been in a sport like this while my body was going through puberty, I wouldn't have been so preoccupied with it. Nobody told me what was going on. I felt it was my fault my body changed. I was told I had no self-control. The change is emotional as well as physical, and the emotional feelings manifest themselves in food."

When her daughter, Jessica, began skating, she sent her to a nutritionist to avoid a repeat of her own childhood pain. Yet Kramer found herself inflicting other abuses. "Look at all these girls your age and they're doing more," Kramer would snap at Jessica. "All I care about," answered Jessica, "is what I do."

Kramer confesses to having pinched her, punched her and screamed at her. "I'd say hateful things, all because of skating. I don't feel like I was living through her. It wasn't that. I think it was because there is nothing like seeing your own kid go out there. No higher high, no scarier scare."

She finally realized that history was repeating itself. The craving for success that had driven her own mother to lock the kitchen door had seized Kramer too. She would do anything to push her daughter to win. Skating for the joy of it, as Jessica wanted, went against everything Kramer had learned in life. Winning was the only truly respected virtue. And in skating, there is no simpler indicator of success than body type.

The inevitable evolution of the sport's appetite for ever thinner, ever younger skaters was on display at the 1994 U.S. Championships in the shape of Michelle Kwan, an eighth grader from Mary P. Henck Intermediate School in Torrance, California. She was in third place after the technical program, and ten rows of reporters in the press room of the Joe Louis Arena in Detroit wanted to know what music would accompany her long program. She leaned hesitantly toward the microphone, her eyebrows arching and her mouth twisting sheepishly like a child who hadn't read the homework assignment. "Ummm," she stammered, shrugging and giggling and looking at her coach, Frank Carroll, seated beside her.

"*Man from Snowy River*," Carroll told her.

"*Man from Snowy River*," Kwan repeated into the microphone. "And..." Kwan giggled again and looked at Carroll once more. She had been rehearsing to this music every day for months. She had no idea what it was.

"*East of Eden*," Carroll prompted.

If Kwan's success at the 1994 U.S. Championships at the age of thirteen left any doubts that ladies' figure skating had become, like gymnastics, a sport for children, the Olympics a month later removed them. Flanking American Nancy Kerrigan on the winners' podium in Lillehammer were two wispy sixteen-year-olds, Oksana Baiul and Chen Lu, neither of whom weighed more than 95 pounds or stood more than 5 feet 1 inch tall.

Size informs every step of a skater's career. At one competition press conference, coach Kathy Casey fielded a question about the progress of her skater, sixteen-year-old Nicole Bobek. Casey didn't hesitate with her answer: "She's learned to handle her growth, and she lost a little weight." End of answer. She mentioned nothing about Bobek's learning new jumps or becoming more graceful.

Coaches become so attuned to their skaters' bodies they can usually detect even the slightest weight gain. When Alex McGowan coached national champion and Olympic medalist Debi Thomas, he knew by watching the height of her jumps if she had gained a few pounds. His current pupil, fifteen-year-old Lisa Talbot, went home to the Midwest for three days during Christmas and when she returned to McGowan in California, he took one look at her and said, "You put on two pounds." She had.

"I always say to them, 'You never see a fat ballerina at the ballet,' " McGowan says.

Though weight and appearance have always counted in figure skating, the sport rewards the lighter skaters more richly than ever because scores now depend so much on acrobatic triple jumps. School figures—the torturously boring exercise of tracing figures in the ice—used to count for 60 percent of a skater's total score, with the technical and free-skate programs making up the rest. Mastering school figures took years, thus skewing competitions in favor of older skaters. Skating dropped school figures from elite competition in 1990; now the two-minute-and-forty-second technical program counts for 33.3 percent and the four-minute free-skate program for 66.7 percent. Triple jumps separate the great long programs from the merely good. Sonja Henie's most difficult jump when she won three consecutive Olympic gold medals from 1928 to 1936 was a single Axel, a jump with one-and-a-half revolutions in the air. Dorothy Hamill won the Olympic gold in 1976 with a double Axel as her flashiest jump. Now a strong long program includes five or six triple jumps, even from the juniors. Kwan won the 1993 U.S. Olympic Festival at age thirteen by landing six clean triples.

Making the jumps means staying light and thin. The less weight a skater has to haul into the air, the better her prospects of completing the jump. Tonya Harding, with her thick, pear-shaped body, seemed to contradict the weight maxim because her jumps were the strength of her skating. She was the only American female ever to land the three-and-a-half-revolution triple Axel. But she landed the triple Axel consistently only when her weight was low. After winning the 1991 U.S. Championships with the triple Axel, she landed only one more in competition for the remainder of her career, at the 1991 Skate America in Oakland.

Though skating doesn't see the traumatic injuries that plague gymnastics, the increasingly difficult skills demanded by the sport have brought their share of stress fractures, broken bones and torn muscles, which is why many in skating would like to see the jumps deemphasized. "I keep saying it's not necessary, that triples aren't everything," says Joan Burns, a top U.S. judge from California. "There are four elements to figure skating: jumps, spins, footwork and choreography. They all have to be good, not just the jumps."

Nevertheless, skating's new archetype, as represented by Kwan, is small, thin and prepubescent, strong enough to launch into the air but light enough to soar high, spin quickly and land softly. When Kwan glided effortlessly across the ice at the 1994 national championships in Detroit, she drew longing glances from older and larger skaters.

One competitor, however, watched Kwan with knowing eyes. Twenty-eight-year-old Elaine Zayak had been in Kwan's shoes once—young, small and extraordinarily gifted. Like Kwan, Zayak was the rising star in a country hungry for its next pixie icon. Then something doomed her career. She grew up.

■ ■ ■

Zayak won the 1981 U.S. Championships at age fifteen and had no doubts about winning it again the following year and the year after that. She was bulletproof. No one could jump the way she could. She finished second at the 1981 World Figure Skating Championships, a remarkable achievement for one so young. She was going to be the best there ever was. She dropped out of ninth grade to train seven days a week, six hours a day. A New Jersey girl who had lost half her foot in a lawnmower accident as a toddler, Elaine was the toast of nearby New York City. The reporters there loved this unlikely skating queen. She talked like a truck-stop waitress, spewing double negatives, laughing from her belly, sharing every notion that crossed her mind.

But at the 1982 U.S. Championships she fell three times and finished third. While the failure rattled Elaine's coaches and parents, it nearly paralyzed Elaine. She was scared to return to the ice, especially at the upcoming World Championships. What if she embarrassed herself again? What if everybody laughed at her? The pressure and fear closed in on her. In her hotel room the day and night before the competition, she cried for hours on end. "Don't make me do this," she pleaded to her parents. "Don't make me go out there and make a fool of myself again."

Elaine's mother cried with her. "Just try," her mother said. "If you don't at least try, you won't be happy." Her father, exasperated, retreated to the hotel bar.

"Okay, Mom," Elaine finally conceded. "But no matter what

happens, whether I skate well or not, this is it, all right? I don't want to compete anymore."

"Okay."

Elaine won, but the euphoria touched her like a breeze, light and fleeting, barely felt. She was relieved more than anything. Now maybe everybody would get off her back. But even her mother joined the chorus: "How can you quit *now?*"

After the World Championships, Elaine returned to school—but for just two hours a day, from eight to ten every morning. It was a joke. She wasn't learning or working toward anything. "But so what," she thought. She had contracts worth $300,000 to skate in ice shows. She had her own fully loaded sports car. Her hometown erected a sign at the edge of town: PARAMUS, HOME OF WORLD CHAMPION ELAINE ZAYAK. Life had handed this daughter of a tavern owner one of the grandest jewels in the figure skating crown. Dorothy Hamill, Peggy Fleming, Sonja Henie. Elaine Zayak's name would be chiseled alongside theirs on the exclusive list of world champions.

But now Elaine wanted out of competitive skating. After doing ice shows for two months, she took off with some friends to Florida and didn't train for two more. She had been skating since she was a toddler as therapy for her partially severed foot and by age ten was training six hours a day, traveling two and a half hours round-trip from New Jersey to a rink on Long Island. At sixteen she was tired. Tired of the United States Figure Skating Association telling her what she could and couldn't say in interviews. Tired of judges calling her parents to suggest she see a dermatologist for a patch of acne on her face—and, by the way, she ought to wear more pink. Tired of hearing about how her parents scrimped to pay the $25,000-a-year tab for her skating.

More than anything, she was tired of everyone harping about her weight. Elaine never looked like a ballerina. She was never going to be Peggy Fleming or Carol Heiss no matter how much she dieted. To make matters worse, she had begun menstruating the year before. Before puberty, girls have 10 to 15 percent more body fat than boys; after puberty, girls have 50 percent more. Elaine was feeling the change. By the time she returned from Florida in early summer, she had gained 15 pounds. No longer the girlish sprite, she found herself in the midst of a whirling battle with her coaches, her parents and her own body. Now more than ever, she wanted to quit. Her parents, upset she was throwing away everything for which she and they had worked so hard, grounded her. "It was basically, 'You don't have a say in this,'" Elaine recalls. "They felt I couldn't make my own decisions." They took away her new car—and Elaine's father infuriated her by driving it himself. Angry and frustrated and feeling that without skating even her own family had no respect for her, she stormed out of the house one night with no clear idea where to go. She ended up at the home of a classmate she barely knew and stayed for a week without telling her parents where she was. "I really didn't even want to hang out with my friends. I didn't know what I wanted to do," Elaine says.

One night Elaine and her friend missed their ten-thirty curfew and the girl's parents locked them out. The world figure skating champion huddled in a New Jersey backyard all night, sleeping on the grass like a vagabond.

Inevitably, her parents and coaches wore her down and she returned to the rink. It was already August. The competitive season would begin in October. And her weight had climbed to 125 pounds. "I felt like I was normal size," she recalls. "To me, it just didn't look like I was fourteen or fifteen anymore...You gain weight in those years even if you're not eating much. You gain weight because you're physically becoming a woman. My father didn't understand that. He goes, 'That's bullshit.' "

Elaine couldn't open the refrigerator door without her parents quizzing her. She tried Weight Watchers and Diet Center. She biked. She hired a nutritionist. Her coaches weighed her every week, exhorting her to lose more. But the weight wouldn't come off. Desperate, Elaine tried amphetamines, given to her by a classmate. She succeeded only in making herself sick.

So she conceded the battle. What else could she do that she wasn't doing? She began to eat in secret. The more she was told not to eat, the more she ate. In her mind she was claiming control for the first time in her life. Her sport, like gymnastics, was all about control: coaches' control, parents' control, physical control, emotional control. Her coaches could order her back into training, her parents could take away her car, they could forbid her to date—they could dictate everything in her life, but they couldn't dictate what she ate. She would eat whatever she pleased. Eating was a rebellion, but it was also a refuge. As world champion, she knew she was expected to win every competition through the 1984 Olympics, still two years away. Food became a drug, dulling her anxieties.

Because she couldn't eat at home, she stuffed herself at convenience stores and delicatessens. Once, when she tried to buy a bagel and cream cheese at the deli near the rink, the man behind the counter wouldn't serve her. "Coaches' orders," the man said. Elaine's coaches had instructed him not to sell her anything but tea and coffee. Humiliated, she drove to the 7-Eleven down the road, bought a pint of ice cream and ate it in the parking lot.

Marylynn Gelderman shudders as she recalls how she and Peter Burrows coached Elaine. "Elaine was our first Olympian. I was very young, and we were a very hungry school. Here was one of the most talented people ever to hit skating, and she's eating and growing. So you panic. I think now that I look back on it, I would never do that again. I would handle it very differently." Gelderman doesn't weigh her skaters anymore. Instead, she emphasizes how much easier they can jump and spin when they're smaller and lighter. "Those who want to lose weight, will." She shrugs. "Those who don't, won't."

Elaine tried throwing up after she ate, but she couldn't. By late September, with competitions a month away, Elaine panicked. The extra pounds were straining her right foot, which bore more than its share of weight to compensate for the half-severed left foot. A friend, a Harvard-educated former skater, told Elaine she had lost 10 pounds in one week with diet pills. Elaine flew up to Boston for the day without telling her parents and visited the friend's doctor, who prescribed the pills. What the woman, then a coach in Boston, didn't tell Elaine was that the pills were on the United States Olympic Committee's list of banned substances.

"It was very hush-hush," Elaine remembers. "Nobody knew about it. My mother would just die if she knew I was doing drugs. It's not something you want people to know about, especially if you're national and world champion."

Tipped off by Elaine's dramatic mood swings, Gelderman found out about the pills and pitched a fit. "You won't make the Olympic team if you get tested!" she told the skater. "Get rid of them!" Elaine first waited until she lost 10 pounds.

But plagued by nagging leg and ankle injuries and doomed by her womanly figure, she would never again be the skater who won the World Championships seven months earlier. The press, once so gushing, wrote that she was fat and washed up. "Look what kind of world champion you turned out to be," her father said to her one day. Elaine stopped talking to him. She never won another national title, finishing second in 1983 and third in 1984. She finished sixth at the 1984 Olympics. In the ice shows afterward, she skated in the supporting cast—no Olympic medal, no starring role. She tried going to Monmouth College in New Jersey and she worked in a deli for a while. She tried coaching. Nothing stuck. With only a high school degree, she found few opportunities.

"This sport is so unforgiving," says ABC's Jurina Ribbens. "Finish second and all of a sudden you're a has-been. They don't look at the long term. They should have let Elaine finish third or fourth for a while, then allow her to come back at her own pace. There's too much emphasis on winning and winning young."

■ ■ ■

It began for Kristie Phillips at age four.

The youngest child and only daughter of Terri and Jimmy Phillips in Baton Rouge, Louisiana, Kristie was cute and fearless, the darling of the family. Terri entered Kristie in her first beauty pageant when she was a year old, drove her 25 miles each way to modeling classes at eighteen months and enrolled her in dance school at two. When Kristie was four, she showed the unflappable confidence that would fuel her meteoric rise in gymnastics. She won a statewide beauty pageant, which qualified her for a national competition at Walt Disney World. But when she and Terri arrived in Orlando, they discovered that the competition included a talent segment. Undaunted, mother and daughter sketched a dance number to a borrowed tape recording an hour before the show, and Kristie finished in the top 10 among 120 entrants.

It was not until Terri watched her preschooler in gymnastics class, however, that she knew she had found her daughter's destiny. The girl moved as if she had no spine. She could bend backward until her hands settled on the floor next to her feet, forming a human circle. She could lie on her stomach and arch her back so acutely that her legs formed a roof over her head, like a fishhook turned on its side. And she had a showman's flair that, in the summer of 1976, found inspiration in the magical images of Nadia Comaneci on her television screen. The four-year-old looked up from the TV as she watched Comaneci and told her mother that someday she, too, would be in the Olympics. Terri believed her with the kind of unconditional faith that only a parent possesses. She felt there was something special about her daughter. A devout Baptist, she believed Kristie's extraordinary talent was a gift from God and that the harder the little girl worked and the more honors she earned, the more she glorified His name. Before Kristie was five, she was training four hours a day.

In three years, when Kristie's talents outgrew the local gymnastics club, mother and daughter moved to Belcher, Louisiana, to train with former Olympic coach Vannie Edwards. Jimmy stayed home with the Phillipses' three sons while Terri worked as a housemother to fifteen of Edwards's gymnasts to make ends meet. When Edwards closed his school two years later, Terri and Kristie spent five months at a gym in Thibodaux, Louisiana, then moved on to the Atlanta School of Gymnastics, where Olympian Kathy Johnson had trained. By then Terri's two older sons were away at college, easing the load on Jimmy, a longtime section supervisor at Exxon.

But eighteen months after moving to Atlanta, Terri and Kristie were on the move again, this time to Houston to train with Béla Károlyi, who was fresh off his triumph with Mary Lou Retton at the 1984 Olympic Games in Los Angeles. Kristie and Terri arrived in Houston with soaring hopes that were soon shared by the master himself. Within a year Károlyi was touting the dynamic Kristie as the next Mary Lou. She blossomed under his tutelage, introducing a move on the balance beam that was so difficult it came to be known as "the Phillips." In a variation of the trick she had done as a four-year-old, she rose into a handstand, then arched her back so that her legs and feet came over her head like a ledge, then she fanned her legs 180 degrees into a split. No other gymnast in the world performed this straddle reverse planche.

Károlyi loved Kristie's spirit, the way she played to an audience and forced eye contact with the judges. Nothing scared her, not even the pressure of big meets. At age thirteen she won the prestigious American Cup, beating veteran gymnasts from nineteen countries. The same year, she won the national junior title and might have won the senior title if not for a minimum-age rule. Then she won four gold medals at the Canadian Cup and another four at the U.S. Olympic Festival despite a broken wrist.

Her talent was so dazzling and her promise so bright that two years before the 1988 Olympics, when she was fourteen and still in braces, Kristie appeared on the cover of *Sports Illustrated* under the declarative headline THE NEXT MARY LOU. "At her age, she is beyond anyone we have ever had," United States Gymnastics Federation executive director Mike Jacki told the magazine. "She'll be at her peak in 1988." A United Press International article marveled at her single-minded march toward the Olympics. "Sometimes I miss things that normal thirteen- and fourteen-year-olds do," Kristie told the reporter, "but I know in my life I can't have everything. I knew if I was going to accomplish my goals, I was going to have to make some sacrifices. I can only have what I want most, and what I want most is to go to the Olympics." She garnered so much attention that she was invited onto *The Tonight Show* with Johnny Carson, for which she was meticulously coached on what to say about boys, school and having fun—perpetuating the cheery illusion that a girl

can train all day every day for the Olympics and still have a normal
teenager's life.

Her life, in fact, was veering so far from the Carson image that
Terri sometimes wondered if she was doing the right thing as a
mother by encouraging Kristie to work so hard. But by then she had
become a full partner in Kristie's dream. She wanted the Olympics
as much as her daughter. Though she was often appalled at Károlyi's tactics, she never objected. He was the best money could buy,
after all, and she was paying plenty—$180,000 over six years. If he
needed to belittle and humiliate girls to produce champions, who
was she to argue? "You do start asking yourself, 'Why should I pay
$180,000 to have my kid physically and mentally abused?' I did say
that. But I never said it to Béla," Terri admits.

During a workout a month before competing for the junior title
at the 1986 U.S. Gymnastics Championships, for which she was
considered the favorite, Kristie reached back to adjust her leotard
and blinding pain shot through her wrist. It had begun to hurt five
months earlier, but she was so accustomed to training in pain that
she let it go. Now she couldn't ignore it.

"You know why your wrist hurts?" the doctor asked her. "It's
broken."

Kristie burst into tears. If she took time off to let it heal, she
would miss the national championships, and that was not an
option. These championships were her opportunity to solidify
her position as America's number one gymnast and its best hope
for the 1988 Olympics. She took the cast off after just two weeks,
though the bone had not yet healed. She dulled the pain by swallowing up to twelve Advils and six anti-inflammatory Naprosyns
every day. She won the junior nationals, but afterward she still
didn't take time off to let the wrist heal. The Olympics were less
than two years away, and the quest to get there consumed her life.

She couldn't slack off, not even for a few weeks. When her training hours were increased to nine a day, she dropped out of school. Education, like her injuries, social life and family life, would have to wait. The world for her was only as wide as the corrugated metal box that was Károlyi's gym. She walled herself off from outside distractions to make sure nothing interfered with her mission.

She never suspected her career would be destroyed from the inside, by her own body and the coach she once adored.

Sometime during her fifteenth year, Kristie's body began to change. Despite the intense physical work and delayed menarche, her body grew and rounded. At 4 feet 11 inches, she saw her weight creep from 88 pounds to 92 pounds and then to 98 pounds. Károlyi turned against his star pupil, as if her growth were a betrayal.

"I heard every day I was fat," Kristie remembers, "that I looked like an overstuffed Christmas turkey, that I was big as a house, that I was never going to make it in life, that I was going to end up looking like my mother—which, if you don't know my mother, she's very large—that by the time I was sixteen I was going to weigh two hundred pounds. Béla was saying all this every day."

With the 1988 U.S. Olympic Trials less than a year away, Kristie's fire began to die. The pressure of expectations she had once handled so effortlessly ate at her. She knew she wasn't the same gymnast who had smiled out from the *Sports Illustrated* cover just eighteen months earlier. Her larger body prevented her from performing some of the spectacular moves she could once do so well. And even if she adjusted to her growing body, Károlyi had lost his fervor for her. She no longer fit his little-girl image of the ideal gymnast.

Yet while her career was crumbling like plaster, her family and friends continued planning their trips to Seoul, the site of the Summer Games. When they saw Mary Lou in a Wheaties commercial or dining at the White House, they still thought, "That'll be Kristie." They had to keep believing because only the prospect of winning an Olympic medal could justify the extravagant investments they had made in Kristie's career: separating the family, spending hard-earned money, traveling to meets, sacrificing their own needs for hers. Kristie began to feel the pressure of their expectations gathering over her like storm clouds. She could see all the sacrifices converging toward the summer day when in just a few brief moments in a gymnastics arena she would have to make good on the debts. It was a daunting burden for a child's shoulders.

Kristie turned to food as an anesthetic. The more Károlyi belittled her body and deepened her fear of failure, the more she ate. No longer the sunny little girl who had bounded into the gym three years earlier, Kristie became alternately sullen and surly. Terri didn't know what to do, how to make everything the way it was. Their dream was unraveling so quickly.

When seven months before the Olympics Kristie said she wanted to quit, Terri wasn't surprised. But she wouldn't consider it. "You can tough it out," she told her daughter. Her father agreed. "You've come this far," he said, "you can manage a few more months." Kristie acquiesced on the condition that she leave Károlyi's. Mother and daughter moved to Southern California to train with former Olympic coach Don Peters at SCATS gym. Kristie felt as if she had been released from prison. She returned to school, scaled back her training hours, made friends, enjoyed life—and ruined what was left of her gymnastics career. Heavier and more out of shape than she had ever been, the one-time national champion finished ninth at the 1988 U.S. Championships.

Still, the livelier and looser atmosphere at SCATS restored Kristie's enthusiasm for the sport and she began to think seriously about the Olympics again. She decided her parents were right: she had worked too long to give up now. She also knew that her best chance at regaining her world-class skills and whipping her body back in shape was to return to the more disciplined regimen of Károlyi's gym. Swallowing hard, Kristie moved back to Houston. For two weeks while her mother settled their affairs in California, Kristie lived with a married couple, friends of Károlyi's. Their job was to help Kristie trim her 112-pound body. She claims that Károlyi's friends, at Károlyi's direction, gave her laxatives and diuretics to quicken the weight loss, though Károlyi vigorously denies this.

In three weeks she weighed 92 pounds but had lost strength and energy. At the Olympic Trials, the same reporters who had crowned her queen two years earlier now wrote her off. "The Sept. 1, 1986, cover of *Sports Illustrated* boldly called Kristie Phillips 'The New Mary Lou,'" one wire-service reporter wrote in June 1988. "Now she is almost 'Kristie Who?'"

Kristie finished the Trials in eighth place, one spot short of being named an alternate. She would go to the Olympics as first alternate only if someone got hurt. As Kristie worked out with the team before they left for Seoul, her despair over missing the cut put the other gymnasts on edge. None of the girls would let Kristie set the boards for their vaults or adjust the bars for their uneven bars routines because they feared she might sabotage the equipment to cause an injury. Brandy Johnson recalls hearing both Kristie and her mother assure friends that Kristie would be going to Seoul. "If I had a magic wand," Kristie was heard to say one day, "I'd wish one of the girls would get hurt."

When the team left for Seoul without her, Kristie couldn't pretend everything was going to end happily ever after. That was it. The road she had followed since she was four years old did not lead to the Olympics after all, but back home to Baton Rouge, where she had not lived since she was eight. Now she was sixteen and saw herself as a complete failure. A zero. Without gymnastics she felt she was nothing—less than nothing because she had disappointed everyone who believed in her. Her parents were never going to see a payoff for all the money they had spent on her. She hated gymnastics, she hated herself, she hated Károlyi. She refused to watch the Olympics on television.

"All of a sudden—bam!—it's over," she says. "We're through, and we're stuck with all the bad memories. All we can think about is, I'm never going to make it in life because I'm going to be fat. We think, 'Gymnastics is over and I'm going to be even fatter than I already am.' All these things are going through your mind and you're not even thinking about the goals you accomplished. Our coaches never say, 'Oh, you did this and this and you should be proud.'"

Her body became the symbol of her failure. She spent her days watching television and eating, indulgences she had rarely been allowed. For months on end she didn't so much as walk around the block. By Christmas, less than six months after the Trials, Kristie weighed 125 pounds. She was barely 5 feet tall. When she stood on the scale, she was horrified: 125. Károlyi was right. She was going to be just like her mother. If she didn't lose weight, and lose it now, her life would amount to nothing. She immediately tried to vomit. She couldn't get the food to come up the first few times, but she kept at it and found the knack. Every time she ate, she vomited. She began to binge, using food as an escape from her depression; then, panicked and disgusted, she would throw up. Like most bulimics, she tended not to eat around other people. But by herself she ate whole packages of donuts, bags of potato chips, hamburgers, ice cream, jars of pickles.

She rode this roller coaster alone. She was too ashamed to tell anyone. The bulimia had affirmed what Károlyi had so often told her, that she was weak and worthless. She was reminded, as she hunched over the toilet every day, how far she had fallen from the cute fourteen-year-old who was supposed to end up on a Wheaties box.

One day, alone in her parents' house, she opened a kitchen drawer, took out a pair of scissors and locked herself in the hall bathroom. "I felt I had nothing to live for after gymnastics," she recalls. She pressed one of the blades into the faint veins in her wrist, but suddenly felt gripped by a strong, strange sensation. She felt God was speaking to her. "He was telling me he had something bigger in store for me than gymnastics." She dropped the scissors and cried long, wrenching sobs, as if purging the last remnants of her Olympic dream.

Kristie began to break away from her identity as the star gymnast. But she emerged from one illusory image, only to create a new one. She would become the perky cheerleader and aspiring actress. At Louisiana State University, she looked the part of the pretty Southern belle, her blond hair curling to her shoulders, her lipstick matching her pink nail polish, her voice as thick and sweet as pecan pie. She spent afternoons drinking iced tea on the painted veranda of her sorority house, swapping gossip with her girlfriends. Yet alone in her room she still binged on food and vomited, wracked with self-hatred and disgust. Though she weighed less than 100 pounds, she had the highest percentage of body fat on the cheerleading squad because she had such an unbalanced diet. "That's all I think about, my weight, what I look like," she says. "And I know I'm skin and bones." She talked about seeing a counselor to treat her bulimia, but as with treating her gymnastics injuries, she never seemed to find the time.

Only when asked about her rise and fall in gymnastics does Kristie allow a glimpse of the dark anger behind the cheery mask.

She blames her suicide attempt and her eating disorder on elite gymnastics, where the confluence of a parent's ambition, a coach's unrelenting demands and her own blind loyalty nearly destroyed her. But she catches herself when talk turns to her parents, especially her mother. "It makes me feel good that my mom loves me that much and cares for me that much that she wanted to see me do that great. I love my parents to death. They care so much about me, and I'm so thankful for that."

But her praise has an edge. She later suggests, gently, that perhaps her mother never understood the depths of her unhappiness during her last year in gymnastics and her first year in retirement, when she fell from teen idol to nobody. Her mother's desire to see her succeed was not so different from that of the father who pitches a hundred curve balls to his son in the backyard or the parent who deluges her child with flash cards and brainteasers. But in elite sports, the by-product of a parent's spirited devotion can be expectations so high and pressure so suffocating that they can cripple a girl's self-worth.

Terri didn't know about Kristie's bulimia, which plagued her for more than four years. Terri often did not see what Kristie saw. The mother's recollections of Kristie's gymnastics are airbrushed, the daughter's outlined in black. In the years since her daughter's participation in gymnastics, Terri's perspective on the damage her daughter sustained and her own role in it hasn't changed. She still believes nine hours of training a day were not excessive if a child wanted to be the best. "If they live away from home and the parents are paying a price, then they need to be in the gym for however long they need to be there." She has no regrets about Kristie's dropping out of school. "I didn't like it, but I didn't have a choice. If she didn't go to the early morning workouts, she wouldn't be on

[Károlyi's elite team of six]. But it didn't hurt Kristie because she took correspondence courses."

Where the two completely differ is over Béla Károlyi's character.

"I think, if you want my honest opinion," Kristie says, "he's in it for himself. He doesn't care about the gymnasts. He doesn't care what they go through, what they suffer through, what he makes them suffer through. He cares about the fame and fortune he's getting out of it... When we're at competitions and when we're on TV and he has a microphone on, he's a different person. He's massaging our necks, smiling and laughing and patting you on the back. This is what the public sees of Béla. But it's really the exact opposite."

Terri, however, says if she had another daughter with talent, she would send her to Károlyi because there was no better coach in the world. She dismisses her daughter's suggestion that what she endured was mental abuse: "You're going to get that at any gym with any coach. Though maybe not as bad." She believes Károlyi's humiliations and wild tirades were, in fact, necessary ingredients to producing champions. "You have to be mentally strong to make it."

A dozen or so framed pictures of Kristie as a gymnast line the walls of her mother's living room. To Terri they are a monument to her daughter's accomplishments, but to Kristie they will always serve as a reminder of her failure.

■ ■ ■

It was thirteen years after winning the U.S. Figure Skating Championships when Elaine Zayak attempted an unlikely comeback at age twenty-eight. Her life had become a string of hazy weekends filled with drinking until the clubs closed, smoking too much, eating too much, sliding toward suburban oblivion. "I really hated my life," she says today. Without her parents' breath on her neck, she rekindled her love for skating. She trained for a year, whittling her weight to 116 pounds. She learned to perform a triple loop, a jump she couldn't master at age sixteen.

She stunned the skeptics by finishing among the top four at her sectional competition to qualify for the 1994 national championships in Detroit. She reveled in the spotlight again, signing autographs, offering quotable observations and insights to a press corps that had once dismissed her as immature and empty-headed. "I'm here to show that your life isn't over at eighteen," Zayak told reporters. Certain that the younger skaters wouldn't know who she was, Zayak was taken aback when the mother of sixteen-year-old Lisa Ervin said her daughter started in skating because of Elaine.

"Right," Lisa said, "when I was three..."

"Oh my God," Elaine laughed, "now I really feel old."

Before she took the ice for her long program, her nerves jangled like juiced wires. She felt sick, wondering why she had ever thought she could pull this off. As she warmed up on the ice, she stopped by the railing and hugged her coaches, Marylynn Gelderman and Peter Burrows. Then she glided to the center of the rink, clasping her hands as if in prayer.

She nailed her first combination of two double jumps, then cleanly landed a double Axel. As she launched into her triple loop, the only triple in her program, the crowd held its breath. She spun and landed beautifully, electrifying the Joe Louis Arena. She skated with a soulfulness and grace the younger girls couldn't match.

When she finished her near-flawless long program, the crowd leapt to its feet. Elaine stood in the center of the rink, her face buried in her hands, her shoulders heaving. Gelderman and Burrows whooped and hollered from the railing. She finished fourth, one spot short of a medal. One national judge, watching the competition at home on television, thought Elaine should have won the gold. But the former world champion wasn't disappointed. She didn't care about medals. She had plenty of medals. In Detroit she finally found what she always hoped she would find on all those winners' stands more than a decade before: joy pure enough to chase her fear and reward her sacrifice. This, she felt, was what skating was supposed to be. She had finally stopped fighting her own body. She showed, at least to herself, that a full-grown woman's body deserved a place on the ice.

4

DO IT FOR AMERICA

PRESSURE

■

Few athletes in any Olympic sport—and certainly none so young—face the unique pressure young female gymnasts and figure skaters do. They must distill an entire childhood of training into one perfect performance, and they must do it on the largest stage in the world. Think of the stress most teenagers feel as they pick up their No. 2 pencils and open the first page of the Scholastic Aptitude Test. Yet if they fail, only they and a faceless grader know. And they get to try again. The young women—girls—who compete on the highest levels of gymnastics and figure skating are graded publicly. Their results are broadcast on television and plastered across newspapers. Their most spectacular mistakes are replayed in slow motion and analyzed by experts. They don't get to try again.

In the summer of 1992 one billion people around the world fixed their eyes on gymnasts competing for the highest honor in their sport: Olympic gold. Twenty thousand packed the Palau d'Esports Sant Jordi in Barcelona each night to watch them in person. America's hopes rested on Kim Zmeskal, whose 4-foot-7-inch, 80-pound sixteen-year-old body graced the news magazines' pre-Olympic covers. She was anointed the next Olympic sweetheart before she even arrived in Barcelona. Zmeskal was the most promising of Béla Károlyi's new generation of gymnasts. She grew up in Houston and enrolled at Károlyi's as a youngster. By seventh grade she had dropped out of school in favor of correspondence courses so she could train full-time. She was never the most graceful performer, but she was fast, strong and tougher than any athlete Károlyi had ever trained. Teammate Erica Stokes remembers how Zmeskal would never let Károlyi see her cry or even breathe hard. She could take whatever Károlyi could give.

At fourteen Zmeskal became the youngest senior women's U.S. champion in history. A year later she became the first American to win the all-around gold at the World Gymnastics Championships. Now, in the summer of 1992, it was time to win it all. Those other competitions, however prestigious, were summer stock in the minds of most Americans. The Olympics were Broadway.

Two minutes into the first event of the all-around competition, Zmeskal stepped out of bounds during her floor routine—the routine that had earned her a gold medal as world champion just months before. That was it. She was finished. Her shot at the Olympic all-around title was gone. That one step dropped her twenty places in the standings, too deep to recover, a decade of work swallowed by 2 inches of blue mat.

Even lesser, almost imperceptible, mistakes can spell doom in gymnastics. The margin for error is as thin as a judge's pencil. The gap between gold and silver in the all-around at the 1992 Olympics was 12/1000 of a point. A bobble, a hesitation. Most sports build in a cushion for failure, an opportunity for redemption. Runners who slip in the starting blocks and swimmers who get a slow jump can make up for their mistakes during the race if they are fast enough. Pole vaulters and high jumpers are allowed three attempts to clear a height. A long jumper gets six jumps to register his best distance. A tennis player gets two serves, a batter three strikes, a quarterback four downs. Gymnasts and figure skaters get one shot. A rut in the ice, a moment of doubt, can shatter a life's dream in an instant.

■ ■ ■

No two women shouldered more pressure in an athletic event in recent years than Tonya Harding and Nancy Kerrigan as they arrived in Lillehammer, Norway, for the 1994 Winter Olympics. Neither could floss her teeth without Connie Chung or *Inside Edition* reporting it in meticulous detail. ("Earlier today, Nancy Kerrigan was seen holding what witnesses said was mint-flavored waxed floss and heading to the seclusion of an Olympic Village restroom. More as the story develops. Back to you, Dan.") Harding's ex-husband, Jeff Gillooly, was interviewed on the tabloid TV show *A Current Affair* every night for five nights. Harding's mother was interviewed by everyone. Kerrigan was interviewed by CBS Olympic host Greg Gumbel. Connie Chung interviewed Harding. Gumbel interviewed Chung about interviewing Harding.

No news organization from the *New York Times* to the *National Enquirer* could resist the story. In coffee shops and office buildings and living rooms, Americans chose up sides. No sports story in history had ever captured the country in exactly the way this one did. It had glamour, intrigue, jealousy, betrayal and two young women at its center who personified opposing American archetypes: the girl next door versus the girl from the wrong side of the tracks. The anticipation of their duel on the Lillehammer ice created the largest television audience ever to watch an Olympic event. Its 48.5 rating far exceeded the previous Olympic high of 33.3, set when Mark Spitz swam to his seventh gold medal in 1972. (One rating point equals 942,000 households.) The telecast drew the fourth-highest rating of any program in American television history, placing it in the company of the finale of the *Roots* miniseries. The competition had taken on the mien of an extravagant morality play, with Nancy and Tonya like cartoonish Wrestlemania characters representing Good and Evil, complete with costumes: Nancy in elegant black and white, Tonya in bordello red.

For the two skaters the unrelenting attention encumbered the pressures they already carried into the Winter Games. The 1994 Olympics were Kerrigan's last chance to erase the memory of her disastrous performance in the 1993 World Figure Skating Championships, when as the favorite she fell apart and finished fifth. Her nerves had always been suspect, and to triumph in Lillehammer before the world's largest audience and under the most intense scrutiny would secure her place among the all-time clutch performers in sports. And if she fought back to win the gold medal after the pain and shock of being attacked at the National Championships in Detroit, she would rise to almost mythic superstardom, dwarfing past Ice Princesses.

The 1994 Olympics were Harding's last chance too. She had thrown all her hopes for the future into this one precarious basket, dropping out of school in tenth grade to concentrate full-time on skating. "I know I'm going to do this," she told reporters in Detroit. "This is my last year as an amateur...Nothing is going to stop me." The words carried more an edge of desperation than one of confidence. They helped answer the question that begged to be answered as the bizarre story of the attack on Kerrigan unfolded: What would drive someone to risk everything—career, reputation, freedom—for a *skating title*? Even if the blow to Kerrigan's knee had kept her out of the Olympics, there were still Oksana Baiul, Surya Bonaly and Chen Lu standing between Harding and an Olympic medal.

But for Harding, skating was all she had. Skating was hope. It was a lottery ticket out of her trailer park life, away from the memories of her mother beating her with a hairbrush for missing jumps and her stepbrother trying to molest her. Without success in skating, Harding was looking at a life of rented apartments and used cars, weekly paychecks and faceless anonymity. The botched attack on Kerrigan was the work of panicked people grabbing for one last shot at riches and fame.

But the Olympic medal not only rewards, it transforms. The champion becomes an icon, a living symbol of a nation's feminine ideal. She moves into a new version of herself, her beauty and grace magnified, her flaws diminished. As a real-life fairy princess, she is welcome everywhere from the White House to *The Tonight Show* to Hollywood premieres. Like Peggy Fleming and Dorothy Hamill, she can spend the rest of her life trading on her magical name.

Harding risked everything for a chance to become America's sweetheart, though even if she somehow won the gold, the country would never embrace a skater so antithetic to its fairy princess fantasies—which made the attack on Kerrigan all the more sad and pathetic. Harding and Gillooly were like John Steinbeck's Okies, who strapped their life's possessions to a shabby truck and headed for the riches of California, only to discover their sacrifice had been for naught. The paradise for which they had sacrificed everything never existed. Like so much in Harding's life, the attack that was going to secure her future backfired. It only served to make Kerrigan a more popular and even saintlier star. And it meant shouldering a heavier load on the ice, adding America's scorn to her own burden of desperate hopes. After hiring lawyers, filing lawsuits and putting up with the media invasion of her life so she could compete in Lillehammer, Harding arrived completely unprepared— everything from not having trained enough to not having brought the right skate laces. She cracked spectacularly under the pressure, finishing eighth.

Kerrigan, on the other hand, rose to the challenge. If not for the inspired performance of the gifted world champion, Oksana Baiul, Kerrigan would have won the gold. After nearly a year of therapy with a sports psychologist who eased her fear of failure, she triumphed over her nerves and skated beautifully, almost flawlessly. She showed in those six minutes on the ice how sports can evoke the best in the human form and spirit. Kerrigan found a strength and calm in the midst of the international media frenzy that transformed the wailing young woman clutching her knee in the hall of Cobo Arena to a powerful, controlled athlete performing as if alone on a pond. The pressure that destroyed Harding elevated Kerrigan exactly in the way Americans had hoped it would. The Ice Princess in white triumphed, as if in a fairy tale.

While the attack on Kerrigan was an aberration, it had its roots in a system that plays favorites and whose obsession with beauty, class and weight conspires against the basic equation of most athletic endeavors: Talent + Hard Work = Success. Harding knew that no performer going into the 1994 U.S. Figure Skating

Championships was a surer bet to win than Kerrigan. She was clearly the heir to Peggy Fleming, Dorothy Hamill and Kristi Yamaguchi, despite a less-than-scintillating personality and dull, snippy interviews. But like savvy political managers, coaches Evy and Mary Scotvold covered Kerrigan's flaws with clever packaging. They lifted her like a real-life Cinderella from the working-class, hockey-playing, beer-and-pretzels Kerrigan clan to American Ice Princess, a stunning young woman with designer costumes, movie star looks and balletic choreography. "You must not mistake who the judges are and what their tastes are," Evy Scotvold says. "You're trying to appeal to them, that's for sure. You're not trying to appeal to your own taste. If you don't have the right taste, learn it. But don't show them your bad taste."

Before the 1992 Olympics, Evy Scotvold persuaded Kerrigan to get her gapped and stubby teeth capped. If she didn't get them fixed, he told her, it was going to cost her a lot of money in endorsements. She and her parents resisted, arguing that Nancy's teeth were perfectly healthy. But Scotvold prevailed—and it paid off. Bronze medalist Kerrigan scored as many endorsements as gold medalist Kristi Yamaguchi. Heading into the 1994 Olympics, Kerrigan already had deals with Evian, Campbell's soup, Reebok and Seiko. She was named one of *People* magazine's "50 Most Beautiful People."

Kerrigan's agent, Jerry Solomon of ProServ, also represented tennis star Gabriela Sabatini and two-time world gymnastics champion and Olympic silver medalist Shannon Miller, but Kerrigan dwarfed his other clients for sheer marketability. She had what it took to please sponsors still uncomfortable with women athletes who were too, well, athletic. Kerrigan had beauty, glamour, girl-next-door sexiness and an Olympic medal. "Most of the time when an advertiser uses an athlete, they show the athlete doing the sport, then cut to a model using the product," Solomon explains. "Even with Gabriela they do that, as beautiful as she is. But she's not as feminine as Nancy. They can show Nancy eating soup because she's so attractive and feminine. She's perfect for companies that want a female audience. She's not a jock type."

Solomon's observation cut to the heart of skating's popularity and in particular the popularity of skaters like Kerrigan. Figure skating is that rare sport in which a woman or girl can be powerful and agile yet not be labeled a jock, which for women is still considered a negative in many circles. Skaters don't show their muscles or their sweat. They wear makeup and sequins and even have a beauty consultant backstage at competitions. Skating offers the wholesomeness of sports without the aggression, the beauty of feminine athleticism without the hazy overtones of lesbianism. The athletes are starlets in blades, with agents and fans fluttering about them.

Even gymnasts, Solomon says, can't match the appeal of skaters. According to him, Shannon Miller looked too young to attract mainstream advertisers. Women can't relate to a girl who is 4 feet 7 inches tall and weighs 70 pounds. And gymnasts don't have the sex appeal of skaters. Solomon was unable to squeeze from Miller's 1992 Olympic silver medal anything like what he got from Kerrigan's bronze that same year. (Which makes the gymnasts' extraordinary sacrifices all the more remarkable: If Miller can't cash in, what hope is there of a reasonable payback for any gymnast, save the rare exception of a Mary Lou Retton?)

Going into the 1994 U.S. Figure Skating Championships, whose top finishers would comprise the Olympic team, Kerrigan seemed to have everything, including the affection of the judges. "Nancy's not from a high-class background," one judge told the *Washington Post,* "but she's a lovely lady. She was raised as a lady.

We all notice that." No one felt the bias toward Kerrigan more sharply than Tonya Harding. Kerrigan represented everything Harding could never be. Kerrigan had the endorsements. The magazine covers. The designer dresses. The Olympic medal. And Kerrigan had beaten Harding at every competition in the previous two years. Harding had nothing but a national championship, earned in 1991, and what did that bring? Raised hopes, a six-page story in *Sports Illustrated* that detailed her childhood and marital troubles, and a fan club that collected nickels and dimes at a mall to help offset her training costs.

Image-making and politicking were the game within the game, and Harding never learned to play. She refused to learn, despite the best efforts by her coaches. Yes, she came from a family with little money and education, but she wasn't the only skater from the working class. Kerrigan was as blue collar as a dime-store clerk. Nicole Bobek too. Harding's unforgivable sin in the skating community was not that she had no class or taste but that she refused to allow anybody to give her some. She wore hideous homemade costumes. She sported a ragged bleached-blond ponytail, garish makeup and fake fingernails. She had a pear-shaped body with heavy legs and arms that she accentuated with sleeveless skating dresses.

In her way, she reveled in the outlaw image. She was neither deferential to nor sociable with the skating community whose approval she needed to win. She smoked despite severe asthma. She trained only sporadically and let her weight drift, even though she knew her success rested almost entirely on landing the difficult triple Axel jump. She drove trucks, brandished a gun, swung a baseball bat at a motorist, filed restraining orders against her abusive husband, divorced him and then reconciled as if nothing had happened. When Harding won her first national title in 1991, she snubbed the formal champions' dinner to shoot eight ball with her friends in the hotel bar. During the week of the 1992 World Championships in Oakland, she refused to eat in the skaters' dining room at the hotel, where the meals were free. Despite complaints of financial problems, she ordered room service every night, which she had to pay for herself.

She did nothing to enhance her image during a tour through Europe with the other winners in the 1991 World Championships, where she finished second. Harding said she would go only if her husband, Jeff Gillooly, went with her. As each skater was allowed one guest, Gillooly went. Yamaguchi and Kerrigan, who finished first and third, respectively, went by themselves and roomed together. At the stop in Rome the local skating club arranged for a special tour of the Vatican. When the team leader, an International Skating Union official from the United States, asked who wanted to go, all but Harding raised their hands.

The team leader took Harding aside. "You know, Tonya, this is a special tour of the Vatican you might never get another chance to experience," he said.

"What," Harding asked, "is the Vatican? Some sort of religious place?"

The team leader, flabbergasted, tried to explain that it was also a place of great art, of Michelangelo's *Pietà* and the Sistine Chapel.

"Who's Michelangelo?"

As the rest of the group boarded the buses for the Vatican, Harding and Gillooly headed out to buy T-shirts.

When Harding reached the 1994 U.S. Championships in Detroit, she was convinced that no matter how well she skated, Kerrigan would always stand between her and the shiniest medal. Only the top two finishers in Detroit would go on to the Olympic Games the following month. And since Kerrigan had a lock on first place, all the other skaters in the competition knew they were fighting for second. Competitor Nicole Bobek went so far as to tell the *New York Times,* "I imagine if she doesn't do well, the judges will hold her up."

"They're not going to keep Nancy Kerrigan off the Olympic team," agreed Elaine Zayak's coach Marylynn Gelderman. "That would be stupid. Everyone accepts that would be stupid. I would be shocked if they ever would do anything as dumb as that."

Harding knew no such allowances would be made for her. She would have to make her own allowances. She had good reason to feel the skating community was against her—mostly by her own doing, though she could never see that—and panicked at the possibility of not making the Olympic team. She had not finished any competition in 1993 above third and now she had to finish in the top two at the national championships to reach the Olympics. She had been chasing this rainbow since she was four years old and this was her last chance at landing the pot of gold. At the next Olympics in four years, she would be too old.

The afternoon of January 6, 1994, the day before the start of the competition, Kerrigan glided around Cobo Arena with six other skaters in her practice session, but she might as well have been alone. In a white lace costume that suggested both First Communion and Victoria's Secret, she drew all eyes. When the session ended and Kerrigan headed down a hall for the locker room, a man in black attacked her from behind, hitting her leg just above the right knee with a club. She dropped to the floor, screaming in pain and fear. The man sprinted down the hall and crashed through a locked door, disappearing into the snowy street.

While Solomon could look at the attack in terms of money— the offers for movies, books, endorsements poured in by the hour—Kerrigan the athlete saw no silver lining. If she was not able to compete, her hard work in recovering from the disastrous World Championships a year earlier would have been for nothing. Because of skating's beauty pageant flavor, one sometimes forgets that skaters are still athletes, as competitive and driven as any quarterback or point guard. To watch as skaters slap the ice shavings from their thighs after yet another painful and inelegant fall is to understand the stoutheartedness that the sport demands. It takes no small amount of courage to glide alone onto a wide expanse of ice and subject oneself to public judgment and the risk of public failure. All the charm school manners and waterproof mascara in the world cannot save the skater who cracks under the pressure.

And at no time is the pressure more staggering for an athlete than during the final stretch of her quest for an Olympic medal, driving otherwise normal people to madness, as one skating mother put it. Christopher Bowman once returned to the locker room at a competition to find his skate blades bent and scratched; someone apparently had beaten them against the radiator. To this day, Bowman's coach, Frank Carroll, never leaves his skaters' bags unattended. Mothers have been known to slip coins into rivals' boots, hoping to cause enough discomfort to disrupt the girls' performances. Pairs skater Tracy Prussack had her skates stolen and her car vomited on. At the Pacific Coast Sectional Championships in 1994, a competition that would determine who would qualify for the U.S. Championships, one young skater received an anonymous special delivery letter at the rink, calling her names and making fun of her skating in an apparent attempt to rattle her.

The mind games are as common as the physical sabotage. Mostly it's the little things, like Surya Bonaly performing a spectacular but illegal back flip right next to Japanese competitor Midori Ito during practice at the 1992 Olympics, drawing accusations that she was trying to psych out Ito. Skaters tell of spreading damaging rumors about other skaters to prey on their emotions. Even Kerrigan got in her digs at the 1994 Olympics. To her first Olympic practice with Harding, she wore the same white costume she was wearing on the day Harding's ex-husband had her clubbed.

The jabs sound petty and silly, but when the pressure to win is so great and the difference between winning and losing so slight, skaters try to gain any advantage they can. All the training and sacrifice, the money spent, the dreams invested, the education lost—they all eventually come down to six minutes on the ice, a heavy load to carry on a pair of ¼-inch-thick blades.

■ ■ ■

Debi Thomas stood on the ice in the Calgary Saddledome as the final skater of the 1988 Olympics, as much a symbol as an athlete. She was the first African American to win the U.S. Championships, which she did in 1986 and 1988, and the World Championships, which she won in 1986. Muscular, smart and outspoken, Thomas had come to symbolize the outsider crashing skating's country club ball. She tweaked skating tradition by wearing a white unitard for her technical program at the 1988 Olympics, but she had performed too well and was too popular a skater for the judges to deduct points. She was pretty but not a beauty queen, graceful but not balletic. She carried onto the Calgary ice not only the hopes of a nation looking for its next Dorothy Hamill but also the hopes of African Americans looking for role models for their daughters. Thomas filled the slot perfectly: while she marched toward the Olympics, she began her freshman year at Stanford University, the first stop in fulfilling her dream of becoming a doctor.

Thomas also felt the expectations of the Northern California skating community, which wanted a homegrown champion. Local judges monitored her practices to make sure she would be ready for Calgary. Her coach demanded she drop out of school for the five weeks before the Olympics to concentrate full-time on her training. She had already signed on with International Management Group to represent her in what would be a financial bonanza if she won the gold.

The pressure to succeed turned skating into a job for Thomas, an eight-hour shift, five to six days a week. What she loved about skating—the sensation of flight, the swirling sense of freedom—had been boxed up and stored with other childish fancies. Skating had become work, grim as a gray suit. Too much money was at stake and too many sacrifices had been made, draining the sport of any fun. "I remember telling my mom, 'I don't even want to go,'" Thomas says. She had wanted to take a week off after winning the national championships in January, then gradually work up to a performance peak the following month in Calgary. Her coach wouldn't hear of it. He wanted her working every day for a month. "But you can't stay at a high for four weeks," Thomas says.

In Calgary, Thomas and her two teammates marched in the Opening Ceremonies, then flew to Colorado to train by themselves until a few days before the competition, sacrificing the camaraderie of the Olympic Village. "It didn't even feel like the Olympics," Thomas recalls. There was no time for the "Olympic Experience." Thomas had gone to Calgary for one purpose, to bring back the gold. "I remember thinking at one time, 'If you don't skate well, you're going to die.'"

Defending Olympic champion Katarina Witt had skated well in her long program but had left enough room for Thomas to beat her. At the edge of the rink Thomas's coach, Alex McGowan, exhorted, "Do it for America!"

Do it for America? "Christ," Thomas thought, *"America?"*

She stood in the center of the rink waiting for her music, from Bizet's *Carmen,* to begin, all the pressure and expectations narrowed like a laser onto the spot where she stood. Suddenly Thomas knew she didn't have it. "The old me would have said, 'You have got to get your act together right now. You don't have time for this crap. Do it!' But I gave in. I thought, 'Well, maybe my body will just do it because of the training.' But your body doesn't automatically do things just because you've trained eight hours a day. What makes you really come together under pressure is determination and focus and toughness. And I didn't try to do it."

When she botched a combination of triple jumps fifteen seconds into the four-minute program—she hadn't missed a jump in practice all week—she gave up. She couldn't do what she had come to do, which was to skate the best performance of her life and win the gold. She turned her triple jumps into doubles, her doubles into singles. She finished third, behind Witt and dark-horse Canadian Elizabeth Manley.

In what should have been the crowning moment of a remarkable career—she did, after all, earn an Olympic medal—Thomas felt only horror and shame. "It was like one of those tortures in Dante's Inferno. I just wanted to get it over with. I don't remember much of it. I've blocked a lot of the Olympics from my memory."

Up on the victory stand, when she accepted her medal, she felt as if she had let down her coach, her family, America and all African Americans who looked to her as a role model. Thomas wanted to quit after the Olympics, but her coach and agent pressed her to compete at the World Championships the following month. "They thought if I won, then the Olympics wouldn't mean as much. Everyone was thinking in dollar signs," she says. "I sort of suffered through Worlds. That was even more of a disaster. The one thing I do remember is skating my long program at Worlds and

I'm screwing my stuff up right and left, and I had the biggest smile on my face because I was just, like, 'You'll never have to do that again.' "

Though she is married and flourishing in medical school at Northwestern University in Illinois, those four minutes at the Olympics still haunt her. Six years later she has yet to watch a tape of her performance. She skated a few years in ice shows while attending college, then left skating for good in 1991. Since then she has skated twice—one time at an outdoor arena in Chicago with friends from med school and the other in the frozen fountain in the park across the street from her apartment. She skated like a child, trying jumps, fooling around. "It was really fun," she remembers. "But I could never go to a rink to skate. When I go to a rink and see people training, I just get chills. I sit there and I think, 'I can't believe I did that for twenty years.' "

Thomas says she has healed most of her wounds and shed the past. But she knows others who haven't. "It's nice when I run into people I used to skate with and I see that they came out okay, because there are some people with a lot of emotional scars. A lot of them just never really realized that life does not revolve around skating. They're still hanging on to it. They never saw that there was something more. I realized after the Olympics that my life wasn't over just because I didn't skate well."

■ ■ ■

Pressure is like a virus that affects each person differently. For some, it's a challenge to be met, something that energizes and emboldens. It brings out their best because they feel most alive when they're risking everything and pushing themselves to the edge of their capabilities. Mary Lou Retton, for example, flourished under the pressure of the Olympics and never blinked in the limelight that has followed her ever since. The greatest athletes, such as Joe Montana and Chris Evert, possess a confidence that won't allow losses to destroy them. They hate losing but don't fear it.

But for most, pressure is an enemy to be beaten back, draining rather than invigorating. To lose a competition is to lose the best part of themselves, the part their parents and coaches reward so lavishly with praise. The child who trains eight hours a day at a sport can't always distinguish where she starts and her sport ends. Her worth as a child is gauged on her performance as an athlete. So the fear of failure is the fear of losing all that is worthy in her. One figure skater pulls out clumps of hair; others develop ulcers and eating disorders. Gymnast Amy Jackson scraped her arms with razor blades and tacks. "We find places to put the pressure when we can't fit it in the gym anymore," says Kathy Johnson, another gymnast and a 1984 Olympic medalist.

Gymnasts and figure skaters, however, withstand another layer of pressure unknown to most other athletes. They must be perfect, not merely excellent. Their bodies must be perfectly lean. Their hair must be perfectly coiffed, their behavior perfectly polite, their movements perfectly precise. Both sports grade on a scale that begins at perfection—6.0 for skating, 10.0 for gymnastics—and drops with each mistake. There was a telling photograph in the *New York Times* after Shannon Miller won the silver medal at the 1992 Olympics. As her coach, Steve Nunno, scooped her up in a hug, Miller's legs were together and ramrod straight. She had assumed perfect form even in a moment of celebration.

The quest for perfection drove elite gymnast Karen Reid to perform ever-lengthening obsessive rituals. Before she left her bedroom for practice each day, she would touch certain objects that her mother, father and grandmother had given her as gifts. "Thank you," she would say as she touched each one. Then she began touching them not just when she left for practice but every time she left her bedroom, even if just to retrieve a sweater. She kept adding more objects until the routine stretched to minutes instead of seconds. At the gym she would say certain prayers before certain routines; the wording of the prayers, in which she asked God to protect her family, had to be precisely the same each time. She felt that God would help her in the gym if she was perfectly disciplined in her prayers. During calisthenics, she performed exactly two repetitions of each exercise beyond what the coach required.

The inevitable mistakes in her gymnastics only deepened the obsession with her rituals, as if she could rise to perfection only if everything in her life was perfectly ordered. Finally she reached the breaking point and forced herself to stop.

"I felt the pressure every single day," says Reid, now eighteen years old. She quit gymnastics at sixteen because of back problems. "There was always pressure to look so young too. You always wanted to look like a little girl, a perfect little girl. It was like a sin to grow up. If someone got their period, it was, like, 'Oh my God, you started! I hope it goes away!'

"Gymnastics was always in my mind. Even on my day off, all I thought about was conserving energy so I could do well at practice the next day...I did gymnastics for eleven years and I ask myself, 'What did I get out of it?' The answer is, 'Nothing.' "

■ ■ ■

The obsession to win and keep winning can create monsters of those who stand to lose the most. Tonya Harding was an aberration, but in her drive to succeed she wasn't much different from the father who relinquishes custody of his daughter so she can live with her skating coach, the skaters who smash the blades of rivals' skates, the young women who surgically reshape their noses or breasts or who starve themselves into bony swans, the mother whose daughter's suicide attempt isn't evidence enough that her bid for success has come at too great a cost. As breathtakingly beautiful as the sports can be, beneath their kittenish exteriors beats the heart of a tiger looking for the best, the next, the new, the one.

Pressure weighs on young athletes not only during certain select moments but every day. They hear it in the urgent corrections from their coaches. They feel it in the sidelong glances of their teammates. But most of all, when they look to the bleachers at the edge of the gym or the rink, they see it in the hopeful eyes of their parents.

5

WE ALL BECAME
J U N K I E S
P A R E N T S

■

Bill Bragg's eyes followed his seven-year-old daughter, Holly, as she spun and glided across the ice. Bragg was a fixture at the rink inside the Fashion Island Mall in San Mateo, California, a suburb of San Francisco. He hunched over a Formica lunch table, absently taking quick draughts from a Diet Coke he had bought at the Pups on a Pole in the food arcade behind him. A baseball cap rode low on his forehead, his faded ski jacket zipped against the cool rink air. His journey here had begun in 1976 when he watched Dorothy Hamill win the Olympic gold medal. He decided right then if he ever had a daughter she would be a figure skater. Bragg himself had been a swimming coach, but swimming held no magic. It couldn't turn milkmaids into princesses. To him, skating was more than a sport. To succeed in skating was to succeed in life. It was a road to riches and recognition, and perhaps more important, it was a road to respectability. Skating offered a life of restaurants with cloth napkins, hotels with marble lobbies, a life where a girl from the wrong side of the tracks could be somebody.

A few mothers chatted together at another table, but Bragg sat apart. He wasn't the storybook picture of a skater's father any more than he had been the storybook picture of a hero's son. Bragg's father played on Duke's 1938 Rose Bowl team, then continued his heroics in World War II: when his plane was blown in half, he flew it to safety, inspiring the song "On a Wing and a Prayer." The young Bill Bragg, walking in this formidable shadow, advanced from prep school in Providence, Rhode Island, to Virginia Military Institute, where he was captain of the swim team for two years. After he failed the eye test to become a pilot, he worked for the Army in South America, married, had four children, then divorced while they were still young. After he joined United Airlines as an airplane inspector in Northern California, he married again and had a daughter, whom he promptly enrolled in skating when she turned four.

At the start Holly hated it. For six months she complained while her father cajoled, bribing her with dollar bills for landing ten jumps in a row. "We as parents see what's on the other side," he said. "When they fall and they're cold, they don't see what we see down the road for them." When Bragg and his wife split up, she took Holly to live in a shelter in San Francisco, but six months later, with her life in flux, she decided she could no longer raise the girl and Bragg took custody. Slowly Holly fell in love with the ice, and she and her father spent every afternoon at the rink. When

Bragg was laid off from United and could no longer afford lessons, he still scraped together ten dollars every day during the summer to pay for two public skating sessions, keeping father and daughter at the rink from noon until 10 P.M., with breaks for dinner and sometimes a bargain matinee movie. "I was going through tough times," Bragg said, "but I got Holly to the rink every day."

A year after taking custody, Bragg lost his apartment. He moved into his 1981 Chevy station wagon and Holly bounced from one friend's house to another. They lived on food stamps, unemployment checks and handouts from churches and friends. Still, Holly skated. "I heard complaints from other parents that Holly was skating too much and they were saying, 'You don't have the money.' But I see it as she's staying out of trouble and she's always around winners," Bragg said. Holly's coach, former pairs skater Tracy Prussack, tried to help Holly when she could, taking payment from Bragg when he had it. The vendors in the food arcade kept Bragg and his daughter fed with pizza and hot dogs and Orange Juliuses, knowing they'd get paid eventually.

When Holly's mother found out her ex-husband was living in his car, she took him to court to regain custody. She did not support Holly's skating and indicated she wouldn't take her to the rink if Holly lived with her. So Bragg made a decision. Rather than see his daughter give up skating, he proposed to the court mediator that neither he nor his ex-wife have custody of Holly. Instead, he wanted to hand her over to Prussack, her thirty-one-year-old coach. The mother, who had a two-month-old baby and was still struggling financially, objected. But after three hours of arguing with the mediator and Bragg, she agreed to let Holly choose. She chose skating. In November 1993, Holly moved in with Prussack, now her legal guardian and full-time coach. Holly has not seen her mother since.

Bragg found work as a ticket agent at United at far less than his previous salary, not enough to get an apartment. He slept in his car at an Interstate 92 rest stop and showered at a 24-Hour Nautilus gym where United employees enjoy free trial memberships. He still goes to the rink every day to watch his daughter, though it is Prussack who takes Holly to school, holds her hand crossing the street and tucks a blanket around her at night.

"I've seen such a difference in Holly—" Bragg began proudly, but interrupted himself when he saw Holly was about to begin her program to James Brown's "I Got You (I Feel Good)." "Watch this!" He fell silent, transfixed, smiling at the ease with which his little girl skated. She had promise, everyone said. A natural. She already had mentioned to Prussack that maybe she would be like Olympic champion Oksana Baiul because Baiul also lived with her coach.

Only when Holly finished her routine, with a coquettish flip of her blond hair, did Bragg pick up his thought. "I've seen such a difference in Holly," he repeated. "She's such a little lady now. As parents, you've got to think, 'What's best for your child?' I'd be very selfish to keep Holly in my situation." His eyes fell on the face of his daughter, who was listening intently to Prussack's instructions. "Even though," he continued softly, "I fear I'll lose her."

Tracy Prussack understood what drove Bragg to sacrifice everything—even the love of his daughter—so the girl could skate. Prussack's parents divorced as Prussack and her brother were rising through the ranks of pairs skating. The father, a neurosurgeon, thought the children were skating too much and refused to pay for their training. Undeterred, Prussack's mother moved into a condominium on $300-a-month child support payments. When the bank repossessed her car, she drove a $200 station wagon with a chain holding the hood in place. With little money for clothes,

Prussack's mother bought her children only skating costumes and equipment. Once, during a trip to Los Angeles for a competition, she announced to her children she had no money for lunch. Tracy took out her lucky ten-dollar bill, which her coach had given her for landing a double Axel jump. She handed it over to a cashier in a paper hat. Her lucky ten dollars fed her family at McDonald's.

Prussack and her brother were ranked fourth in the country in 1979, a good bet to make the 1980 Olympic team. During a physical fitness test at an Olympic training camp, Prussack had to jump next to a wall to determine her vertical leap. She caught her foot in a hole in the wall and so severely tore a muscle in her leg that she could no longer skate on the elite level. She was seventeen and her career was over. Kitty and Peter Carruthers—another brother-and-sister pair, ranked lower than the Prussacks—took the Prussacks' place at the pre-Olympic Skate America competition. They finished second, then went on to win the silver medal at the 1984 Olympics. Just like that, the Carrutherses, not the Prussacks, grabbed the fame and riches for which both teams had sacrificed so much. In one instant an injury zapped an entire career, a lifelong dream, with all the ceremony of a computer suddenly erasing a program.

Now Prussack had another shot at success through Holly, though she didn't take Holly to make her a champion. She knew she was Holly's best chance at a decent life.

Prussack hobbled on her skates toward Pups on a Pole to buy coffee as Holly spent the fifteen-minute break teaching a friend some jump or other on the ice. Holly virtually lived at the rink now because Prussack spent so much time there. In January 1994, Holly accompanied Prussack to the U.S. Figure Skating Championships in Detroit, where they slept in a hotel with marble floors and ate in restaurants with cloth napkins. Bragg waited in San Mateo, huddled against the January chill under blankets in his backseat.

■ ■ ■

Almost every successful child athlete rides to the top on the shoulders of a parent undaunted by sacrifice and extremes—whether this means sending a child far away to train, mortgaging a home to foot the bills, taking a child out of school so she can train longer hours, abusing her physically or verbally for not performing, or even giving up custody. All skating and gymnastics parents worth their salt own four things: a car, an alarm clock, a checking account and a vision—sometimes their child's, often their own. They rise before dawn, drive dark highways and sit for hours in cold rinks or sparse gyms. Parents act as chauffeur, nutritionist, nurse, benefactor, cheerleader, masseuse, maid, politician. They work the judges and the coaches, currying favor, questioning decisions. One skating coach had to install a second phone line in his house just to handle all the after-hours calls from parents.

Many parents watch every minute of their daughter's training, sitting elbow to elbow with other driven parents. Cliques take shape. Hierarchies form. The parents of the most successful and most veteran girls wield the power, interpreting for the others the coach's body language, predicting the outcome of competitions, anointing (or dismissing) the up-and-coming stars, declaring the competence of one judge or another. Some play mind games by spreading rumors to destroy a rival athlete's reputation and concentration. They can plant seeds of anxiety by repeating a coach's critical remarks about another woman's daughter.

"I'd sit and watch and find myself getting into the trap with the moms," recalls Chris Reid, whose daughter trained at Béla Károlyi's. "I'd look at these mothers in the beginning and say, 'I'll never do that.' It's a dog-eat-dog thing, everyone groping and grasping for that coach's attention."

At Károlyi's the parents' lounge buzzed with gossip and grous-
ing. Rising star Kristie Phillips's mother, Terri, ruled the roost in
the mid-1980s. She sat in the second seat from the window along
the right wall, and God help the parent who didn't know that was
hers. She helpfully informed mothers who couldn't watch practice
every day that their daughters had gotten into *big* trouble with
Károlyi that day. She grumbled about any gymnast who pulled
Károlyi's attention from her own daughter. While her husband and
teenage son stayed home in Baton Rouge, Louisiana, Terri defrayed
costs by renting a house in Houston and taking in gymnasts whose
families lived outside Houston. The girls were told they couldn't
bathe after Kristie retired for the night because the bathroom
adjoined Kristie's room and she could not be disturbed. "Terri was
very likable," recalls one mother, "but she'd cut your throat behind
your back."

The women gossiped about everyone—this gymnast was
anorexic, that one's mother neglected her, another's beat her.
They frequently speculated about one coach at Károlyi's who was
reputed to have slept with several of the mothers—and did, in fact,
end up moving in with a mother whose daughter was one of his
most gifted pupils. The stories took on lives of their own. Martha
Traylor, mother of a Károlyi gymnast, insisted that the coach and
the mother were taking drugs and informed everyone that she had
turned their names in to the Drug Enforcement Administration.
No arrests were ever made. Yet she continued to allow her daughter
to be coached by this man, who, one supposes, could have caused
the girl serious harm if he had been coaching while on drugs. "If
you took her out, they'd never let her back," Traylor explains.

Parents become so immersed in their daughter's sport that it
becomes their own. We all are familiar with the Little League dad
who goes ballistic when his kid loses or the tennis mother who sits

on the sideline at every match as if keeping vigil. But the parents of an elite athlete take the cliché one step further, since their sacrifice and investment can bring such potentially greater glories—or greater losses. Parents have always lived through their children to some extent, but these live in fear their daughters will be expelled from the gym, so they say nothing when the coaches belittle their children or push them too hard. "We should as parents be able to make sure they're treated properly, I guess, but everybody's afraid to do it," says another Károlyi mother, Chris Fortsen. "I guess I wasn't a very good mother, because I just kind of took it."

On the one hand, the parents puff up like peacocks. "When my daughter made the Olympic team," says Carrol Stack, "I told her, 'You didn't make the Olympic team. I did.'" Yet on the other hand, many neglect their own health and family as they heap all their energy on their rising star. Skating rinks and gyms are filled with rumpled, often overweight women gathering the belongings of perfect little girls decked out in hair bows and lipstick. It's as if some mothers become invisible in the blinding light of their daughters' talent. Terri Phillips so worshipped her daughter she had a picture of Kristie painted on the side of her van.

No parent sets out to destroy a girl's life. Yet so many lose their way, seduced by the possibilities. Parents speak of being swept into a maelstrom of competitiveness and ambition so intense they often use the word "insane" to describe their behavior at the time. What begins as child's play, as a way of filling long afternoons, mutates into a tense dance between daughter and parents. Parents fear that if they're not supportive enough, their child will complain years later, "Why didn't you make me stick with it? Maybe I could have made the Olympics." But they also fear being too fervent, that they will stand accused of stealing their daughter's childhood. The parents of a gifted child have an unenviable, almost impossible, task.

They must encourage without pushing. Protect without hindering. Give praise but not too much—a daughter shouldn't be made to feel her performance determines her worth.

Too many parents simply are not knowledgeable or sophisticated enough to walk this line, to keep their eyes on their child's welfare and nothing else. Immersed in this aberrant subculture of elite sports, they lose perspective. With so many of the parents treating their children like commodities, it begins to seem normal; and no matter how harsh a parent might be, he or she can always rationalize by finding a parent who's worse. The gymnastics and skating federations do little to prepare parents for competition at the elite level. They don't warn them about eating disorders, ambitious coaches or cutthroat politics.

"I always considered the parental role as one of a buffer," says Kathy Anderson, whose daughter Hillary rose to the elite ranks while training at an unheralded gym in Newington, Connecticut, then went on to compete at Stanford. Despite pressure from coaches, Anderson limited Hillary to twenty hours of training a week—the rest of the U.S. national team trained between thirty-five and forty-five hours. As Hillary's coaches howled about lost training time, the Andersons left every Christmas for a week's vacation in Vermont. Kathy made sure Hillary ate well and kept up with her schoolwork. In the spring before the 1992 Olympics, when Hillary realized she was at best a long shot to make the U.S. team, she decided she would have deeper regrets if she missed the spring dance rather than the Olympic Trials. Her mother applauded her decision. "When I watched the Olympics, I was thankful my child wasn't there," Kathy says. The sacrifices for that brief shining moment were too great.

Hillary scored 1300 on her SATs and earned a full gymnastics scholarship to Stanford—approximately a $100,000 value over four years. By the end of her second year at college, Hillary had yet to be injured. One can only assume that her moderate training and balanced diet were responsible—a formula so basic and reasonable that it has found no place in the obsessive world of elite gymnastics.

Yet only the extremists win. While Béla Károlyi is unforgiving and relentless, he has also produced more Olympic gymnastics champions than any coach in history. So the choice becomes: Do you want your child to win, or do you want your child to stay healthy?

Few parents learn from those who have gone before; the girls' careers are too short. By the time parents realize their mistakes, their daughters have retired, the parents themselves have moved on and new parents have come in to play out the same old script. "I would never do it again," says Laura Irvin, mother of another Károlyi gymnast. "When my daughter said she'd never let her own daughter do gymnastics, I felt like a failure. All we wanted was a perfect life for her."

Chris Reid has similar regrets. She recalls how much her daughter dreaded Sundays, even though it was her day off from Károlyi's. "She once told me, 'I hate Sundays because the next day it starts all over again.' Had I known then what I know now, I never would have put my daughter in gymnastics. It's too damaging. People would say, 'Why in God's name did you keep your child in that sport?' Well, the child wanted it. At the time, it seemed it would crush her if we took her out. But I also saw how the sport began to wear down her self-esteem, how she started to walk with her shoulders rounded, as if she was worthless." Back injuries ultimately drove Chris Reid's daughter out of gymnastics at age fifteen.

Even knowledgeable parents have lost their way. The sight of one's child on a victory stand with a medal gleaming from her chest can turn a parent's head. "The first competition one of my daughters won, we were hooked," says Wendie Grossman, whose twin girls, Amy and Karen, rose through the skating ranks in the late 1970s. "God, did we get hooked. You just think, 'Wow, this is the greatest high you can find.' I really do believe it's a high. There's a rush that comes when you have a competitive skater go into a rink. It's just an amazing feeling. It's like horse racing. That's your horse. That's your prized possession. That's your showpiece. And when they do well, it's easy for a parent's need for recognition, for filling unfulfilled dreams, to surface...We all became junkies for our kids' success. You get a little bit of it and you're hooked. You want more and more, and you push your kids, and you push yourself. And you spend money you don't have."

When the Grossman girls skated, the yearly bill came to about $20,000 for both of them. By 1995, one elite skater could expect to pay about $30,000 a year for coaching, equipment and travel. One beaded costume could cost $1500. Boots went for $600 and blades for another $300. The top coaches charged between $75 and $90 an hour. There are more bills for ice time at the practice rink, airfare and hotel rooms for competitions, costumes for practice. There are bills for choreographers, music rights and mixing, ballet lessons. Many skaters' careers have been financed through second mortgages. Often a father takes on second and third jobs while the mother manages the skater, ferrying her to practice at 5 A.M., then to school, then back to practice, and in between ordering boots and blades, listening for music to accompany her daughter's freestyle programs, planning her meals, arranging her trips to competitions, monitoring her progress. "When a kid is up on the podium," Wendie Grossman concludes, "they ought to give the parents the medal."

All this work, money and sacrifice for—what exactly? A child's sense of accomplishment and self-esteem? The joy of mastering complex skills? In a perfect world, yes. Linda Leaver, Olympic gold medalist Brian Boitano's coach, stresses to parents that if they can't make their sacrifices an unconditional gift to their child, they shouldn't sacrifice at all. "They shouldn't be doing this for an end. They should be doing this for the process. There are so many things that can prevent a child from getting what you sacrificed for. But if you pursue the sport simply as a tool to becoming a better person—to learning about goal-setting, discipline, increasing self-esteem—then you can't go wrong."

Unfortunately, we don't live in a perfect world. "I'll be honest with you," says Carrol Stack, whose daughter competed on the 1988 U.S. Olympic gymnastics team. "The more money you put into it, the more you want to see. It gets to the point where it's real vicious. I think it's bad. I think it's real bad what I did. I think it's real bad what other parents did. You get so competitive and you want...you want your kid to be the best, and you're going to push, scream, yell and holler—'Hey, I paid for this.'" Stack admits that she bribed her daughter to go to practice. She threatened her with spankings when the bribes didn't work. She once refused to give her medicine for the flu because it made Chelle tired and interfered with her training. When Chelle was ten years old and running a 104 temperature, Carrol took her to the state meet in Dallas anyway. Chelle slept in the car the whole trip and fell asleep that night during dinner. She slogged through the meet the following day by taking swigs of Pepto-Bismol from her gym bag between rotations. Carrol once helped the mother of another ten-year-old dab the girl's chicken pox with makeup so no one would know she was sick. But the girl's fever soaked her in sweat during the meet and the makeup dripped down her body in streaks. The girl was asked to leave—but not before having exposed a hundred other little girls to the virus.

When Chelle didn't work hard enough, Carrol told her she was humiliated to be her mother, leaving the girl in tears. "I'm stronger than she is," the mother says. "Unfortunately."

By 1988, with the Olympics looming, the Stacks—who had moved from Philadelphia to train in Houston with Károlyi—were spending $750 a month on Chelle's gymnastics. Three months before the Olympic Trials, Chelle told her mother she wanted to quit. She couldn't take it anymore. Carrol wouldn't hear of it, saying, "I put this much time and effort into this and, by God, if you think I'm going to let you quit now, you're crazy. If I have to literally go out there and get up on the beam with you, you're going to do it. If I have to beat you every day, you're going to do it."

Chelle fell during her uneven bars routine during compulsories at the Olympics. Her big moment was a bust. Károlyi was furious, Chelle was upset, and her parents were devastated. "I went back to the hotel and cried," Carrol recalls. "I mean, I bawled. I just couldn't believe it was over. It was finished. That was it. It was a big letdown. We went through everything and this was it? Everybody had thought she was going to be the next Mary Lou, and she didn't even make the finals. There was no glory."

Carrol Stack is recounting her daughter's short career over tea at the Chinese restaurant a few doors down from the pet shop she and her husband operate in a shopping center off Highway 1960 and Interstate 45 in Houston. Though Chelle had often announced her desire to quit, she had stayed in elite gymnastics at her parents' urging until she broke her knee at age eighteen.

Two years later her mother is still coming to terms with the end of both her daughter's elite career and her own dreams. "It consumes you," she says of the sport. "It's your every thought. You sit there before a meet and you dream of their routines before they do them. After the meet you replay them. I could do every routine she did in my mind."

The years in the gym left Chelle with toes so gnarled she can't wear high heels. She has eighteen hairline fractures in her knee. She courted digestive problems by drinking whole bottles of laxatives to keep her weight down after hitting puberty. Her mother fears her daughter will suffer arthritis at a young age because her bones took such a beating for so many years. Still, the Stacks voice few regrets. Frank Stack concedes they would have been better off putting Chelle in tennis or golf because at least then she could have made some money.

"But real regrets?" Frank says as he rings up a Baggie of fish at the pet shop. "No. She came out healthy."

■ ■ ■

Parents of a gymnast or figure skater looking for a return on their investment would be better off stashing the money in their daughter's college fund. The payoff in gymnastics is almost non-existent. Mary Lou Retton and Nadia Comaneci are the only gymnasts who have made a substantial living off their sport. Olga Korbut, the 1972 gold medalist from the former Soviet Union, enjoys a modest life as a coach. Olympic silver medalist and two-time world champion Shannon Miller, who once had the same agent as skater Nancy Kerrigan, couldn't land endorsements outside the gymnastics world. Gymnasts, explained agent Jerry Solomon, don't have the sex appeal that figure skaters do. They're too young and robotic.

The payoff in skating is more substantial—as long as one wins a medal at the Olympics. But only a handful of skaters even *make* the Olympics. A country can send, at most, three female singles skaters to the Winter Games—and then only if that country had a skater finish in the top three in the previous year's World Championships.

At the 1994 Olympics, for instance, the U.S. could send only two skaters because no American woman finished higher than fifth in the 1993 World Championships. Because the Olympics are held every four years—except in 1994, when the Winter Games were held just two years after the previous competition to set up the Winter and Summer Games on staggered, biennial schedules—the United States can send no more than nine female singles skaters to the Olympics over the course of a decade. Nine! And only those nine have *any* chance of making decent money from the sport. A skater with no Olympic credentials has no chance. She can join the ice shows, but the pay scale for those in the supporting cast won't come close to matching the investment she and her parents have made.

. . .

It is not only the financial balance sheet that comes up short at the end of a girl's career. The personal losses also mount. Too often parents don't notice until too late that their preoccupation with their daughter's sport has damaged their family.

Wendie Grossman and her husband moved to Long Island from Virginia when their twin girls, Amy and Karen, were twelve years old. They found a rink first then looked for a house nearby. Their priorities were understandable: the rink was like a second home. Wendie had her baby shower at the rink. She nursed her newborn son there. Skating enveloped their lives. Wendie made matching red velvet dresses for the girls' first competition and later spent hours hand-beading their glittery costumes. She drove through paralyzing ice storms so the girls could train. She had blades sharpened and boots fitted. She found and cut the music for their programs. "It was really twelve years of my life completely devoted to seeing what I could do to make my kids' career work," Wendie says. Religious education was a low priority. "There was just no time for God," Wendie recalls. "Skating was God. That's what we prayed to: First Place."

Amy Grossman was one of the hottest young skaters on the East Coast for a time. But Karen struggled, putting in the same effort as her sister while enjoying fewer rewards, and she grew frustrated. She knew that her father, an aggressive Harvard-educated investment banker, and her mother hoped for more. "There's so much invested in your kid winning," says Wendie Grossman more than a decade later. Having returned to school for a master's degree in counseling, she now winces at the pressure she once applied to her daughters.

"Kids pick up on winning and losing real fast. There's one winner and everyone else after that is not the winner. We couldn't say, 'Coming in fifth is great, I'm so proud of you.' Five! Five is not a number that wins. It's very hard to be thrilled that your kid came in fifth, even though she skated her best. You have to be a very sophisticated parent, interested in the well-being of your child and not interested in your own competitive spirit, to say, 'You came in fifth. You skated a great program. I'm so proud of you.' That didn't happen. Not in our family."

If Amy came in eleventh and Karen thirteenth, Amy lorded it over her sister. The competition within the competition permeated the Grossman household, exacerbated by two intense parents. Amy and Karen barely spoke to each other. Wendie's marriage was distant and unhappy, held together only by the couple's shared passion for their daughters' skating.

"It was very hard to have two siblings in the same house in the same sport," Wendie says, "but to have identical twins... We didn't plan it. We were rather seduced into it. They both loved it, they both thought it was great in the beginning. And then as the drama started to unfold about the competition and who was first and who was third, or eleventh and thirteenth, we were unable to stop the damage...

"We're talking kindergarten kids [when they began skating]. Kindergarten children start skating and measuring themselves according to each other and then the rest of the world. Where else do we ask kids to start measuring themselves like that? It's incredible. It's not like playing a musical instrument, where you develop this capacity and you mature and you enter a competition when you're fifteen or seventeen."

Karen quit skating at age thirteen, tired of competing against her sister and trying to fulfill her parents' expectations. "I saw how easy it is for parents to live vicariously through their child, and it's a burden for a child, living for her parents' hopes and dreams," says Karen, now twenty-eight years old. She says her father especially had a difficult time when she left skating. "He had worked very hard in his life to have distinction, so it was very hard for one of his kids to be just a kid."

Karen's departure from skating did nothing to dampen the Grossmans' fervor for it. As Karen went off to boarding school, her parents focused on Amy, who was trying to move up in the ranks. Each time a skater wanted to move up to the next level—preliminary, juvenile, intermediate, novice, junior and senior—she had to demonstrate a proficiency in school figures and freestyle moves before a panel of three judges. When Amy took the test to qualify her to compete as a junior, she failed. She took it again. She failed again.

"We were devastated," Wendie remembers.

Amy's career as a singles skater was over, just like that. She was a beautiful freestyle skater but had no feel for the slow and meticulous school figures, still required then. When Amy chose to try pairs skating, for which she wouldn't need school figures, the Grossmans agreed to send her to Southern California to train with respected coach John Nicks, who matched her with a partner. Amy was fourteen. Though she was a gifted student, she stopped going to school full-time in favor of two to three hours of group tutoring at the rink. After five months Amy's partner quit. The Grossmans, never comfortable with Amy's leaving regular school, brought her home. Amy found a partner in New York and flourished. The pair won the Eastern Championships in the junior division and was selected by the United States Figure Skating Association to represent the U.S. at the 1982 World Junior Championships in Germany.

When Wendie opened the embossed letter from the USFSA informing her of Amy's invitation, she thought, *"We've made it."* She and Jerry both traveled to Oberstdorf, Germany, for the competition. All the work and sacrifice had culminated in this moment, with their daughter representing the United States on the ice. Seeing Amy's name in lights at the rink in Germany filled the Grossmans with pride and satisfaction. Amy and her partner finished eighth, a triumph for a team that had skated together for such a brief time. A few weeks later they won the bronze medal at the national championships.

Several months later Amy was diagnosed with a degenerative disk caused by the throws and lifts required in pairs training and competition. She had to quit skating. She was seventeen. She followed her sister to Choate boarding school, but remained a year behind Karen as a result of having missed so much school. The two would have little to do with each other. It wasn't until their late twenties that they reconciled their differences. Both graduated with honors from Ivy League schools.

Wendie and Jerry Grossman divorced. As for Matthew, the little brother, he took tennis lessons. "He hates skating," Wendie says. "I think he sensed the obsession. And I could see how the obsession could be easily transferable to another child because I was getting as hot and heavy into [Matthew's] tennis, and I knew who was who hanging around. The only difference is that I don't particularly love tennis. And I adored skating." At nineteen he is, according to his mother, a genuinely wonderful young man. "Somehow he has come out of this as the nicest kid."

Somewhere in her home in Long Island, where she lives with two dogs, Wendie still has most of her daughters' skating outfits. She still has stacks of old *Skating* magazines and videotapes of her daughters' competitions. "The past few years have been tough," she says, referring both to the divorce and her daughters' departure from skating. "I went back to school, so I filled myself up with that. And I had Matthew, and I put my energies and focus into that." She still loves skating and watches as many competitions and shows as she can. In the TV room on this autumn day, she pops a recent tape of Amy skating into the VCR. Her daughter glides across an empty rink like an angel.

Wendie is still transported by the grace of the sport and the joy of watching her own child. "I still think she's one of the most beautiful skaters I've ever seen," Wendie says. "I always wonder if things might have turned out differently with a different partner or a different coach. It's a question of luck and timing. To reach this level of sophistication and grace is a great achievement and sometimes the kids don't feel they achieved very much because they didn't win an Olympic gold medal.

"The rewards are few in terms of medals and high visibility, considering the sacrifices put in. But I don't regret the years I put into it. I feel we had more plusses than negatives. We traveled; we learned about winning and losing; the kids learned to be disciplined; we met many wonderful people.

"Sometimes I'd like to adopt a kid and do it all over again."

■ ■ ■

Most parents, like Wendie Grossman, wade into the waters of obsession incrementally.

Amy Jackson's father dove headfirst.

By the time Amy was six years old, she already had her first press clipping. A story in her Pennsylvania hometown newspaper, the *York Dispatch*, began, "Amy S. Jackson stands only 42 inches off the floor, but she's a good bet for the 1992 Olympics." It ended with a quote from her father, Bill: " 'Our goal is for her to have a happy childhood. We don't want to push her so much she burns out.' "

Yet as Amy's talents blossomed, bursting to life one after another, Jackson pushed for more. He had Amy take aptitude tests when she was four years old and, convinced of her superior maturity and intelligence, started her in kindergarten a year before her playmates. She began competing on the YMCA swimming and synchronized swimming teams at age four, practiced with the Yorkettes gymnastics team at five and learned Tae Guk E Bo kicks at karate school at six. Bill took karate classes at the same school and delighted in his tiny daughter's fiery spirit. The two were inseparable, the slight man with the glasses and nagging allergies and his blond tomboy daughter. Carol, Amy's mother, floated in the background like a vapor, transforming from chauffeur to cheerleader to cook as the need arose.

When at age six Amy qualified for Class 4 gymnastics, the

lowest competitive level, Bill took her out of swimming to devote more time to gymnastics. He was convinced his child was a prodigy. He saw how neighbors marveled when she ripped across the lawn in a blur and launched into a roundoff back handspring. She practiced her balance beam dismounts off the backyard bench. She once jumped into the Main Street parade at Walt Disney World and turned cartwheels for a block.

Still just six years old and in only the third meet of her life, Amy finished third in the all-around competition at the state level, impressing the Pennsylvania gymnastics community and cutting the tethers to whatever reservations Bill Jackson had about his daughter's talent. "What a boost to the ego to have a child like that," Jackson says today. "I was a stage father. No question." He had not competed in sports as a child in Hogansville, Georgia, the heart of the rural South. He found baseball and basketball boring and was forbidden by his domineering father from playing football. Bill was twelve when his father died, and he assumed responsibility for his mother, grandmother and younger brother until he left for college and, afterward, served eight months as a corpsman for the Third Marine Division in Vietnam.

He marveled that his unremarkable Hogansville roots had produced the extraordinary creature who, he believed, would someday ride through ticker tape parades in red convertibles. He dreamed of the Olympics as he watched Mary Lou Retton rivet the nation at the 1984 Summer Games. More important, he watched her coach, Béla Károlyi, whom Jackson considered "the god of gymnastics, the man who could take your child out of obscurity and into fame and fortune."

When Amy was eight, Jackson decided she had gone as far as she could at the YMCA, but he felt she was not yet ready for

Károlyi's. So he found a new job in Atlanta as a nurse anesthetist and moved the family there, enrolling Amy at the well-respected Atlanta School of Gymnastics, where both Kathy Johnson and Kristie Phillips had trained.

For Amy, gymnastics would never be the same. She immediately moved up to Class 3, where she was the youngest of the competitors in her first meet. For the first time she would have to perform compulsories, which are routines of required skills in the uneven bars, balance beam, vault and floor exercise; and optionals, which are routines of the gymnast's own choosing in each event, with only a limited number of required skills. Jackson saw this meet as a test of his daughter's mettle. He wanted Amy to announce her presence as the newest star on the scene, the one the others would have to chase. When she finished second, an incredible triumph in Amy's mind, her father offered no congratulations. In the car afterward, he spoke sharply into the rearview mirror, his eyes locked on his daughter's face in the backseat, "Next time you can win it," he said. "Next time I know you can do it." Stunned, Amy said nothing.

Amy's gymnastics career consumed her father's attention. When she had trouble mastering the handstand on the uneven bars, Jackson made her do push-ups at home to strengthen her upper body. When her handstand pirouettes on the bars drew her coach's criticism, Jackson bought a single parallel bar and mounted it on a stand low to the ground in the living room. He sometimes had her practice her handstand pirouettes until her arms shook. For Amy, both the father who had been her closest pal and the sport that had been her favorite game disappeared that first summer in Georgia.

In 1985, less than two years after arriving in Atlanta, Jackson decided Amy was ready for Károlyi. She prayed he would change his mind. Even at nine years old, she understood that moving to

Károlyi's raised the stakes in a game that already frightened her. "I was kind of worried that my father was so excited about it," Amy recalls. "I was scared, scared of learning new things, scared I wasn't going to be good enough, that I wouldn't be able to do anything to please him. I was already thinking of quitting." But she never told anyone. Later, when she became terrified of the vault after Julissa Gomez broke her neck, she still said nothing. "I always did what I was told. I was so scared of what my dad would do if I said anything."

Károlyi gushed over Amy when she arrived in Houston and placed her in coach Rick Newman's group of young hopefuls. Jackson kept close tabs on Amy's workouts at Károlyi's through his wife's phone reports from the daytime sessions and his own observations at night. He drove directly to the gym after work to join his wife in the viewing room. Amy would glance at her father after every skill, and he would coach her with hand signals, indicating her legs weren't straight or her back wasn't arched enough. Her father's appraisal meant more to her than her coach's because her father's penalties for mistakes were much stiffer. If she had a bad practice, she had to hear on the ride home how much this training was costing him and how important it was to make the Olympics. Amy says he had worked himself into such a fit of anger after one practice that he pulled her hair in the car; when he let go, her head knocked into the door window.

"He just got caught up in it all," Carol Jackson says. "We all got caught up, to the detriment of our children. That's the way it was." Sometimes Carol ached for her daughter but said nothing. In the midst of her husband's explosions, when Amy's eyes locked on her mother's, Carol would look away. She knew she should speak up for the girl, but she felt powerless, and deep down she craved her daughter's success as much as her husband did.

Amy kept winning through Class 2, beating the likes of future world champion Kim Zmeskal when they were ten-year-olds. Yet one night after dinner, while her mother cleared the table, Amy screwed up the courage to tell her father she wanted to quit. For two hours he yelled at her, saying she was too good to quit. Her mother kept her eyes on the dishes. When a short time later Amy won the junior division of the prestigious American Classic at age eleven, she seemed on her way to stardom whether she liked it or not. Jackson's excitement was boosted even further when Károlyi summoned the family into his office one day after Amy's triumph. He patted her blond head and said the words that Bill Jackson had longed to hear: "Well, you are the next one."

But at the U.S. Classic a short time later, Amy finished second by two-tenths of a point. It was the beginning of the end. Károlyi's enchantment with her wore off quickly as he laid his hopes on the tough and tiny Kim Zmeskal. Amy hit puberty at age twelve and soon towered over her teammates. She hated the gym more than ever. She faked illness by pouring cups of water into the toilet to simulate the sound of vomit. She faked injuries. Usually, her father made her go to practice anyway. So Amy would sabotage her workouts at the gym. Girls who didn't listen or messed up their routines were sent off to do conditioning exercises as punishment. Amy deliberately got into trouble so she could do exercises instead of her routines. If she wasn't doing routines, she couldn't make mistakes for which her father could berate her.

Even Jackson began to understand what was happening. Amy was used up, her body was betraying her, and Károlyi had moved on to the next rising star. The god of gymnastics was not going to turn Amy into Mary Lou Retton. He wasn't even going to try. The dream was over. "If the Károlyis are not going to pay any attention to her, what's the use?" Jackson told his wife. But by now Carol

had invested too much of herself to let Amy quit. Carol switched
her daughter to another gym in Houston in the hopes that a change
might regenerate Amy's enthusiasm. Instead, Amy's gymnastics
declined and Carol returned her to Károlyi's. A few months later,
two weeks before her thirteenth birthday, Amy walked out of Károlyi's gym in the middle of practice one day and never returned.
Her father wasn't around to talk her out of it. He had filed for
divorce and moved to South Carolina five months earlier.

When asked about Amy five years later, Károlyi had no rec-
ollection of her. "I'm not surprised," Bill Jackson says. "There's
no room in his memory or his heart for someone he considered a
quitter."

Amy tried out for cheerleading at Westfield High School in
Houston, just blocks from Károlyi's gym, but was kicked off the
squad when she failed science. She joined the drill team but refused
any role that would bring attention to herself. She joined student
government but wouldn't run for office. Her grades slipped. Amy
didn't want to be good at anything ever again. The price of success, she had learned in her young life, was pain, abandonment and
inevitable failure. She preferred to be invisible, a nothing.

By her junior year she had left the drill team for the company
of the school outlaws—the diffident, ambling crowd of kids who
smoked cigarettes in the bathroom and marijuana in the parking
lot. Amy pierced her nose and got a tattoo of a shamrock on her
abdomen. When she watched the 1992 Olympics, for which she
had invested her childhood, she felt no pangs of longing. "I didn't
want to be there at all," she says. "I didn't want to think about all
the work I'd have to do to get there. I don't think it's worth it."

It wasn't until her senior year, when Amy was caught smoking
on campus, that a school counselor suggested she see a psychologist. She had stopped brushing her hair. She barely bathed. Her

clothes looked as if she had pulled them from under her mattress. "I didn't feel I was worth anything," she remembers. She had also begun cutting herself.

It began after a fight with a boyfriend. She pulled a tack from her bedroom wall and ran the point across her arm until it bled. At school she hid her hands under her desk and cut herself with an open staple. Sometimes she scraped herself with a straight razor, leaving raw red patches. If her mother noticed the marks, Amy would say she had fallen while playing soccer. Once, Amy squeezed blood from a cut, dipped her finger in it and wrote a note to her boyfriend. "I didn't know how to deal with the pain inside," Amy says. "But I knew how to deal with physical pain."

The psychologist referred her to a psychiatrist, who diagnosed her as a manic-depressive due to child abuse and abandonment— the abuse from gymnastics and her parents, the abandonment from her father. The doctor prescribed sleeping pills, therapy and eventually Prozac, the controversial antidepressant.

After two weeks on Prozac, Amy awoke one night with a plan. She was sick of cutting herself and had figured out what she needed to do. The next morning she showered, fixed her hair and carefully applied makeup. "I looked real nice that day," she recalls. "I guess I was feeling, like, 'This was it. I might as well go out looking good.'" On her way out, she slipped a huge bottle of aspirin from the kitchen into her backpack. At lunch with her boyfriend, she excused herself from the school cafeteria with a paper cup of Coke, went to the bathroom and swallowed four handfuls of pills, about 150 in all. Her boyfriend noticed the half-empty bottle when she returned to the lunch table and rushed her to the school nurse.

After doctors pumped her stomach, she recovered in the hospital for two days, then was transferred to Baywood Mental Hospital. She stayed two weeks, though she was given a three-hour pass one afternoon to attend her high school graduation. She spent the summer of 1993 in therapy and in the fall enrolled at Blinn College, a junior college one and a half hours from Houston, then moved back with her mother to attend North Houston Community College. She stopped cutting herself and no longer takes antidepressants. For the first time since she was thirteen, she has no man in her life. She broke up with her last boyfriend after he pushed her against a bathroom wall and cut her back on the toilet-paper dispenser. "I'm happy now," she says. "It's weird, because I haven't been happy for so long."

She rarely sees her father, who lives in Lexington, South Carolina, with his second wife and her son. She resents him for what he did and feels he still doesn't recognize how much damage he caused. Not true, Jackson says. "I'm a failure as a parent. I know that. I was a crummy father. To have an Olympian, oh man, what a thing to have happen to you. She was on course and it consumed our relationship.

"What I'd tell other parents is it's not worth it. It's just a sport. Don't do it. Don't do it at all. Enjoy your children as they grow up. It was child abuse what we did, what the coaches did. It was the psychology of war: stripping people of their egos so they can go out and kill somebody. I did it and I was wrong. The only thing I don't apologize for is wanting her to do as well as she could do. But how do you draw the line between encouraging and pushing? I certainly couldn't."

■ ■ ■

The parents who relinquish control fail their children as surely as those who hoard it. Parents who turn their children over to coaches and surrogate families expose them to potential mistreatment, including a parent's darkest fear, sexual abuse.

The potential for sexual abuse when men coach young girls is real. "The more you reduce the number of controls in a family situation, the more likely [abuse] is going to happen," says psychologist Greg Briehl, who has counseled young tennis players damaged by sexual relationships with their coaches. The very traits that make young girls good gymnasts or figure skaters—obedience, reticence, pliability, naïveté—also make them prime targets for sexual abuse. The USGF instituted what one official calls "a pretty pro-active program" in the early 1980s to fight sexual abuse after several coaches were accused of molesting their athletes. One coach was relieved of his national coaching duties after a complaint to the USGF, a complaint later bolstered by another gymnast, who came forward with her own accusation that the coach coaxed her into having sex with him when she had just turned eighteen. She said he also turned two athletic massages into sexual encounters. Neither gymnast pressed charges, and the coach had long since retired when the second gymnast confronted him with her memories years later.

A rarely acknowledged danger, however, lurks in the living rooms and bedrooms of an athlete's home away from home. A young gymnast who leaves home, for example, often moves in with the family of another gymnast. Parents must believe that the family to whom they've entrusted their daughter will protect and nurture her. But the parents, hundreds or thousands of miles away, can't know for certain.

One girl was fourteen when the father of a fellow gymnast, with whom she stayed several nights a week to avoid the long commute to her family's home, began molesting her. He was also molesting a friend of hers, another gymnast who often stayed at the house.

The first girl was molested for four years, from her freshman year to senior year in high school. When as a sophomore she injured her knee, dislocated her elbow and hurt her back, she pleaded with her mother to let her quit. But she had said the same thing so many times that her mother figured she was just talking again. She told her to stick with it.

The abuse finally came to light when the girls took part at school in a written survey on sexual abuse. Because the survey was anonymous, this young girl answered the questions truthfully. A classmate saw what she wrote and told the principal, who summoned the police to the school. She immediately admitted what the man had done to her. Her friend at first denied anything had happened, then also confirmed the abuse. Both wrote long accounts for the police, who trapped the man into admitting the abuse by having the first girl call him at work from the police station.

The other girl's mother refused to allow her daughter to testify. So the first went to court alone during her freshman year at college. She was battling an ulcer, brought on by stress and by the four to five Motrins she had been taking every day since she blew out her knee two years earlier. Sometimes her stomach and throat hurt so much she couldn't eat and could barely swallow. The year was a blur. She was taking Zantac for her ulcer, going to therapy, trying to keep up in class, competing in gymnastics and flying across the country for depositions and the trial.

The man pleaded guilty to one count of sexual assault against her and no contest to a second charge involving her friend. He was sentenced that summer to twelve years in prison. As of 1994 he was still out on bail pending an appeal.

■ ■ ■

Nearly a year after moving in with her skating coach, eight-year-old Holly Bragg still had not talked with her mother. "If you make it to the Olympics, I'll guarantee you she'll be there," Holly's father said to her. Still living out of his Chevy station wagon at a highway truck stop in San Mateo, Bill Bragg visited his daughter twice a week at the new San Jose Ice Center, where her coach had landed a job as skating director. But his car was starting to give out and he could no longer coax it over the East Bay hills to the rink in Dublin where Holly also trained several times a week. He had no money to fix the car and wondered what he'd do when it broke down.

"Oh, but it's not so bad, really," he said. "Not as bad as it sounds. And anyway Holly's still skating. We've faced so many roadblocks that you think she shouldn't be skating ever again, and then the roadblocks are taken away to keep her skating. You should see her. Doing double jumps, almost doing double Axels. Pretty good at eight."

During the summer Holly spent a week training with Olympic gold medalist Kristi Yamaguchi and Yamaguchi's coach, Christy Ness. Bragg cornered Kristi one day. "You've been working with my daughter for a few days now. How would you compare yourself at eight to her?"

Kristi arched her eyebrows. "Oh my God, Holly is so much better than I was." Bragg nodded and smiled. Overhearing the exchange, Christy Ness gently interrupted. "It's not how good you are when you start," she said, "but how good you are when you finish."

Sometimes that fate is not shaped by athlete, coach or parent but by a system rife with politics and favoritism. Sometimes a young woman is doomed before she begins.

6

THE GAME WITHIN
THE GAME

POLITICS AND MONEY

■

The dark concentration and tension of the last few months of training had fallen away from Kim Kelly's face. Her eyes seemed lit from behind. "Welcome," the announcer boomed over the cheering crowd inside the Baltimore Arena, "the 1992 United States Olympic Team!"

Kim and five other gymnasts waved their flower bouquets to the fans as they paraded across the floor at the end of the U.S. Olympic Trials. After falling short at the Trials four years earlier at age fourteen, the youngest gymnast at the meet, Kim had staked everything on making the Olympics in 1992. She put off entering the University of Alabama so she could train full-time, and she became a slave to a strict diet that pared 10 pounds from her squarish frame. She worked longer hours than she had ever worked in her life. But at that moment, with the cheers washing over her and with her parents near tears in the stands, Kim Kelly felt like a sailor finally spotting land.

She had been in gymnastics since she was six years old, first at a park and recreation program near her home in King of Prussia, Pennsylvania, then at a local gym. When she was thirteen, she joined the nationally respected Parkettes gym in Allentown, 63 miles from home. She and her mother made the commute six days a week for two years. Then, when Kim's training schedule grew more intense, mother and daughter moved to Allentown, boarding in the home of an elderly widow. Stephanie Kelly worked as a medical transcriber to pay their living expenses and as a secretary at the gym to pay for Kim's training. Her youngest son was just entering high school, a daughter was graduating high school and another daughter was entering college. Stephanie wouldn't be around to guide any of them, relegating the responsibilities to her husband. She stayed with Kim in Allentown for four years, usually driving home once a week, once every other week if Kim had a competition on the weekend. She missed all of her son's high school years, justifying the sacrifices by believing Kim needed her more. Her daughter loved the sport so passionately and had a chance to achieve something special. The family hadn't staked their fortunes on Kim's making the Olympics, even though Kim was clearly a contender. She had competed on the U.S. national team on the junior and senior level for seven years, and represented the United States at the 1989 World Gymnastics Championships.

"We were not naïve, stupid people," Stephanie says. "We took our goals one year at a time. The Olympics is such a stupid, unrealistic goal. If you're in it for the Olympics, you're stupid. You're in it for all the wrong reasons." But when a judge told Kim in 1991 that she had a great shot at making the team, she postponed college for a year to train full-time.

In 1992 the United States Gymnastics Federation had laid out a clear selection process for the Olympic team. The U.S. Gymnastics Championships would count 30 percent toward qualifying for the team and the Trials would count 70 percent. The seven gymnasts with the top combined scores would make the training team: six would compete in the Olympics, one would be the traveling alternate. Polished and fit, Kim finished sixth at the U.S. Championships and fourth at the Trials, making the team with room to spare. As everyone understood it at the Trials, the training team would be those six who waved at the crowd in Baltimore plus Michelle Campi, who didn't compete at the Trials because of a fractured elbow but had finished among the top six at the U.S. Championships.

Kim didn't care who else was on the team or how they got there. She was on it. She and her coaches had ignored the whispers that at eighteen Kelly was too old and that her womanly body didn't present the right image. When Kim finished the Trials, her coaches, Bill and Donna Strauss of the Parkettes gym, marked her triumph by giving her a pendant in the shape of the five Olympic rings. In their excitement, neither Kim nor her coaches heard the USGF's political machine whirring to life, its blade spinning in their direction.

■ ■ ■

Politics in gymnastics and figure skating is the politics of image. In sports where the results depend on the perception of a performance as much as the performance itself, playing the political game well can make or break a career, as Tonya Harding learned. The coach and athlete who curry favor with the powers that be and conform to the proper body type and image enjoy clearer paths to the victory stand than those who don't. In gymnastics, the federation officials wield most of the power. In skating, the judges do. Judges are both god and guide. They nudge skaters down the "right" roads, advising them on everything from music to mascara.

The relationship between judges and skaters is more informal than one might expect in such a large, international sport. Judges regularly call the parents and coaches of a skater to suggest she wear more blue, or grow her hair long, or lose a few pounds. One judge reportedly suggested to a top skater that she get a nose job because her nose was "distracting." Another encouraged a skater to get breast reduction surgery. Nothing is too personal in skating if it bears on the skater's career. It all matters. At the 1993 U.S. Figure Skating Championships, there was speculation that judges lowered scores for flamboyant Nicole Bobek, then fifteen, because she didn't fit the desired image. She carried a reputation for having a wild streak—as evidenced, the judges decided, by the four earrings she displayed in one ear. "They're sending her a message to tone it down," a skating insider told the *Washington Post* at the time.

"There's a certain amount of feeling that goes into who wins," says Nancy Kerrigan's agent, Jerry Solomon. "There's a concern about what people think. About how you do in practice. About what you say to the press. It's all going to have an impact on whether someone gives you a 5.8 or a 5.7."

Despite a rule book the size of a phone book, judging in figure skating is an imperfect science, mostly because its practitioners are human but also because they are still unpaid volunteers who advance in rank through a system that rewards conformity and political savvy as much as knowledge. This message is made clear to aspiring judges when they begin as "trial judges." Trial judges sit in the stands behind the real judges and score the skaters. At least 80 percent of their scores must match the real judges' scores for the United States Figure Skating Association to consider them for certification. Not surprisingly, trial judges often try to get a feel for how the real judges view the field of skaters even before a competition begins, thus improving their chances of matching scores.

The real judges are also under pressure to keep in line with the majority. A committee reviews every judge's marks from every competition during the year and questions those who have disagreed too often with their colleagues. Such a standard, while it weeds out incompetents, pressures less confident judges to follow the political wind rather than trust their own eyes and risk standing alone. Pairs coach Keith Lichtman recalls a judge rushing toward him during a practice session at the World Junior Championships one year. She was shaking and near tears. "Where should I put these teams?" she asked Lichtman, who had a team skating in the competition. "She was completely confused," he says. The pressure to conform can also encourage cheating. At the 1994 U.S. Championships in Detroit, for example, one judge reportedly was caught on videotape glancing over at another judge's marks after each pair performed during the junior ice dancing compulsories.

Trial judges are also subject to a process called peer evaluation. A minimum of eight real judges rate the trial judges on a scale of one to six on such traits as punctuality, ethics, appearance and rapport with skaters, coaches and other judges. The National Football League, the National Basketball Association and Major League Baseball would prompt an insurrection by the referees and umpires if appearance and amiability became job requirements. The players and coaches would revolt too. More than anything else, a competitor wants an arbiter who is fair, competent and unflinchingly principled, no matter how personally unpleasant or unsightly he or she might be. But in figure skating, image is so important that even the Zamboni driver wears a tuxedo.

Because judges reward conformity and tradition, coaches pressure their young girls to model themselves after the reigning princess—say, Nancy Kerrigan—because her look and style are what the judges want at the moment. If a girl is of stockier build than Kerrigan, she must lose weight and reshape her body, whether it makes her a better skater or not. If Kerrigan is winning with classical music and balletic choreography, then skaters know that safe and conventional programs are likely to win out over daring and imaginative ones. Certainly there are judges who stand alone against the crowd, but the system discourages it. A judge who stands alone too often will no longer be a judge.

Some coaches and even some parents use a judge's insecurity— or ego—to their benefit. They lobby the judges on their skater's behalf. "I'm absolutely positive that it does work if you're wining and dining judges and bringing them in, buying them dinners and stuff. But it's up to the individual judges to spot if they're being played for suckers or if it's genuine," says Alex McGowan, Debi Thomas's coach.

At the Olympics in Lillehammer, Kerrigan's coach Evy Scotvold was seen after practice one day chatting and laughing with Margaret Weir, the only American on the women's judging panel. It's doubtful they were talking about Kerrigan—she hardly needed a boost—but the appearance of a coach and a judge fraternizing just days before the most important competition of the skaters' lives would not go unnoticed by Kerrigan's opponents. Scotvold dismisses the suggestion that he works the judges. He doesn't do it, he says, because he doesn't need to. "Very frankly, when you're a coach who's been around and been successful, you're well known.

When you stand at the boards [at the rink's edge] and those judges see you're standing there with a skater, that skater is already doing better than all those other skaters are. So you don't have to do things." In other words, the reputation of a coach can enhance or diminish a judge's opinion of a skater.

Parents frequently call local judges at home after a competition to ask them to explain their marks. One coach recalled how a mother from his club was notorious for cornering influential judges at competitions to lobby for her daughter. During a practice session at the national championships one year, as the woman made a bee-line for a judge, the mother of a rival skater purposely intercepted the judge and kept him occupied until his bus arrived to take him back to his hotel, leaving the other mother seething.

Coaches sometimes ask colleagues who might be particularly close to a judge, and who don't have an entrant in the event, to put in a word for their skater. Some include judges on their Christmas card list. "One judge, if you told her she looked good in her jeans, she loved you," says Keith Lichtman. The skaters themselves, at least the savvier ones, quickly learn how to play the game. When Debi Thomas was breaking into the upper echelons of skating, she switched membership from a Northern California skating club to the Los Angeles Skating Club. Her reason: more national and international judges happened to live in Southern California and belonged to the L.A. club, thus improving her chances of getting a "home judge" on a judging panel during competitions. It is generally accepted that judges score skaters from their own clubs more favorably because they know the skater so well and because a high-ranking skater enhances the reputation of the club.

As a matter of course, a skater and her coach will invite a local judge to the skater's rink to evaluate her program before a competition. One skater reportedly sent a tape of her program to twenty-four judges across the nation before the 1986 U.S. Championships to solicit feedback. Most skaters genuinely want the input; they respect the judge's eye and appreciate the judge's willingness to share his or her time and expertise. Others do it merely to stroke the judge's ego, agreeing with every suggestion, then rolling their eyes when the judge leaves and changing nothing in their programs.

"Judges are supposed to be unbiased," Debi Thomas says, "and if you believe that, I have a bridge to sell you."

To be fair, the judges' job is almost impossible. They determine winners and losers without the benefit of a measuring stick. Yes, each skater must successfully execute certain required elements in each program, but the rest is as subjective as evaluating art. Judges are charged with quantifying grace and beauty—and they must do it in one minute. In the sixty seconds following a skater's performance, a judge must make sense of the notes he or she has scribbled during the program, subtract fractions of points for mistakes and rank the skater not only in relation to those who have already skated *but to those who have yet to skate*. Unlike in gymnastics, where a score emerges from a (supposedly) hard-and-fast point system based on execution and level of difficulty, skating's scores are all relative. Each of the nine judges must rank the skaters—one through fifteen, or however many skaters are competing—as they perform. These rankings are called ordinals. A judge cannot give the same score to two skaters because he or she cannot give the same ranking to two skaters.

If, for example, a judge gives one skater a 5.9 (out of a possible 6.0), that judge is leaving room for only one other skater in the rest of the field to score higher. If two skaters perform better, tough luck; only one can finish ahead of the 5.9 skater on that judge's scorecard. This is why judges watch the skaters practice for days before the competition. Though part of the skating judge's oath reads "I will free my mind of all former impressions," the job doesn't allow it. He or she must already have a pretty good idea of how the skaters compare to each other. Otherwise, how can a judge possibly give a score to the first competitor? The judge who has no clue about the competence of the rest of the field cannot know whether the first skater was better or worse than most. And if there are twenty or thirty skaters in a field, how can a judge remember how No. 12 performed by the time No. 25 comes along if he or she has seen each skater's program only once?

In the three or four days of practice before a competition, the skaters doll themselves up like Estée Lauder cover girls, hair in French braids and ribbons, bodies in backless costumes of gold lamé and black spandex. They know they are being watched—by rival coaches and skaters, by a smattering of fans and by the judges, who are already sorting the skaters into three categories: those who look likely to win a medal, those who are long shots and those who have no chance. The official competition may not start for a few days, but the real competition begins in these practice sessions.

The flaw in the system is clear: the playing field isn't level on the day of the competition. Judges leave little room for upstarts to have the performance of their lives, and they prop up recognized stars who have an off night. One example of the system's failure came during the 1994 U.S. Championships. Judges for the pairs competition watched the team of Karen Courtland and Todd Reynolds skate cleanly in practice all week. But at the competition Courtland fell three times and tripped her partner once. Another team, Rocky Marval and Natasha Kuchiki, skated beautifully with no major errors. But Courtland and Reynolds still somehow drew higher marks than Marval and Kuchiki, winning the bronze and earning the last spot on the Olympic team. Michael Rosenberg, the agent for Marval and Kuchiki, exploded.

"They were screwed!" Rosenberg raved to reporters in the press room that night (after prudently instructing his clients to take the high road and not criticize the judging). "It's a fucking travesty! This is everything! This determines who goes to the Olympics, which changes their lives forever. They kept Rocky and Natasha from going to the Olympics and kept them from potential fame and fortune. They weren't beaten, they were jobbed."

Most concede, however, that judging is a bit less political today than a few years ago, now that school figures have been dropped from competition. Instead of three parts to a competition—figures, short program and long program—there now are just two. In the old days, judges could rank a skater so low in the figures portion of the competition that she couldn't win a medal no matter how well she skated in the short and long programs. And the judges could make the ranking without fear of second-guessing, since the press generally didn't cover the tedious event. In essence, the skater would be out of medal contention before she even got to the short program.

To this day, Marylynn Gelderman contends that Elaine Zayak's scores in figures were based on whether she was in or out of favor at the time. "When she was ranked fourth [in figures] at the World Championships, she should have been about seventh," Gelderman says. "And when she was ranked thirteenth, she should have been about seventh. But when she was fourth, they loved her, and when she was thirteenth, they didn't like her, whether it was because she had failed them at the time or she had put on weight."

But, says four-time national medalist Caryn Kadavy, the dropping of figures has hardly eliminated the politics in judging. "It's still judged so much on whether people like you or not."

And whether you have a name.

Judges have been known to suffer temporary blindness when a

reigning champion falters on the ice. Evy Scotvold saw this at the 1992 Olympics when his skater, Paul Wylie, skated flawlessly yet lost the gold to Viktor Petrenko. Petrenko had been first or second at every competition going into the Winter Games; Wylie had been erratic while trying to juggle skating with his full course load at Harvard. Even though most observers thought Wylie skated better than Petrenko at the Olympics, Petrenko won, based partly on his track record.

"It's unfair, but we all know how it works," Scotvold says. "So in a sense, we could never hope for a gold medal for Paul in '92. We could only hope for a medal. It's unfortunate, but it's so hard for a judge to come up with a perfect, accurate judgment in four minutes while they're trying to take notes, mark down what the skater did and still see everything. It is so hard. So you have to forgive. It can't be done much better than that.

"So judges have to have an idea of what a person is like before they judge them…It might sound imperfect, but it's as humanly good as we've been able to come up with, and all of us who have been around know so…So there is fairness to it in that everybody knows this is how it works. The only thing that would be unfair is if they suddenly decided they're going to do it differently and they didn't tell me. For example, we can play cards and if you want to cheat, that's fine, but you've got to let me know it's fair to cheat. But if you're the only one that's allowed to, well, you see what I mean.

"So you deal with the system on that basis. If you want to be the champion, you're going to have to soundly drub [the reigning champion]. If it's even, you've got to presume that you're going to lose."

. . .

After Kim Kelly and her coaches arrived home from the Olympic Trials in Baltimore, they received a letter from the United States Gymnastics Federation officially informing them that the selection process had been revised. The Baltimore six and Michelle Campi were not *necessarily* the Olympic team. They might be, but they might not. The federation wanted the team to include a sixteen-year-old gymnast named Betty Okino, a stunningly talented athlete who was too injured to compete in either the U.S. Championships or the Olympic Trials. Okino, long-legged and elegant, had won a silver medal on the uneven bars at the World Championships in the spring, despite having surgery weeks before to screw a bone in her lower right leg back together. A month later, after complaining of back pain, she was diagnosed with stress fractures in four vertebrae in her lower back and had to miss both Olympic qualifying competitions. Doctors had told her to rest for ten weeks, but with the Summer Games less than ten weeks away, she had returned to the gym within a week, wearing a brace, popping anti-inflammatory drugs and swallowing eight Advils a day.

Pain shot down the backs of both legs. It hurt to breathe. But she had dreamed about the Olympics since she was nine years old. She was going to find a way to be there. And the USGF was going to help her. Okino, like Károlyi teammate Kim Zmeskal and Oklahoma City's Shannon Miller, was a star. The International Gymnastics Federation had recently recognized a move she introduced on the beam—a triple pirouette—as "the Okino." She had a name. And names carried weight with international judges.

The federation announced another "trial" for the six gymnasts who had triumphed in Baltimore, plus Campi and Okino. From these eight, the six Olympic competitors and one traveling alternate would be chosen. One gymnast would go home. What's more, the USGF decided to hold this unprecedented event at Brown's

Gymnastics in Orlando, Florida, which happened to be the home club of Wendy Bruce, who had finished last among the six "Olympians" in Baltimore.

The federation still wasn't finished with its maneuverings. It decided that the "trial" in Orlando would not be judged. There would be no scores, no way to quantify the performances. The gymnasts wouldn't know at the end of each event how they were faring. Instead, the *coaches of the competing gymnasts* would simply observe the athletes, then gather in a room and vote on who should be on the team.

Even Béla Károlyi, who stood to benefit from getting his gymnast Betty Okino on the team, howled at the unfairness and inanity of the selection process. "If there are no rules, or the rules change depending on who is telling them to you, it is crazy," Károlyi told reporters. "It is absolutely outrageous." Gymnastics was subjective enough with real judges. Now the federation was taking away scores altogether and selecting the team on the votes of seven coaches who were fighting to get their own gymnasts on the team and who had alliances with each other. Károlyi had three gymnasts competing: Betty Okino, Kim Zmeskal and Kerri Strug. Rick Newman, who had worked for Károlyi for ten years, had Michelle Campi. Steve Nunno, who had worked for Károlyi for a year, had Shannon Miller. Rita Brown, who owned the gym where the meet was held, had Wendy Bruce. The only coaches with no edge among their colleagues were Kelli Hill, who trained Dominique Dawes, and Bill and Donna Strauss, who had Kim Kelly. Who knows what sort of lobbying and vote-trading went on behind closed doors? Getting an athlete into the Olympics can transform a coach's career. It boosts a coach's business, not to mention his or her ego.

Rita Brown, especially, had a lot riding on Wendy Bruce's success. Another of her athletes, Brandy Johnson, had left her less than two months before the 1988 Olympics to train with Károlyi. When Brandy made the team, Károlyi got the credit. Says Brown, "I had something to prove—that yes, I can produce an Olympian."

"There was definitely lobbying done ahead, and certain individuals went out and were seeking votes," Donna Strauss contends. "It's just sad that that's how the Olympic team did get selected." Perhaps there is a more ridiculous, more unjust way to select an Olympic team, but one doesn't come immediately to mind.

The men's Olympic team, by contrast, was set in stone by the end of the Trials. If someone was hurt, bad luck. If someone had an off day, bad luck. "Let the chips fall where they may and get on with your life," men's program administrator Robert Cowan told the *Baltimore Sun*. "I don't want three guys sitting around a pre-Olympic training camp hoping for someone to get hurt."

Though it seemed as if the officials for the women's program were making up the rules as they went along, they had actually made provisions in December 1991 for this unusual second "trial." An ad hoc committee made up of federation officials and coaches, including the Strausses and the Károlyis, approved documents that detailed the team selection processes for the World Championships and the Olympics. But the language about holding a second "trial" to allow top-ranked injured gymnasts a chance at making the Olympic team was sufficiently unclear so that it took the coaches by surprise when the federation invoked it the following summer.

The coaches reacted so viscerally to the second "trial" because they had come to expect the worst from the USGF, which was by turns paternal and petty, protective and cruel. The federation still had the feel of a small-town council that could massage the rules into any desired shape, even if, as in this case, its decision to hold the "trial" was completely legal. It still managed, despite tremendous growth, to operate much like the small, insular organization that began in 1963 in Tucson, Arizona, inside the kitchen of former national champion Frank Bare.

Bare was thirty-two and selling insurance when a group of college coaches asked him to serve as executive director of the new federation they were starting to usurp the Amateur Athletic Union, which they felt didn't promote gymnastics. With an $8000-a-year salary, Bare worked seven years before he finally wrested control of gymnastics from the AAU and the federation was officially sanctioned by the International Gymnastics Federation. With one secretary and a part-time printer, Bare set up shop in an office building, just in time to field the flood of new members in the wake of Olga Korbut's triumph in the 1972 Olympics. What had been an overwhelmingly male sport—all thirty-eight participants in the first U.S. Gymnastics Congress in 1965 were coaches of men's teams—was now shifting dramatically toward females. Nadia Comaneci's performance in the 1976 Olympics sparked another huge rise in enrollment at gymnastics clubs. The tiny organization grew from 7000 mostly male athletes in the mid-1960s to 58,000 mostly female athletes in the 1990s. Total membership, including judges, administrators, coaches and club owners, has now climbed to 160,000.

Yet the federation's management hasn't kept pace with its growth. Some of the highest-ranking managers have little formal education to guide them in their particular duties. Steve Whitlock has almost no background in physiology and body mechanics, and yet he heads up the federation's education and safety department, formulating certification programs for coaches and establishing safety guidelines. He studied music and psychology in college, taught gymnastics classes at Wayne State, was gymnastics director for a Michigan school district's recreation department, and operated his own gym near Detroit for fourteen years. "I picked up an

anatomy course here and a physiology course there, but most of
what I know I learned as a coach," he says. Kathy Kelly became
technical director of the women's program on the basis of her background as a secretary in the federation's offices and her involvement
as a parent of a gymnast. "If you would tell somebody in Europe
that the person leading a country like the United States of America
has no gymnastics background, no coaching background, nobody
would believe it," Károlyi says, shaking his head. "And even today,
I don't believe. I don't believe."

■ ■ ■

The federation defended the second "trial" to skeptical reporters
by pointing to world champion decathlete Dan O'Brien. In a stunning upset at the U.S. Olympic Trials for track and field, O'Brien
missed a pole vault and didn't make the team. Reebok was already
running Dan vs. Dave commercials, trading on the expected showdown between American superstars Dan O'Brien and Dave Johnson in Barcelona. USGF executive director Mike Jacki considered
O'Brien's absence from the 1992 Olympic team absurd and suggested the U.S. track team adopt a selection process similar to that
for women's gymnastics.

What Mike Jacki didn't understand was that preserving the
integrity of the sport took precedence over winning, not because
the other federations were nobler or less obsessive about winning,
but because they understood that at the heart of competitive sports
is the dictum that an athlete must prove his or her value with every
new competition. Barry Bonds isn't waved to first base simply
because he is acknowledged as one of the best hitters in America.
He has to step up to the plate and earn his status again and again.
And if an athlete is injured, bad luck. It's the nature of sports that

athletes must perform on demand, whether or not they are in top condition at that moment. The NFL doesn't reschedule the Super Bowl because Joe Montana pulls a hamstring. In sports, justice might not always be served, but fairness usually is.

In Orlando, neither was in great supply. The eight gymnasts gathered at Brown's gym to train a week before the "trial." The tension mounted as the competition drew near. Kim Kelly did not train flawlessly that week, but on the day of the event, she completed all eight of her routines—compulsories and optionals on the uneven bars, balance beam, floor and vault—without a major error. She performed so well that at day's end, she called her parents from her hotel room at seven-thirty in the evening. "Mom! I did it! I hit eight for eight! I'm an Olympian!"

"Are you sure?" her mother asked warily.

"Mom, there's no way I didn't make it. They're meeting right now and the Strausses said they would call me."

When Donna Strauss took her place at the long conference table in the Park Suite Hotel, she felt as confident as her gymnast. She felt that some of the injured athletes had watered down some skills and hadn't performed "picture perfect" routines, as the federation had told the coaches they must in order to unseat a gymnast already named to the team. "The injured gymnasts definitely were having some problems," Strauss remembers. Others who watched the competition, however, say Betty Okino and Michelle Campi looked strong and showed no signs of their injuries. The press was not allowed to observe the "trial," eliminating any nonpartisan evaluation.

At the hotel each coach was permitted to make an argument in support of his or her gymnast but were instructed by the federation lawyer, who conducted the meeting, not to comment on any other gymnasts. Rita Brown and the federation's Kathy Kelly insisted later that all the coaches respected this directive. But Donna Strauss clearly recalls that negative comments were made about her gymnast regarding the issue that would eventually doom Kim Kelly: body type. And even though some who watched the two-day event say Kelly was the weakest gymnast of the eight, most also mention her body—Kim was 5 feet 1 inch tall and weighed 102 pounds at the time.

"There were direct statements of 'We prefer not to have mature body types. We want to walk onto the floor in Barcelona petite and strong,'" Strauss says. Kim Kelly was the only gymnast who had breasts and hips. Even Wendy Bruce, though at nineteen a year older than Kim, had the straight body of a child. Bruce herself said later, " [Kim] looked like a woman. She had boobs and a butt. It's not her fault, that's just the way her body was shaped."

"Her physical shape was not what it had been optimally through the season," Rick Newman says in defense of the coaches' concern about Kim's body. "The aesthetics of how they look, their athletic appearance, is important when you're being judged internationally. It's a fact."

Brandy Johnson, the former U.S. champion who trained and coached at Brown's gym, shakes her head when asked about Kim Kelly. "Kim did not fit the part," she says bluntly. "She wasn't that little thin gymnast. If Kim was more the mold, she would have made it. I'm basing that on my knowledge of gymnastics and my experience. I was totally appalled."

Károlyi contends Kim was the weakest gymnast in the group but condemns the process that eliminated her. "Why did she have to perform the second trial?" he asks. "It was a dirty, dirty joke." In the meantime, Károlyi fought for his own gymnasts, as he should have, promising that Betty would get stronger by the time of the Olympics and that her international reputation would sway

Olympic judges. Clearly, the decision was not based on the performance of the athletes on the day of the "trial." It was based on everything except that, it seems. Some coaches even admit to having paid little attention to the other gymnasts at the "trial" because they were so focused on their own athletes, not to mention their own careers.

After about an hour of discussion, each coach wrote down seven names on a slip of paper. The federation lawyer at the head of the table tallied the ballots on the spot and announced the team. Kim was out. Bill and Donna Strauss could barely speak. Kim had proven herself three times, passed every test, and none of it mattered. The room was silent as the Strausses rose to leave. "Everyone here has to live with his own conscience," Donna Strauss told her colleagues, "and some of you will have a difficult time doing that."

As Kim lay in bed watching TV and waiting for the phone to ring, Bill and Donna Strauss knocked on her door.

"Kim," Donna Strauss said, "they cut you."

Kim thought they were teasing her. The Strausses had to tell her three times before the news sank in. Then she collapsed on the bed, shaking with tears. "What did I do wrong?" she asked. "What did I do wrong? I did everything they asked of me."

Stephanie Kelly got the call at ten-thirty. "It was the worst moment of my adult life," she says. "Kim was positively hysterical and here I was in Pennsylvania not able to do anything. I didn't go to bed that night." She finally got USGF official Kathy Kelly on the phone at three in the morning and screamed at her, "How can you do this? Have you no conscience?"

Kathy Kelly says she felt terrible for Kim, but the decision was out of her hands. "If we're going to blame someone for Kim's heartache, we all get the blame because not one of us stopped to think [back in December] about the one athlete left at home." She says she begged the United States Olympic Committee for an extra credential so Kim could go as a second alternate but says she was refused. The federation offered to pay Kim's way as a spectator, which she ultimately accepted.

At the training camp in France two weeks before the Games, Michelle Campi tore a hip muscle and couldn't compete. The remaining six comprised the Olympic team. If one more gymnast went down with an injury, the team was doomed, which was the risk the coaches and federation took when they removed a healthy Kim Kelly to make way for an injured athlete. In fact, Kim would have been the healthiest gymnast on the team. Wendy Bruce had torn a ligament in her thumb two weeks before the Baltimore Trials, then tore it further before the Olympics. She needed a cortisone shot to get her through the competition, and surgery immediately afterward. When Dominique Dawes went down with a sore rib cage from Schlatter's disease—a temporary and steady pain in certain bones due to growing—and didn't train for two days in France, Kathy Kelly appealed to Dawes's loyalty and patriotism. "I told Dominique how much the team needed her," Kelly recalls. When doctors assured Dominique she wasn't risking long-term damage by competing, she resumed training.

In Barcelona, Kim kept her distance from the American team, girls she had known since childhood. One day as she waited to be interviewed inside NBC's studio, a production assistant ran Kim's name through the athletes' computer and discovered she *was* credentialed after all, no matter what Kathy Kelly said. On her own, Kim picked up her athlete's pass, sought out her room in the Olympic Village and inside found a duffel bag of Olympic merchandise with her name on it. It was like a loopy dream. She had beaten Wendy Bruce at both the U.S. Championships and the Olympic Trials and somehow Wendy Bruce was competing at the Olympics and she wasn't. Betty Okino had taken part in neither competition and Betty Okino was down there on the floor of the Olympic arena and she wasn't. "To deny a kid forever of being an Olympian, when she earned that spot, I just don't see how this is what we stand for," Donna Strauss says. "It's not the American way."

But the worship of winning is. Kim Kelly wasn't at the Olympics because U.S. coaches felt she didn't blend in with the sleek line of pixie girls the judges and the public love so much. Her adult body broke the fairy princess spell the little girls created, and they cut her loose.

After the Olympics, Kim Kelly had the five Olympic rings tattooed just inside her bikini line, where only she would ever see it.

■ ■ ■

For Kim Kelly, the fallout from being kept off the Olympic team was purely emotional, the shattering of a lifelong dream. But for other athletes, not competing in the Olympics—or failing once there—can also mean losing forever their shot at a financial bonanza that grows more lucrative with each Olympiad, especially for figure skaters. Only in the world's biggest boxing matches is more money on the line for one athlete for one night of work than it is for an American female skater at the Olympic Games. Agents say a gold medal is worth about $10 million in endorsements and appearance fees, as corporations have jostled in recent years to hitch a ride on skating's booming popularity.

Companies such as Seiko, AT&T, Evian and Bausch & Lomb have shifted money away from tennis and into figure skating. Sara Lee plunked down $1.4 million to sponsor fourteen skating events in 1994, in addition to paying a $40 million sponsorship fee to the United States Olympic Committee to use the Olympic rings logo on their packaging. Even traditionally "male" products are discovering skating: Chrysler sponsored the 1994 U.S. Championships. "Figure skating," John Bennett, a senior vice president at Visa, explained to *New York* magazine, "is the closest you can get to sex in the Olympics."

Television ratings consistently outdraw the mainstream sports. In the fall of 1993 an eight-month-old tape of the World Figure Skating Championships drew ratings just a tenth of a percentage point below those for a live broadcast of the much-anticipated Indiana-Kentucky college basketball game. The 1992 Olympic skating competitions outdrew both the final game of the World Series and the deciding game of the NCAA basketball championships that year. Even non-Olympic skating events have become a cash cow for television. When CBS lost the rights to broadcast NFL games in 1994, the network packaged skating into made-for-television quasi competitions to fill the void. These were the sequined equivalents of the phenomenally successful Skins Games in golf, another brainstorm of a television executive. (The biggest names in golf compete for huge payoffs on each hole, where one putt could be worth $200,000 or more.)

It was testimony to the skaters' popularity that CBS quickly ran into problems with agents and federations who wanted to protect their financial turf. French star Surya Bonaly pulled out of the made-for-CBS Ladies' Outdoor Skating Championship just days before the event in October 1994. She also backed out of another CBS event, the Nikon Skating Championships, a week later, as well as four competitions run by Dick Button's Candid Productions. The French federation threatened not to reinstate her eligibility for the 1998 Olympics if she skated in these professional competitions and tours, which are unsanctioned by the International Skating Union. National federations have the option of offering a one-time amnesty to skaters who have forfeited their amateur status by skating in unsanctioned events. But the French federation's concerns might have been more than bureaucratic. The federation had contractual obligations with a French television network that wanted Bonaly for its events.

"It's chaos," CBS executive Rick Gentile told the *Chicago Tribune*. "Figure skating is just like baseball or hockey [where in the fall of 1994 all play came to a halt because the owners and players couldn't reach an agreement on finances]. It's unbelievable." With Bonaly out and Oksana Baiul suddenly canceling because of unscheduled knee surgery and with a block of air time to fill, CBS transformed the Ladies' Outdoor Skating Championship into the Men's Outdoor Skating Championship, and it indefinitely postponed the Nikon Skating Championships.

But CBS soon landed back in the headlines by announcing the richest skating competition in the history of the sport, which it called "Ice Wars: the U.S.A. vs. the World," conjuring visions of pro wrestling or of Don King hawking his latest heavyweight bout. For a press conference at its studios, CBS summoned three skating beauties, Nancy Kerrigan, Oksana Baiul (suddenly recovered from knee surgery) and Kristi Yamaguchi, to perch on high director's chairs. In their black miniskirts and black hose, with their legs demurely crossed, they looked like Bachelorettes One, Two and Three from *The Dating Game*. The manufactured competition would pit the American team of Kerrigan, Yamaguchi, Brian Boitano and Paul Wylie against Baiul, Katarina Witt, Viktor Petrenko and Kurt Browning. The winning team would split $1 million. The losers would go home with handsome payoffs, as well as a thank you for showing up.

Sitting in the director's chair in front a packed room of reporters and photographers, Kerrigan seemed as uncomfortable under the spotlight as ever. "I'm trained to be a skater," she said afterward, "I'm not trained for this." In explaining why she turned down a multimillion-dollar offer to skate against Tonya Harding, Kerrigan said, "Money's not that important to me. I'm from a hard-working family. I'm not looking for an easy way out." But under the guidance of her agent, Jerry Solomon, Kerrigan was cashing in as if her medal were an ATM card. She had an exercise video coming out soon and a Christmas tour with singer Aaron Neville, in addition to her skating appearances and many endorsements. And to keep the money coming, Solomon needed to keep Kerrigan in the public eye, no matter how much she disliked it. He and CBS executives booked her onto the Conan O'Brien late night talk show after the press conference to promote "Ice Wars," and Solomon landed her a featured layout in *McCall's* magazine. She was also writing a children's book and promoting her own exercise video. "You get people who come along now and then, like Peggy Fleming and Dorothy Hamill," Solomon says. "And Nancy is the next one in line." If she isn't, it won't be for lack of effort on Solomon's part.

Agents have become so close to the skating community in the last five years or so that they can be found at any social gathering of the top skaters. Several of the top agents even date their clients. The relationship between agent and skater, especially when the skater is so young and the agent so confident, is one rife with the possibility of exploitation, as are so many of the complicated relationships in the spectrum of elite competition.

But none bears down more heavily on a girl than the one between her and her coach.

7

WHATEVER
IT TAKES

COACHES

■

The surest hands for molding girls into gymnastics champions during the 1980s belonged to the Romanian-born Béla Károlyi. As the son of educated parents, Károlyi angered his father as his restless, competitive nature pulled him away from his studies and onto the playing fields. At the age of seventeen he was junior national champion in the hammer throw and a novice boxer. When the young Károlyi announced that he would pursue athletics instead of enrolling in the engineering program at the local university, his father disowned him and threw him out of the house. With no place to live, Károlyi slept at a steel mill where he found work, then at a slaughterhouse where he slipped scraps of meat into his pockets for dinner. But within a year he was accepted at the five-year Physical Education University in Bucharest to study coaching.

Early in his studies Károlyi flunked a required gymnastics class. Angered, he devoted himself so completely to learning the sport that he made the college team and caught the eye of Márta Erőss, another driven gymnast. After Márta and Béla graduated first and second in their class, respectively, they married and, with little money, started a gymnastics school in Vulcan, a small coal-mining town in central Romania. They were perfect counterparts: Béla was gregarious and mercurial, Márta shy and levelheaded. But both shared a staunch work ethic, an obsession with winning and a zealot's respect for order and place. Their gym was the laboratory where they set out to distill the human form and spirit to its purest elements. If they could clear away the human flaws and limitations—pare away the fat, elasticize the limbs and spine, numb the pain, control the nerves—they could create a body light and fluid as a ribbon rippling in the wind. They could deliver the ultimate promise of athletics: to reveal the gods within.

They soon found a match for their ambitions in a dark-eyed six-year-old named Nadia Comaneci, plucked from her kindergarten class after Károlyi saw her turning cartwheels in the playground. With Nadia as his centerpiece, Károlyi developed the training system that would produce seven Olympic gold medals, fifteen World Gymnastics Championships medals and, after he defected to America, seven U.S. national champions in ten years. The system was based on militaristic control. His gymnasts lived in dormitories at the gym in Romania, trained seven to eight hours a day, fit in a few hours of school and ate only what the Károlyis fed them. There was no talking or fooling around inside the gym. The only proper response to Károlyi's instructions was a nod. He trained them like boxers, like little men, introducing rigorous conditioning and strengthening exercises to their workouts, transforming their bodies into muscled machinery. Károlyi insisted on small young girls for his team, not only for their pliability and resilience but for the little-doll look he believed enchanted the spectators and swayed the judges.

That's what he was counting on when his young, unheralded team arrived in Montreal for the 1976 Olympic Games.

Károlyi knew he had a special talent in the fourteen-year-old Comaneci, but she was just a faceless chorus girl behind the stars of the Olympics, namely the Soviet team, anchored by 1972 Olympic darling Olga Korbut. But Károlyi wasn't worried. He relished the underdog's role. He delighted in devising clever strategies to manipulate the crowd, the judges, and the rival coaches and gymnasts to his team's advantage. At competitions he played the actor, smiling and winking when pressure was highest to keep the other coaches off balance, or dramatically throwing a tantrum over one gymnast's score in the hopes of influencing the score of the next. ("The floor," he explains, "that was my battlefield more than even the kids' battlefield.")

In Montreal the challenge was to draw attention to his team and away from the Soviets. The day before the competition, the gymnasts performed in a "podium workout," a rehearsal of their routines before fans and judges. The Soviet team was introduced first and marched into the arena to thunderous applause. The home-country Canadians marched in next to another huge ovation. The spectators became so engrossed in watching the Soviets and Canadians, who had started to work out on the apparatus, that they barely acknowledged the introductions of the Chinese and Czechoslovakian teams.

"And now," the announcer boomed, "the national team from Romania!"

In the hallway behind the entrance, Károlyi didn't move.

"Mr. Professor," Nadia said, "they are calling for us."

"We're waiting. Just waiting a bit."

The announcer repeated the introduction a little louder. Károlyi didn't budge. When he saw Olympic officials scurrying toward him, he ordered Nadia to stand inside the bathroom door and come out only when he gave her a signal. The officials tried to hurry him onto the floor. "I don't know English," Károlyi said, shrugging—prompting a flurry of elaborate gestures from the officials. "Oh," Károlyi said, "somebody is in the bathroom. Sorry." The announcer repeated the introduction a third time. Károlyi peeked into the arena. By then the spectators had turned their eyes toward the entrance, wondering what had happened to the Romanian team. Károlyi smiled and signaled for Nadia to return. He waved to the announcer.

"And now, finally, ladies and gentlemen, the young team from Romania!" The crowd cheered as Károlyi's line of tiny girls in matching red bows marched onto the floor with the precision of a bugle corps. While other gymnasts sat on benches to pull off their warm-ups or wait their turn on the apparatus, Károlyi's girls lined up in perfect formation at the beam, their first event. Each completed her routine as precisely as if in the real competition, then resumed her place in line. No sitting, no talking, no fooling around. By the time Nadia mounted the beam, the tiny Romanian dolls had riveted the crowd's attention. They had never seen such perfect little gymnasts.

When Nadia finished her dazzling routine with a stunning dismount, the fans roared. "That was like hell broke down," Károlyi recalls. The papers the next morning proclaimed Nadia THE NEW QUEEN OF MONTREAL. The judges took notice. Days later Nadia validated Károlyi's conviction that with enough sacrifice, hard work and well-orchestrated public relations, he could create perfection. Károlyi's star pupil made Olympic history by scoring the first perfect 10 on her way to winning the all-around gold medal. "I would say that Nadia never in her life [would] receive a perfect ten without this careful, strategic preparation of the event," Károlyi says today.

Károlyi thrived on the attention that followed him back home to Romania. He already had his next generation of gymnasts working toward the 1980 Olympics, where he could solidify his position as the world's greatest gymnastics coach. But when the government began to assert more control over his training center and his gymnasts, Károlyi protested so vigorously that his funding was cut. He was collecting enemies inside the Romanian sports federation, some of whom protested that he pushed his athletes too hard and was maniacal about control. Károlyi's position as national team coach eroded further when his gymnasts failed to beat the Soviets at the 1980 Summer Games in Moscow. Whether his concerns were real or imagined, Károlyi began to fear for his safety in his homeland. During an exhibition tour in the United States in March 1981, Károlyi, Márta and the Romanian team choreographer, Geza Pozsar, slipped away from the Romanian delegation and disappeared into the New York streets. Under his arm Károlyi carried a stuffed bear bought for his seven-year-old daughter, Andrea, who had been temporarily left with an aunt in Romania.

Despite their credentials, the Károlyis couldn't find coaching jobs. U.S. coaches felt that American girls would never stand for the grueling demands of the Eastern Bloc training system. Too many hours, too much pain, too little freedom. But the skeptics underestimated both Károlyi and the lengths to which prepubescent girls would go to please their parents and coaches. After brief stints as a longshoreman and custodian in Los Angeles, Károlyi landed a coaching job through a gymnastics acquaintance at the University of Oklahoma and was finally able to send for his daughter. When he was invited to work in a new gym in Houston months later and found it closed down upon arrival, he borrowed money and reopened it himself, attracting students through homemade signs stapled to telephone poles. Within eighteen months he was coaching five hundred students and changing forever the face of U.S. gymnastics.

■ ■ ■

In Károlyi's small, cluttered office off the lobby of his steamy corrugated-metal gym, the walls are jammed with photographs of his gymnasts: Mary Lou Retton, Julianne McNamara, Kim Zmeskal, Betty Okino, Nadia Comaneci. All smiles. Behind his desk hangs a poster of Kristie Phillips with an inscription to him and Márta: "I love you both and want to thank you from the bottom of my heart." The shelves sag under the weight of shiny trophies. Károlyi's vision of the world is encapsulated in mementos within those four walls, all happy endings, triumphant smiles, warm hugs. If girls have left his gym unhappy and damaged, as so many (including Kristie Phillips) have done, it's done nothing to diminish Károlyi's sunny opinion of himself. He dismisses the failed gymnasts as weak, stupid, lazy, bitter or the sorry victims of overzealous parents. He dismisses the criticisms directed at him, dating back to his days in Romania, as the work of jealous rivals or disappointed gymnasts and parents.

When his gymnasts lost, he imagined evil plots. He is convinced to this day that the Soviets planted soldiers in the crowd at the 1980 Olympics in Moscow specifically to jeer his Romanian gymnasts, causing his team to lose the gold medal. At the same

Olympics he saw a conspiracy among the judges to make sure the top Soviets beat Nadia Comaneci. He claimed that the Romanian government and gymnastics federation kidnapped his entire team, including Nadia, after the 1976 Olympics when he grew too successful. Károlyi's ego and ambition lost nothing in the journey to America. He threw himself into producing little champions where almost none had existed. Before Károlyi imported his training system in 1981, the best showing by the U.S. women in a World Championships was Marcia Frederick's gold medal on the uneven bars in 1978. They had never won a medal at the Olympics. Since 1982, American women have won thirteen individual medals and two team medals at the Olympics. And they've racked up thirteen individual medals and one team medal at the World Championships. Károlyi's Mary Lou Retton was the first American to win the all-around gold medal at the Olympics, in 1984, and Kim Zmeskal, a Houston native who trained with Károlyi from the time she was six years old, was the first American to win the all-around gold at the World Championships, in 1991.

As Károlyi established himself in the United States as the top coach, some of the same symptoms Westerners had denounced in the Eastern Bloc system—the blank faces, the abnormally small bodies, the bandaged ankles, broken wrists, and compressed vertebrae—were beginning to appear in American gymnasts. Yet the more American champions Károlyi produced inside his gym in North Houston, the softer the complaints. Those in the U.S. gymnastics community who did criticize the alarming control Károlyi wielded over his girls and their parents—and the disturbing consequences of that control—did so halfheartedly. They understood the ripple effect of Károlyi's success: enrollment at gymnastics schools boomed after Mary Lou Retton won the gold in 1984, sponsorship dollars poured into the federation, and television networks battled for the rights to broadcast competitions. Everyone, even coaches who despised Károlyi, benefited. Two cherished American values came crashing against each other in the debate over Károlyi: the protection of our children versus our will to win.

"We have to figure out what our goals are," says Olympic medalist Bart Conner, who considers many of Károlyi's detractors hypocrites. "If we want a team that looks nice in their uniforms, that isn't under all this stress, that isn't playing with pain, that isn't risking injury, then we're not going to win."

If there was any doubt that the most important mission of the country's Olympic movement was not to instill life lessons on fairness and sportsmanship but simply to win, it was confirmed in 1988. After disappointing results at both the Summer and Winter Games, the United States Olympic Committee appointed a much-publicized task force, headed by New York Yankees owner George Steinbrenner, to figure out how the United States could win more medals.

Parents from all over America continued the journey to Houston to lay their daughters at Károlyi's feet. His unwavering confidence in the right way to train their children was a soothing relief to those who were confused and intimidated by the subculture of elite athletics. His dictatorial manner created an almost cultish devotion, at least for a while. "I thought Béla was God," says Carrol Stack. "I was afraid of him. If you go to Béla and say you have this problem, he tells you how rotten your kid is, how she won't do anything. You get lectured and go home and tell your kid how rotten she is."

Though Károlyi has never been particularly gifted in teaching the technical nuances of the sport—Márta and his assistants fill those gaps for him—no one can match his almost magical power to inspire. "I think he could take a basketball team and if he knew what he was doing technically, he could motivate them to win a championship," says Steve Nunno. Károlyi is mesmerizing to watch, speaking with his entire body, hands flying, brows bouncing, eyes dancing. His smile is like a drug to his gymnasts, doled out just frequently enough to leave them craving more.

"You would do anything for that smile, that pat on the head," Kristie Phillips says. And there is no creature on earth more desperate for approval than a girl inching toward puberty. Studies show that a young girl's self-esteem plummets much more dramatically than that of a boy at a similar stage in life. Self-conscious about her looks and sensitive about her body, in particular her weight, she is a mass of insecurities looking for an identity. She is the perfect clay with which coaches can create the ideal gymnast.

No one was better at exploiting a girl's insecurities than Károlyi. Westerners had heard about his cruelty, but they had seen only the television persona, the jovial bear of a man with the smiling eyes and droopy mustache who enveloped his tiny gymnasts in joyful hugs. And even in Houston, where he transformed little girls into champions, few saw how many other little girls were sacrificed in that quest.

"This looks like you," he once said to Michelle Hilse as he plucked a cockroach off the floor. Michelle was thirteen when she moved to Houston by herself to train at Károlyi's. Shy and emotional but a hard worker, she was branded weak the first time she cried in front of Károlyi. He called her an idiot and kicked her out of the gym. "As soon as you show tears, as soon as he knows that's your weak point, forget it," Hilse says. "Crying was just the way I let out my emotions. It wasn't that I was giving up or I was a loser, but they wanted everybody to fit a certain mold and react in a certain way." For a time she actually took encouragement from his daily tirades against her. "If he ignored you, that was worse. You were written off, weren't worth anything." But soon she began to believe what he told her. She thought she was stupid, a loser. He was kicking her out of the gym more and more for failing to master certain skills, and he finally told her she should leave permanently, a devastating blow despite her misery.

Károlyi once gripped Chelle Stack by the back of the neck and walked her to her mother's car in the parking lot, calling her pathetic and no good. Chelle's offense? She wouldn't raise her legs high enough during a warm-up jog because she feared reinjuring her hamstring. He called Erica Stokes a pregnant goat as she began to go through puberty. Betty Okino was a pregnant spider. Kristie Phillips was an overstuffed Christmas turkey. Károlyi belittled and ignored his girls for one reason: he got results. He winnowed out the weak and prodded the strong. Julissa Gomez left with her confidence shot. Erica Stokes left with an eating disorder. Kristie Phillips left feeling suicidal. Chelle Stack left resentful and disappointed even though she had reached the Olympics. Danielle Herbst, Tricia Fortsen, Karen Reid, Alicia Ervin, Amy Jackson, Laurie White, Cindy Sauer—the list goes on—all arrived fresh, young and hopeful and left disillusioned and often broken.

But the bodies stacked like cordwood outside his door did nothing to dull Károlyi's appetite for more champions. He was successful in great part because he had no conscience as a coach. The Communist system instilled in him an extraordinary ability to close his eyes to everything beyond the strict borders of his responsibilities. Once, on a hunting trip with several of Romania's political leaders, Károlyi saw a bear suddenly charge a forest ranger. Károlyi had been forbidden to shoot bears because only certain dignitaries were allowed that privilege. As the bear descended on the ranger, Károlyi kept his gun at his side. The bear ripped open the man's torso, and he died almost instantly. The decision not to shoot presented no moral quandary for Károlyi. To shoot would have meant stepping beyond the rigid boundaries of his place within the hunting party. "There were very, very, very strict rules," Károlyi says. "We grew up with it and we knew that there was not too much to get around it, and you'd better obey it. You do not even question in your mind."

It is his ability to compartmentalize feelings that has enabled Károlyi to forge champions from the bodies of little girls. He never frets over any problem he has created for his gymnasts outside the gym—whether it be a destroyed self-image, disordered eating, lifelong debilitations or depression. Fixing those problems is somebody else's responsibility. Fixing their Yurchenkos and full-twisting dismounts is his. Eating disorders, for example, fall outside his responsibility. He does not believe coaches in any way foster the disorders, and so he denounces any suggestion that he ought to educate himself and his athletes about the dangers. He sees eating disorders as he sees most everything, as a reflection of one's strength or weakness. Those who vomit are simply too lazy to lose weight through diet and exercise. "Gosh, sorry, but I have to tell you, they are selecting the cheapest way to satisfy everything," Károlyi says, poking his finger in his mouth. He says Erica Stokes was his only athlete with an eating disorder, which he wasn't aware of until she retired from gymnastics. He denies having suggested to Kristie Phillips that she take laxatives or diuretics to lose weight. He says Nadia never had a problem, though she dropped 40 pounds in two months to make a comeback at the 1979 World Championships. And eleven years later, when she escaped to the United States, a story in *Life* magazine further suggested she was bulimic. "Her appetite for food is voracious," wrote Barbara Grizzuti Harrison. "She eats her own food and [her companion] Constantin's too. After each course, she goes to the bathroom. She is gone for a long time. She comes back, her eyes watery, picks her teeth and eats some more. She eats mountains of raspberries and my crème brûlée. She makes her way to the bathroom again. When she returns, she is wreathed in that rank sweet smell."

Chelle Stack drank laxatives when she went through puberty, but Károlyi didn't know that either. He dismisses studies concluding that gymnasts have a higher rate of eating disorders than the general population and is angered that gymnastics has been blamed in the death of Christy Henrich. Despite devoting his life to coaching young girls, he seems to know nothing about the psychological and emotional issues of adolescence, especially as they pertain to weight and body image.

"People, wake up!" Károlyi says. "Christy Henrich, bless her heart, she was not even close to gymnastics at the time she was getting deeper and deeper in the whole tragedy. It was exclusively her and her family...How great an imaginary scapegoat, the ones who five years ago and four years ago mention that she is overweight. I mean, wake up people and blame the right area. The ones who are really responsible for the human tragedy of those kids are the parents, the mom and dad and the family. They are the ones feeding them. Sure, the coaches are making remarks about overweight. But it is normal in every sport, doesn't matter, wrestler, boxer, you name it."

Like eating disorders, injuries barely brush Károlyi's conscience. A USA Gymnastics official who asked not to be named says Károlyi's gymnasts often would have to sneak medical treatment. "Béla would get angry if they were hurt," the official says. Károlyi had a deep distrust of medical trainers, who he felt babied his athletes or scared them with too much information about their injuries. "With or without injury they have to compete; they must compete without any kind of doubt," Károlyi says. He once insisted that the United States Gymnastics Federation tell one particular medical trainer not to talk to his gymnasts about their injuries; he would pass along whatever information he thought they needed to know. He rushed the gymnasts back in the gym sooner than doctors recommended, rationalizing that the doctors were simply concerned with liability. "I take the liability because I'm the one who must get the technical and physical performance from the kids as soon as possible. If I'm not doing it, nobody else is going to do it."

Kristie Phillips, for instance, trained for three years with a fractured wrist because Károlyi didn't feel it was serious enough to warrant full rest. Nearly ten years later the wrist barely bends. More recently, a gymnast went to a Károlyi-recommended doctor with a painful heel that Károlyi insisted was only bruised; he wanted the gymnast to continue training for an upcoming meet. Without having the gymnast take off her shoe, the doctor miraculously diagnosed the heel as a bruise. Similarly, before the 1991 World Championships a Károlyi doctor diagnosed Kim Zmeskal's wrist pain as a sprain, leading Károlyi to suggest on national television that the injury was more in Zmeskal's head than in her wrist. It turned out Zmeskal's problem was a fracture of the distal radius, or growth plate—a common injury among elite gymnasts but one with which Károlyi's doctor was apparently unfamiliar. "If Béla wants a kid to be injured so she doesn't go to a meet, she's injured," a federation official says. "If he wants a girl not injured so she can compete, she's not injured."

When Chelle Stack was fourteen, she broke two toes while practicing on the balance beam just hours before the Chunichi Cup in Japan. Whether she was nervous or unfocused, she kept jumping off the balance beam in the middle of her routine and broke the toes when one foot landed on the other. As Károlyi watched what he considered an utterly undisciplined, unprofessional display, the veins in his neck looked as if they would snap. "You look around this arena and if you find one person who is acting so out of control, so outrageously crazy like you are acting, then you show me," Károlyi barked at the girl. "I have to single you out in the whole gymnastic world as the craziest person I've ever seen and the most uneducated." Károlyi calls Stack's falls from the beam and the subsequent injury "the most embarrassing thing I ever been through in my thirty-five-year coaching career."

Károlyi still wanted her to compete, so the doctor on site shot the foot with Novacain as the meet began, though Károlyi later denied he knew anything about Chelle's medical treatment. With little feeling in her foot, she stumbled on all of her events and Károlyi screamed at her. When the pain crept back midway through the meet, Chelle took another shot of Novacain. Chelle says Károlyi ignored her the rest of the trip. By the time she returned home, her foot and ankle were black and blue from the pounding. "This is when I began to hate Béla," says Stack's mother, Carrol.

The quick fix was normal procedure in Károlyi's stable. When Dianne Durham, one of Károlyi's stars in the early 1980s, pulled a hip muscle away from the bone during the American Cup, she couldn't lift her leg. A doctor offered her a shot of Novacain so she could keep competing. She declined. "I'm not stupid," she says today. "When that Novacain wore off, my leg would have been behind my back."

Injuries had no place in Károlyi's carefully designed formula for producing a star every four years. He built his program around the girl with the most talent. "Your top athlete is a very strange little creature," Károlyi explains. "Of course, I never studied psychology, but through the years these little guys taught me. We paid our dues on own mistakes, praising our little guy and cheering and clapping and showing our enthusiasm and babying them. And those are the ones who turn around and show disappreciation, ignorance and even arrogance. They take advantage of your sincere urge to show your appreciation. Give them everything in the world and surely you're getting a big, big, big, big slap. She is the first to turn her back."

So Károlyi constructed a training environment that kept his star athlete questioning her worth. In selecting five other gymnasts to train with her, he carefully chose each to play a specific role. Perhaps the most torturous position was that of the secondary star: like the understudy in a play, the girl was just talented enough to present a threat to the star's status. Nadia had Teodora Ungureanu, Dianne Durham had Mary Lou Retton, Kristie Phillips had Phoebe Mills, and Kim Zmeskal had Betty Okino. The four remaining gymnasts were "the crowd," as Károlyi called them, chosen as much for their personality traits as their talents. One girl from "the crowd" was always chosen as his pet. She might be the least talented, but she possessed the qualities he wanted to reinforce in his star: hard work, discipline and stoicism. Károlyi would praise her lavishly and hold her up as an example, angering the more talented gymnasts, who resented the favoritism. Anger, Károlyi knew, was a powerful motivator. He had built his own career on it. "My worst enemies, those are the ones who pushed me further," Károlyi says. "I've seriously considered writing each one a thank-you letter…The worst time of my life [as a coach] was the smooth period of time when I had nothing to fight against."

He would play all six girls like chess pieces, every move designed to toughen and sharpen the queen. He would pit them against each other. "If someone else wasn't getting a skill and you got it, or if someone fell and you didn't, it made you feel good," recalls one gymnast. Károlyi would shun one girl in order to teach another a lesson. He'd make one gymnast do extra work for a teammate's mistakes. Girls like Michelle Hilse had to absorb not only the taunts of her coach but sometimes the contemptuous looks of her teammates. "You're so young and you're trying to gain your identity from all these coaches and from your peers," Hilse says. "And if your peers are competitive with you and they want you to fall on your face, it's not very good." Károlyi would also have a group of younger gymnasts, his next generation of stars, training at the gym to keep the pressure on his top six. He'd also use the next generation of gymnasts as insurance. When his older gymnasts left after the Olympics, another crop of highly trained girls would be coming in to secure his job and keep his gym the best in the country.

Károlyi's system has backfired several times. He ignored and belittled Dianne Durham enough to drive her from the gym temporarily. Károlyi still managed to produce his star that year, as Durham's departure gave secondary star Mary Lou Retton room to blossom. His system failed spectacularly, however, with Kristie Phillips. She burned out a year before the 1988 Olympics after Károlyi had touted her as the next Mary Lou. When Kristie's name is mentioned, Károlyi nods knowingly. He says he learned from the experience, because over the years he's figured out exactly what destroyed Kristie: her parents.

"I never had this type of ingredient on the floor, a child who basically acted completely on the influence of her parents. It was totally strange. But I did not see that very well at the time because that was the very first [gymnast he had who was dominated by her parents]. Even after '88 when the whole thing went wrong for her, I did not see completely the whole picture. But now I do because unfortunately we have more and more monsters on the floor, the ones who are driven exclusively by the parents, and not for their own desire. I have to tell you honestly that was one of the reasons in '92 I said, 'That's it.' I don't want even to see that anymore."

On the day the United States won the team bronze medal and Shannon Miller, coached by rival Steve Nunno, was leading all competitors in the competition for the individual all-around title at the 1992 Olympics in Barcelona, Károlyi still managed to steal the headlines. He announced his retirement. He had decided to retire before he arrived in Barcelona, and what he found there confirmed his decision. The Dream Team, America's superstar basketball squad, represented a shift in the Olympics toward crassness and undisciplined showiness that Károlyi could not tolerate. "Those ignorant animals," he says. "Watching those animals walking in, acting like kings of the trash pile, signing autographs for other athletes who should be proud of their selves... That disgusting element of the Dream Team over there, showcasing them like monkeys. Everybody clapping because here the miracle of the world are coming. They so much humiliated everybody around there, including me. I felt humiliated knowing there is no appreciation of anybody else's work, for the ones who put their young lives on the line to be here. It was the Olympic Games of the bigshots, of the millionaires, of the Magic Johnsons. In other words, it's not mine anymore. I ask myself, 'Am I too old? Too conservative? Am I a dreamer?' I just don't fit anymore with that."

His decision to retire was reinforced, too, by the failure of his star, Kim Zmeskal, who as world champion had been touted as America's best hope. In the first five seconds of the competition, in the compulsories, she fell off the beam on a simple back handspring. "She knew and I knew at that moment the whole Olympic medal was gone," he remembers, "just like somebody turns a bucket of cold ice water over your head." Later she stepped out of bounds in her floor exercise, two stunning mistakes for a gymnast as steady as Kim. Some say she was overworked, underweight and in pain from training with an injured left wrist. But Károlyi bats away any hint of blame and instead accuses the USGF of destroying Kim's confidence by purposely scoring her low at both the 1992 U.S. Gymnastics Championships and 1992 U.S. Olympic Trials. The American judges, Károlyi says, failed their "patriotic duty" in not boosting Kim's scores at those competitions in deference to her position as world champion.

"The old European way of looking at things is that the ones who are national heroes, the ones who are the pride of the nation, got to be preserved and got to be supported," Károlyi says. "But American judges are eating up their own stars like hyenas." To support his argument, he points to the 1994 U.S. Championships, in which Dominique Dawes beat the reigning world champion, Shannon Miller, out of all five gold medals. It was a shockingly lopsided victory, on a par with a pitcher's throwing a no-hitter. Károlyi cannot accept that Dominique was better on that day, nor that the judges could rightly ignore Shannon's more impressive credentials.

"A big, big vicious wheel is turning and rolling, and they rolled over [Shannon] so brutally that it was just disgusting...I think this is the very nasty human urge to see the king die, to see the king down, to see the leader suffering. We've seen the whole society do this. That's an American mentality, which is part of the whole hidden human urge which people here have more opportunity and freedom to express than anywhere else in the world. There is not one President since I've been here in ten years who is not blamed and not dragged in the mud after a short period of time."

Károlyi knows firsthand of what he speaks. During the 1992 Olympics, journalists who had once been charmed by his lively interviews and passion for the sport blamed him for turning U.S.

gymnasts into dull-eyed zombies. The sight of American girls looking more wan and miserable than the Russians prompted letters of
concern to the USGF and drew scathing commentaries in newspapers across the country. Some of Károlyi's gymnasts stepped forward to defend him. "He loves his gymnasts as much as he loves
his own kids," Nadia Comaneci says. And Phoebe Mills: "He's
very loving. He would never do anything to hurt his gymnasts."

Károlyi wasn't solely to blame for the disturbing state of the
1992 Olympic team, at least not directly. Most of the American
girls at Barcelona had been trained by others. Yet each coach
there owed part of his or her success to Károlyi. He introduced to
America the now-common practice of holding two workouts a day
and training six days a week. He implemented a more structured
and less forgiving training system, spawning a new generation of
American coaches who screamed, taunted and demanded absolute
subservience.

One was his wiry, high-strung assistant, Rick Newman.

■ ■ ■

"My coach's desire to win seemed stronger than mine at times…"
wrote Danielle Herbst in a paper for her high school English class.
"In times of pressure, which not a day passed without…I was
yelled at, screamed at, and had things thrown at me…Somehow,
my coach had convinced himself, and constantly reminded me,
that I was a fat imbecile, a bloody idiot, no good and worthless."

Danielle trained with Rick Newman from age ten until she
burned out at age thirteen. She became so insecure about herself
during her time with Newman that in sixth grade she made her
mother meet her in the parking lot during lunch so she wouldn't
have to face her classmates in the school cafeteria. Even two years

after she left the sport, Newman's insults lingered like a virus. "You feel ugly because you're used to being a pole and now you've got boobs and hips. You're filling out, and it's like you're going through a meltdown."

Newman, some say, wasn't abusive until he began working at Károlyi's. Barbara Sauer liked Newman so much at his previous gym that she switched her daughter to Károlyi's when he was hired. "But Rick changed when he moved to Károlyi's," she says. His job was to groom a handpicked group of young gymnasts—called the "Hopes" team—who would replenish Károlyi's revolving stable of six super-elites. During the heyday of Károlyi's gym in the 1980s, Newman's hands shaped future stars as much as Károlyi's did.

Outside the gym Newman was a soft-spoken, mildly introverted man who played tennis in his off hours, adhered to a vegetarian diet and enjoyed a lively nightlife. (He once partied so hard the night before a Class 2 meet on the road that he was too sick to coach his gymnasts the next day.) Inside the gym he was a brilliant technical coach who laid the foundation for the careers of Kim Zmeskal, Erica Stokes and World Championships team member Hilary Grivich. Many of Károlyi's gymnasts credit Newman with teaching them the skills that launched their rise into the national rankings. He submerged himself in the Károlyi system, in which even the lowest-level coaches adopted the master's biting demeanor. ("Use your head for once!" a coach snapped when his six-year-old gymnasts headed for the wrong water fountain during a break one recent day at Károlyi's.) "It was basically an atmosphere where Béla set the tone and set the pace of the workout," Newman says, "and if he chose to be very aggressive in his development of the kids, then basically I followed suit."

Newman had Károlyi's temper and withering sarcasm but

none of his charm. "The yelling went a little too far," Erica Stokes says. "It got a little overboard. It was probably the verbal abuse that eventually put him out the door. Béla didn't know a lot of the words, so maybe it took him a little while to realize what Rick was saying." Chris Reid's daughter Karen was on Newman's "Hopes" team with Kim Zmeskal and Hilary Grivich. "He could be so cruel to the children, calling them 'fat,' 'you idiot.' I used to think, 'What is this going to do to my daughter when she starts dating? Will she choose an abusive partner?' She was always trying to please this abusive man...It's disgusting, all these men with their huge egos dealing with little girls."

Laurie White left Károlyi's at age nine partly because of Newman. "What he said to me and my friends really had an impact," says White, now a gymnastics and cheerleading coach herself. "Rick knew he had us out there [in the gym] and no one else could hear what he was telling us. He succeeded in what he was trying to do—we were great at competitions. But I think it's harmful. As children, we don't have our own value system. We don't know who we are. We're listening to authority figures to tell us who we are. If somebody tells you something so many times, you're going to believe it."

Looking back, Newman says he was immature and had no idea he might be damaging the girls with his insults. "It was part of the game," he explains. "And they were willing participants. I always felt as a coach I couldn't leave any stone unturned...The basic goal was: This athlete expresses a desire to be successful. And if positive motivation will do it every single time, that's easy. It takes no energy from me. But if it didn't work, I would try to do whatever I could to turn around that situation."

■ ■ ■

The attitude is not unique to either Newman or gymnastics, though few sports apply it so bluntly on athletes so young. At the elite level of sports, where the coaches' reputations ride on the performances of their athletes, they will often go to any lengths to squeeze the best from their pupils. "The majority of coaches are teaching because of their egos," says maverick skating coach Evelyn Kramer. ABC's Jurina Ribbens agrees: "The root of a lot of evil in this sport is coaches who are fulfilling their goals through their skaters." One Olympic skater says her coach resorted to physical abuse to motivate her skaters: "We'd practice our figure eights in strips on the ice and the girl next to me had terrible figure eights and she'd get screamed at, hit and her hair pulled. The behavior wasn't considered abusive; it was considered discipline. And we won."

Linda Leaver, who coached Brian Boitano to the 1988 Olympic gold medal, is of a different school of coaching. The mother of two athletic daughters, Leaver nurtured Boitano more than she pushed. She understood that, despite Boitano's remarkable talent, the sport offered no guarantees. If he didn't win a single medal, Leaver wanted Boitano to look back on his childhood and feel he had spent his time well anyway. "The key is to let the child increase his self-esteem," she says. "If you feel good about yourself, you can handle a lot of failures and even use them as trigger points to learning. If you pursue the sport as a tool to become a better person, then you can't go wrong." But she acknowledges that the authoritative, negative approach to coaching is effective with young children. "It works pretty good in the short run. You take kids out of school and they're great for about a year. Then they burn out. They're the ones who beat my kids at age twelve, then disappear. But the short-term success gives a false sense that that is the way to do it. And it's the easy way. It takes more time and energy to create a positive, nurturing environment and allow the athletes to push themselves as far as they're comfortable doing it."

To most coaches, even the sensitive ones, Leaver's view is unrealistic. Kelli Hill coaches national champion Dominique Dawes and has also served as her substitute mother since the gymnast moved in with Hill, her husband and two sons to save her own mother the thirty-minute drive to the gym at 6 A.M. Hill is tough but treats her gymnasts like thinking, feeling people with voices of their own. She has resisted the Károlyi ethos by producing a U.S. champion who does not seem beaten down or dispirited. She drives Dominique hard, but she also nurtures and encourages. "Every day you have to push them beyond what they think they can do," she says. But it requires knowing one's athlete well enough to read her face and her body language for clues to her state of mind. "You watch them. You know when they're well prepared and just need a push. Then I'll say, 'C'mon. You're ready. Let's go.'"

"No human being can drive himself to his zenith, to his finest point," says Nancy Kerrigan's coach Evy Scotvold. "Everybody needs somebody behind them pushing... You hope that you can get your athletes to understand that you're not being mean and hard, that you do these things out of love and caring." Sometimes, Scotvold says, a coach must save an athlete from herself with what he calls shock therapy. "They could really be going south right in the middle of an important event. You start seeing this glaze in their eyes and, boy, you've got to take them and verbally throw them up against the wall and snap them to. Because if you don't, you know they're going to fail." Scotvold says he can't worry about being liked by his skaters. "You don't get skaters because you're a nice person. They come to you for one reason: because you can make them the best skater."

Which explains why parents and their daughters stick with the Newmans and the Károlyis, despite their abusiveness. Coaches hold a revered place in the mythology of American sports. Few figures outside of politics and the military embody the American ideals of manliness and power as completely as our most famous coaches do. Their names—Vince Lombardi, Red Auerbach, John Wooden, Casey Stengel—evoke images of the gritty, hardworking, passionate taskmaster who made men out of his young athletes by putting them through hell, and by doing so inspiring their ever-lasting love and loyalty. These coaches' exhortations are imprinted on the national psyche, reaching beyond sports: "Winning is the only thing"; "Nice guys finish last"; "Show me a good loser and I'll show you a loser." With a heavy dose of tough love, they seem to draw the best from a child when the parents can't, and indeed often assume the parents' role by instilling discipline and shaping values. Coaches seem imbued with the power to transform. A teenage Mike Tyson was plucked from the hard streets of Browns-ville, New York, by Cus D'Amato, a gruff old boxing trainer who assumed legal guardianship. Tyson lived in D'Amato's house in the Catskill Mountains, adhering to his strict rules of behavior and discipline. By the time Tyson was twenty-one, D'Amato had trans-formed the angry and insecure boy into the heavyweight cham-pion of the world. It was only after D'Amato's death that Tyson fell from grace both in and out of the ring. Even as his career began to spin out of control—perhaps because of it—Tyson revered his dead mentor so completely that he named his first-born son D'Amato.

Hollywood has reinforced the mythic image of coaches as physical and spiritual alchemists with portrayals ranging from Pat O'Brien's in *Knute Rockne, All-American* to Gene Hackman's in *Hoosiers*. Movie coaches are the athletic versions of fairy godmoth-ers; they wield a whip instead of a wand but they transform just the same. They're almost always crusty and cross, but with hearts of gold. Crotchety Walter Matthau turns the sorriest baseball team in Little League history into champions in *The Bad News Bears*. Emilio Estevez does the same with hockey players in *The Mighty Ducks*. In *The Karate Kid*, Pat Morita plays a martial arts master who teaches an ordinary boy the secrets of life and winning. Even the Tom Hanks character in *A League of Their Own* overcomes his own sour attitude to help his players discover the champions in themselves. Sometimes coaches are not so much magicians as midwives in an adolescent's passage to adulthood, as is the Nick Nolte character who turns Barbra Streisand's son from childish wimp to mature good guy in *The Prince of Tides*.

Sorting image from reality can be a difficult proposition for parents who invest their hopes in a coach's ability to transform their child. They believe in the myth that endless work and rough language will always strengthen and toughen, and the coaches believe it too. Rick Newman believed it, and the results told him he was right. He coached two American Classic winners and placed nearly a dozen girls on the national gymnastics team. It wasn't until 1989 when he fell in love with Celi Campi, the mother of one of his gymnasts, future Olympian Michelle Campi, that Newman would leave Károlyi's. After they left their spouses and moved in together, Newman became Michelle's de facto father as well as her coach, blurring the boundaries of their relationship and removing whatever space Michelle had maintained between her gymnastics and her life. The gossip in the parents' lounge over the affair reached such a fever pitch that, despite Newman's credentials, including an award from the USGF for his work as Károlyi's assistant, Károlyi told Newman he should leave. Károlyi said it had nothing to do with Newman's treatment of the gymnasts. In fact, if anything, he thought Newman took the job too lightly. ("The purpose of his life was to take advantage of the regular, ordinary pleasures that life was offering," Károlyi says. "I always see him, like, doing a nine-to-five job rather than giving one hundred percent.") Károlyi recommended Newman for a job at his old friend Geza Pozsar's gym in Sacramento, California.

Though Pozsar had coached with Károlyi in the Romanian system and had defected with him, he took a different coaching path once in their new homeland. Pozsar's gym in Sacramento is small and friendly, with parents sitting on bleachers so close to the tumbling mats that their daughters can swing by for a quick hug or an encouraging word. (The sign in the gym window proclaims WE TRAIN THE STARS OF TOMORROW! but in truth when Michelle Campi arrived, she was the gym's only star.) Pozsar's specialty is producing gymnasts skilled enough to compete in college. "To have six gymnasts with scholarships at major universities is worth more than one Olympian," Pozsar believes. Though he pushes his gymnasts hard and they grumble about him, he encourages them to put their education ahead of their gymnastics. When he travels with the girls to European meets, he takes them to the Louvre in Paris, the Prado in Madrid, the National Gallery in London, to expose them to the artwork he loves so much. While Károlyi collects trophies and press clippings, Pozsar collects art and books. He speaks six languages and takes classes in international relations at Sacramento State. He has a bachelor's degree from a Romanian university in choreography and is the premier gymnastics choreographer in America, flying to gyms around the country to design floor routines for the top gymnasts.

On Károlyi's recommendation, Pozsar welcomed Newman, who softened his approach in the laid-back Sacramento environment. He rarely screamed. He worked with girls as young as five but focused mostly on preparing Michelle for the 1992 Olympics.

Sixteen-year-old Michelle was the fairy princess of the gym, lovely, long-limbed and lean. She spoke softly and smiled easily, the perfect young woman. An autographed poster of her hung on the bulletin board at the gym's entrance, serving as a reminder to hopeful fathers and mothers of what their daughters could be. Celi sat in the bleachers in her shower sandals and oversize shirt reading John Grisham novels and chatting with the other parents. But she was more than an observer. She oversaw all of Michelle's meals, arranged her travel, massaged her sore muscles, gave her pep talks. At home sometimes, Newman says, he would have to tell Celi to quit talking about gymnastics because he and Michelle had had enough for the day.

The quest for the Olympics defined their lives together. Michelle was Newman's ticket out of Károlyi's shadow. If he could get her to the Olympics, he would shed the "assistant" label that still followed him. For Michelle and Celi, the Olympics would be the reward for the upheavals in their lives, moving from Florida to Houston to Sacramento within two years and weathering a prickly divorce.

In the summer of 1992 the time had arrived to lay all their time and sacrifices on the line. The three flew into Baltimore the night before the Olympic Trials and immediately went to the arena so Michelle could get adjusted to the equipment. As she launched into a simple roundoff, she lost her balance—she still doesn't know how—and landed on her arm, tearing the tendon away from the elbow and fracturing the bone. After doctors reattached the tendon with a screw, the devastated trio flew home. Because Michelle had finished fourth at the national championships, she was allowed under the rules to compete for a spot on the team at the second "trial" in Orlando. But it was just thirty days away.

Those thirty days when Michelle rehabilitated her arm inside

Pozsar's gym were torturous. "It took probably five years of my coaching life off the top," Newman says. "Celi and I joked that it was the hardest thirty days that we ever spent." Newman and Michelle had to compress all the training they had done in the previous three years. Michelle had to be ready to perform eight routines—four compulsories, four optionals—to perfection. The pressure nearly crippled her. Midway through the month, she suddenly was incapable of performing her Yurchenko vault. "We had two or three workouts in a row when we were on the verge of collapse," Newman recalls. "We tried to encourage her and tried to say, 'Honey, please don't. Just because you're having this one mental problem with this one event, don't jeopardize a career you spent basically seven years working on. Don't throw it away just because you're having this one particular problem.'"

Michelle stayed in the gym day and night and worked through her mental block with the vault. But such intense work in such a short span took its toll. She developed a stress fracture in her hip. Still, she managed to ace her routines at the second "trial" in Orlando and make the team. But during the team's training camp in Europe, less than two weeks before the Summer Games, it became clear she couldn't compete. The pain in her hip was too much. She relinquished her spot to the alternate, but stayed with the team in the Olympic Village and accompanied them onto the competition floor.

She decided to keep training for 1996, even though she would be almost twenty by the time of the Summer Games. In the spring of 1994, just days before the American Classic, which was a qualifying meet for the World Championships Trials, Michelle fell from the high bar practicing her uneven bars routine. She landed flat on her back with a sickening slap. She and Newman figured she had just knocked the wind out of herself. She walked around the gym hoping her body would settle back in place, but then she began feeling nauseous. Her mother and Newman took her to the hospital, where doctors discovered Michelle had fractured three vertebrae; they had to insert a rod into her spine to stabilize the ninth, tenth and eleventh vertebrae. She had to wear a brace for four months.

In the meantime, Pozsar had seen enough. When Michelle injured her back in the wake of her injuries before the Olympic Trials and then the Olympics, he feared for her safety. "You have to know everybody's breaking point," says Pozsar. "When you have repeated accidents and injuries, you're dealing with someone who doesn't understand the breaking point." He abruptly fired Newman, who decided Pozsar got rid of him because Michelle no longer brought any notoriety to the gym. "She ceased to be a functioning asset," Newman says.

He flew to Oklahoma City in search of a new job at Dynamos Gym, owned and operated by another coach who shaped himself in Károlyi's image, Steve Nunno. Nunno had the hottest gymnast in the world at the time, Shannon Miller, and more little girls on the way up. He reveled in the spotlight, especially during competitions on the road, where as coach of the world champion he could melt snow with the white heat of his ego.

■ ■ ■

The girls clustered in jittery knots of three and four by the hotel elevator, waiting. Their hands clutched sheets of hotel stationery, notebook paper, whatever they could grab on such short notice. They snapped to attention like pointer dogs at each *ding* of the elevator. Still, Shannon Miller almost slipped by them. She moved without stirring the air around her. She was seventeen but looked twelve, not only in size but in demeanor. She offered no greetings to the other gymnasts already waiting in the lobby for their bus to Towson State University and a last workout before the start of the

World Gymnastics Cup in Baltimore. Shannon's eyes never left the carpeting as she trailed closely behind her coach.

"What's the world coming to?" Nunno had boomed happily to no one in particular as he burst into the lobby. Broad-shouldered and swaggering, Nunno drew looks even from those who didn't know he was the famous coach of the famous gymnast. He wore a warm-up suit, an overcoat, a scarf, new white Reeboks and—despite being indoors on a gray winter day in Maryland—sunglasses. His hair rose from his large head as thick and stiff as a lawn, with a mustache to match.

He shook open the newspaper with a wide grin. "Seen this?"

The headline read LORENA BOBBITT FOUND NOT GUILTY OF SEVERING HUSBAND'S PENIS. Nunno nudged a female USA Gymnastics official. "What's the world coming to?" he asked again, smiling. Nunno had become so loud that a few of the Russian gymnasts sitting nearby shot annoyed looks his way. *Doesn't he ever shut up?*

Shannon stopped next to her school tutor, Terri Thomas, and stood close, almost touching, her feet together and shoulders hunched. The girls by the elevator edged up to their idol and one by one asked for autographs. Shannon smiled politely and signed with the quiet efficiency of a seasoned celebrity. Yet, in the company of her booming coach, she was less star than satellite. "Shannon Miller," former trainer Jack Rockwell says, "is subjugated to Steve Nunno more than any girl I've ever seen."

Shannon was an extraordinary child from the day she showed up at Nunno's Dynamos Gym as a child. The second daughter of a physics professor and a gymnastics judge, she was bookish and shy. She looked like a bird. But she could weather pain and Nunno's explosive temper without wilting. She had an extraordinary drive to succeed, denying herself food and friends and sometimes sleep to keep up with both gymnastics and school. At age eleven, in a spasm of normalcy, she asked Nunno for Friday nights off to go to the movies with her friends; he convinced her they were trying to sabotage her gymnastics. On her sixteenth birthday she ate a slice of pizza and made herself run an extra mile on the treadmill the next day. She absorbed Nunno's unending criticisms without complaint. "Unless you get a ten, [the performance] is not perfect," she explains in Nunno's defense. "So you always need to keep looking at what you did wrong." Even at the 1992 Olympics, at which she shined brighter than any American star and won the all-around silver medal, Nunno fed her a steady stream of corrections uncut by compliments. "He told me I did great once," Shannon says, "right after the competition was already over." Nunno allows no time to bask in one's moment of glory. Keep pushing, keep working, there are always more medals to be won. When Shannon won the World Championships in 1993, she allowed *International Gymnast* magazine to publish a six-week diary chronicling the training and competition. This was her entry on the day she won the title:

8:30 A.M.—Get ready for gym. Eat and leave at 9:30. Condition and stretch. Beam sets, bars warm-ups. Back to the hotel, have some fruit, rest and do homework. Nap. Lunch at 3:30 and go to the arena for all-around finals. Open warm-up at 4:15: beam, floor, vault, bars. Competition: bars, beam, floor, vault.

9:30 P.M.—Go to an interview. Call Dad for just a minute to tell him the good news, but the local TV and radio stations had announced it already. Dad said that he had heard it on the radio driving back from dropping my brother off at the gym. He sounded very happy.

Her incredible triumph was summed up in five words: "Competition: bars, beam, floor, vault." No expression of joy or pride, no hint at satisfaction, not even a mention of the victory itself. "She's young," Nunno explains. "If she stops to look back at what she's done, she might lose her edge. She's got the rest of her life to look back."

Shannon moves through each day to the steady tick of the clock in her head, rising at 6:30 A.M. to reach the gym by 7:30 and school by 9; it's back to the gym at 3 P.M., then home by about 8 to eat dinner and study until midnight. In eight years with Nunno she has missed only one scheduled workout. He excused her for one day after she broke her elbow and had to have screws inserted to hold the tendon to the bone. If Shannon had to leave town for a day or two to shoot pictures for a leotard catalog or accept an award, she stole the time from school, not gymnastics, and still managed to maintain an A average in honors courses. She used school vacations and plane rides to catch up on missed homework. "It's tough," says Terri Thomas, who was hired by the Edmond, Oklahoma, school district to travel with Shannon after her schedule pulled her away from school so often after the Olympics. "She goes all week without a break. Sometimes she doesn't get enough sleep. Sometimes she breaks down, but it's over in fifteen minutes."

Nunno feels nothing but pride in how he has shaped Shannon's childhood, so much so that he has said he'd like to write a book on how to coach top-level gymnastics without sacrificing the gymnasts' self-esteem. "Shannon has done exactly what she's wanted to do. Everyone in the world wants a place in life and wants to make a little bit of a difference. Kids too. They strive for it. That's why you've got gangs, drugs—they're trying to find some identity... It's unfair of us to ask, 'What did Shannon give up [to do gymnastics]?' She gave up nothing. She did it her way. If there were sacrifices, they were from her family to allow her to strive for an identity. She'll be done with her career at nineteen or twenty and will have the rest of her life to go to the movies with friends. Plus she's made more friends around the world than you can ever imagine. Not close friends, but how many of us still have friends from childhood? I don't."

On the bus from the hotel to Towson State, Shannon fished a book from her gym bag to finish reading for an English assignment. Sitting a few rows ahead, Nunno complained out loud when the driver took what Nunno considered a longer route than necessary. For Nunno, every wasted minute is wasted opportunity. He usually works eighteen hours a day, nine coaching and nine running the two gyms he owns in Oklahoma City and nearby Edmond as well as overseeing a third in Denton, Texas, in which he has a partner. He has more than a thousand gymnasts among the three gyms. He is the Károlyi of the 1990s, the poster boy for a generation of Béla acolytes. Nunno coached under Károlyi for seven months and says he took away only two lessons: how to communicate to his gymnasts and how hard to push them. "I've seen Béla push kids too hard and give up on kids," Nunno says.

But when you watch him in the gym, it's clear he picked up much more. He hollers, berates and bullies like Károlyi. He rules with Károlyi's godly righteousness. He has become the American Károlyi down to the mustache and bear hugs. "We were making jokes," recalls Wendy Bruce, one of Shannon's 1992 Olympic teammates, "that he was even starting to walk like Béla."

If his goal was to replicate Károlyi's production line of gymnasts, he has succeeded. Nunno's gymnasts are as thin, blank and obedient as were Károlyi's Romanian teams. Nunno sees the girls as vessels to fill up with his energy. Before competitions, he holds Shannon Miller by the shoulders and has her look into his eyes to draw power and strength from him. "It's a partnership," Nunno says. "A teamwork situation." So much so that when Shannon earned the number one ranking over Kim Zmeskal on the 1992 Olympic team, even though Kim technically outpointed Shannon at the Olympic Trials, Nunno accepted the victory as his own. His best had beaten Károlyi's best. The student had finally beaten the master. When Károlyi complained to anyone who would listen that Kim had really won the Trials, Nunno exploded. "I'll be damned if somebody is going to take this away from *me*," Nunno told reporters. "Tonight, Béla has to raise his glass to *me*."

Shannon Miller is the jewel in Nunno's crown. As long as Miller is a world champion gymnast, then he is a world champion coach. If she slips, he slips. Even at the extravagantly named World Gymnastics Cup in Baltimore, a meaningless exhibition in which the gymnasts performed in costumes to music, Nunno wouldn't allow her to be anything less than perfect, despite having competed almost nonstop in the eighteen months since the Olympics. Hopping from exhibitions to the U.S. Olympic Festival to the gymnastics tour to the U.S. and World Championships, she caught one cold after another. Her back hurt, only sporadically at first and then every day.

Though doctors couldn't pinpoint the cause, Nunno was certain the pain was not from training too hard. "We don't think the back problem is a common overuse syndrome," he explained during the Baltimore event. "It's just something that probably she did at one point, and we haven't been able to give it enough rest time because of all the competitions she was in last year."

As for the colds, Nunno ruled out fatigue as a factor. Shannon got them simply from being around so many crowds the past year. And if she *were* fatigued, it wouldn't be from gymnastics. "I think school is taking its toll on her," Nunno said. "The junior year in high school is probably the hardest year."

Nunno delivered the explanations like carefully packaged goods, controlling their content as he controls everything from bus routes to a seventeen-year-old girl's life. At the Olympics in Barcelona, Nunno kept Shannon isolated from the excitement and bustle of the Summer Games. Like the other American gymnasts, she didn't walk in the Opening or Closing Ceremonies. She didn't explore the city or even the athletes' village. In interviews afterward, Shannon spun out the same mechanical answers about how much fun she had had meeting athletes from different sports and different countries. But when pressed for specifics, she couldn't come up with anything she had seen or done at the Olympics beyond the competition. "We just kind of went from our little housing area to the cafeteria and then back. And then usually just to training. But still, just on the walk over there you saw some people. You didn't necessarily get to meet and talk. But you could say hi."

Nunno later explained that even if Shannon didn't get much of a flavor for the Olympics, it was made up to her when she arrived home to a parade of 15,000 people and a gift of a new car from the town of Edmond. "The fact that they appreciated her efforts and noticed her, that's what the Olympic Games is to her...The Olympic spirit is to participate. But you don't work that hard for that long to try to attain a goal like that and go just to enjoy the Games. You want to go and do your very best. And the spirit of the Olympic Games is in her heart forevermore."

When Károlyi retired after the Olympics, fourteen-year-old Olympian Kerri Strug left his gym and eventually joined Nunno in Oklahoma City. When she abruptly went home after one unhappy year, Nunno claimed that Kerri had come to him as damaged inventory from Károlyi's. "She didn't believe in herself," Nunno says. "She had very low self-esteem. Of course, she came from that same gym, you know. Everybody I know who ever came from there had the same problem."

Nunno shifts the rest of the blame for Kerri's failure to thrive at his gym onto the gymnast herself: she called home every night complaining about the gym as a way of getting attention from her parents; she always blamed everyone else for her own failures; and she never accepted him as her coach. "I knew that she needed to be home," Nunno explains. "We just agreed that that's what she should do."

Nunno leaves out the primary reason for Kerri's departure. The day before Kerri left for a series of European meets with Nunno's assistant Peggy Liddick, an orthopedist gave her a shot of cortisone for acute pain in one of her abdominal muscles and told her she wouldn't damage the muscle by competing. Despite mounting pain, Kerri competed with Liddick's blessing. By the third meet, she had torn the muscle.

Asked about Kerri's injury, Nunno throws up his hands. "She wanted to make something of herself. And the doctors had given us clearance. They said just take care of it. Pace her. And we did." Kerri's angry mother didn't think having her compete in three meets in Europe constituted pacing. She flew to Oklahoma City and brought her daughter home to Arizona to heal and gain back the weight she had lost at Nunno's. The muscle tear was so serious she couldn't compete for eight months. When she did return in the summer of 1994, she slipped from the uneven bars and crashed to the floor in a twisted heap, her chin on the mat, her back and legs arched over her head. She rolled onto her side crying in pain and was taken from the arena strapped to a stretcher, her neck in a brace. She spent the night in the hospital in serious condition but was released two days later. Just a sprained back. She was back

LITTLE GIRLS IN PRETTY BOXES

in her Arizona gym within a week, popping painkillers to ease the way.

■ ■ ■

Like Nunno, most coaches in the United States have no formal training in coaching. Most learn their sports as competitors, though not necessarily as elite competitors. Anyone can put an ad in the newspaper and declare himself a coach. "Jack the Ripper could walk off the street and coach your child," says Dr. Lyle Micheli, a pediatric orthopedist at Harvard Medical School and former president of the American College of Sports Medicine. "Some of the biggest offenders are the elite coaches. If they have to sacrifice seven kids to get one champion, some will do it." Micheli supports legislation that would require every coach from Little League on up to be certified, as they are in Canada, Australia and New Zealand. He'd like coaches to be educated in basic child psychology and physiology, which might make them less likely to enforce arbitrary weight goals that drive athletes to eating disorders or to demand unnecessary, potentially damaging, training. When a study found that swimmers who swam 10,000 yards a day performed no better than those who swam 5,000 yards, coaches still wanted their swimmers to go 10,000, clinging to the myth that more is always better.

A recent study by Dr. Anthony Kalinowski, a researcher at the University of Chicago, found that the more hours of training *over a lifetime* an athlete put in, the greater were his or her achievements— a finding coaches could use to bear out their belief that more is better. But what Kalinowski also found was that swimmers who competed nationally began training at age ten, while swimmers who competed on the Olympic team began training at age seven.

Yet a Florida State psychologist, Dr. Anders Ericsson, found that the top achievers in sports, music or chess trained arduously for no more than four hours a day. After four hours, "you find a tremendous drop in mood, and a jump in irritability, fatigue and apathy."

Back when sports were exclusively male, coaches didn't need to know much more about physiology than how their own bodies and minds worked, which is vastly different from having to know the anatomy and psychology of children and teenage girls. Women have taken great strides in athletics over the last thirty years, but the coaching hasn't caught up. For the most part, girls still are coached on a male model without regard to bone density, menstrual cycles, growth plates and eating disorders, as well as the very real self-esteem issues that weigh on teenage girls. Research on young female athletes has been accumulating over the last decade, including that generated by a groundbreaking 1992 national conference called "The Female Triad" at which scientists addressed the physiological impact of intensive training on young female athletes. The conference, organized by sports medicine doctors and researchers, hoped to highlight their growing concern that early and excessive training could invite long-term damage. But few coaches in elite gymnastics or figure skating keep abreast of the latest research. Most aren't students of sports as much as they are students of winning.

It would be naïve to think that those who choose to coach female rather than male gymnasts do so because of a particular expertise or interest in female athletics. The fact is that girls' gymnastics is more popular and lucrative. "Girls are easier when they're young," says Kelli Hill, Dominique Dawes's coach. "Their body fat is low, so they still have a little boy's body. And boys aren't as disciplined. I coach girls the same age as my two sons, seven and eleven, and it's apples and oranges."

In a stab at upgrading its coaching ranks, USA Gymnastics has instituted voluntary certification for coaches through its new Professional Development Program, which offers courses on coaching technique and safety. "We are absolutely seeing that the coaches coming into our sports don't have physical education or education backgrounds," says Steve Whitlock, director of education and safety. "Over eighty percent are like myself. They came to the sport because they were athletes."

Steve Nunno says he wholeheartedly supports a certification process for coaches to screen out the unqualified people, who, according to Nunno, "could affect the lives of young Americans." He says the USA Gymnastics's new program is an excellent start, though he has not yet taken any of the courses himself. His views offer a good example of how fractured and contradictory the coaching community is on the issue. For example, Nunno suggests that a basic requirement for being a gymnastics coach should be a college degree. (He himself majored in business administration and earned a master's degree in sports administration, learning gymnastics first by competing, then by coaching under the likes of Béla Károlyi.) On second thought, Nunno says, the coaches should be required to have a two-year associate's degree. Or if the coach is young, then just a high school degree.

In the end, he comes up with two basic requirements: "I think first of all you have to have no criminal record. Second of all you have to be a good citizen."

Which would qualify most of America. The fact is, if a coach is producing winners, his lack of education and compassion draws little attention, much less criticism. The casualties of his coaching disappear so quickly we barely notice. In our microwave, Jiffy Lube, ATM, drive-through culture, it seems almost normal for a girl's athletic career to rise and fall in a blink. We're impatient for results, and gymnastics and figure skating feed our impatience with their production of ever-younger stars. The coach, who has to produce winners to thrive financially, must keep serving up new athletes, hoping one or two will make it and tossing away the rest. The girls are as disposable as everything else today, from razors to contact lenses.

And though parents see their daughter's teammates disappearing one by one, they somehow never make the connection to themselves, envisioning some Hollywood version of success, something brilliant and lucrative. They're feeding at the same trough as the people who buy lottery tickets: though their chances of winning are laughably remote, *somebody* wins—and that provides enough hope to keep them buying tickets. For parents of young elite athletes, the end too often comes as a stunning disappointment, as if they've never heard the mounting rumble of the truck that finally hits them, though it is the same truck and the same blind corner that have crippled so many before them. The shock and grief were summed up perfectly by the mother who wept and raged for eight hours, pounding her fists against the walls of her rented Oklahoma City apartment after her unhappy, bulimic daughter quit gymnastics a year before the Olympics.

Coaches who claim they are paid to produce gymnasts and figure skaters and nothing more are betraying a trust implicit in the mentor-student relationship. Coaches of elite children's sports, by spending the bulk of every day with their athletes, can influence these children more than their parents or their teachers at school. The coaches become role models whether they want to or not. Their words and actions can profoundly affect the long-term physical and emotional health of their athletes, making the job too rife with the possibilities of abuse to allow it to continue unregulated.

Though the gymnastics and skating federations don't have

the muscle to enforce even minimal coaching standards, they can make attendance at certain basic courses a requirement rather than a suggestion. Further, they can insist on the athletes' staying in school full-time until at least age sixteen; those who drop out would lose their eligibility to compete. Ultimately, it is up to the U.S. government to step in and require that every coach secure a license. Licensing won't eliminate the abusive coaches, but it will make it easier for a parent to insist on certain standards of behavior, knowing that the government backs them up.

Whether we see any changes instituted to protect these young athletes hinges on our willingness to sacrifice a few medals for the sake of their health and well-being. Our obsession with winning, with dominating opponents and reveling in victory, is not considered a character flaw. On the contrary, few traits are more admired in this country than hard-driving ambition. And we expect sacrifices to be made in the name of great success. But when the sacrifices mean a childhood spent in the toils of physical and psychological abuse, the price is too high.

8

THE
AFTERMATH

AN UPDATE

■

When the U.S. women's gymnastics team walked onto the floor of the Georgia Dome for the start of the 1996 Olympics, it was clear that a subtle but significant shift had taken place since the 1992 Games. For the first time in twenty years, the majority of the gymnasts on the U.S. women's team were, indeed, women. Three were nineteen years old. Two were eighteen. Only fourteen-year-old Dominique Moceanu and sixteen-year-old Jaycie Phelps weren't adults. On the 1992 team, all were children except one, nineteen-year-old Wendy Bruce.

These 1996 gymnasts were, on average, 17.6 years old, 4 feet

11 inches tall and 92.3 pounds—one year and nine months older, 1½ inches taller and 10 pounds heavier than in 1992. They were a revelation.

They showed that women—albeit very small, light women— could compete at the highest levels in gymnastics. The older gymnasts in 1996 possessed the strength and confidence that had been lacking four years earlier. Shannon Miller, Kerri Strug and Dominique Dawes, the returnees from 1992, were like new gymnasts in 1996. Miller, in particular, confounded the experts. She had gained 19 pounds and grew 4 inches between 1992 and 1996, but instead of letting the growth doom her, she blossomed into a stronger, more beautiful athlete.

"They have more finesse, more composure, more self-confidence," Diane Amos, who coached 1996 Olympian Amy Chow, said of Miller, Strug and Dawes. "I think the older girls are doing this more for themselves, which is what competition is all about. It's no longer their parents making decisions, their coaches making decisions. They're doing it because they want to do it."

Fourteen-year-old Dominique Moceanu grabbed most of the pre-Olympics headlines, landing on magazine covers and captivating reporters with her smile and enthusiasm. But it was the older gymnasts who emerged as stars, flourishing under the pressure of a vocal home crowd in Atlanta. Miller won her first individual Olympic gold medal with a near flawless routine on the balance beam. The event was her thirtieth over the course of two Olympics. In the previous twenty-nine, she had earned four bronzes and a silver in Barcelona and the team gold in Atlanta. Now, in her last event, she finally got to stand on the top step of the victory stand by herself. Dawes won a bronze in floor exercise.

And Kerri Strug, a shy eighteen-year-old veteran from the 1992 team, surprised everyone by blossoming into the biggest star of all.

On Tuesday afternoon, July 23, inside the Georgia Dome, the U.S. entered the team optionals competition in second place behind the Russians and just ahead of the favored Romanians. Right from the start of competition, there was a confidence and poise about this group that had been lacking in previous years. And there was a sense of unity, which had been carefully orchestrated by coaches Mary Lee Tracy and Márta Károlyi. They housed the team 25 miles north of Atlanta, well beyond the distractions of the Olympic Village. They lived, ate and trained together as a true team, not as individuals from separate gyms who happened to be wearing the same uniform.

The togetherness even rubbed off on rival coaches Béla Károlyi and Steve Nunno, who watched and cheered from the sidelines, occasionally hugging each other as one American after another nailed her routines. After the first rotation, the Americans inched ahead of the Russians. After each rotation the lead widened: .472 after the bars, .497 after beam, .897 after floor. The Georgia Dome, with a sellout crowd of 32,000, sounded like a raucous party.

In the final rotation of the team competition, with the U.S. on the verge of winning its first team gold medal, Moceanu faltered badly on her two vaults, falling on her rear both times. Strug was the final American competitor. On her first vault, a Yurchenko 1½, she jammed her landing, rolling her left ankle and landing on her backside. She grimaced in pain as she made her way back to the top of the runway.

"I can't feel my leg," Strug said to coach Béla Károlyi on the sidelines.

"Give me one last good vault!" Károlyi shouted.

"Do I have to do this again?"

"Can you? Can you?"

Strug had thirty seconds to make a decision. She didn't know that she had torn a ligament in her ankle. Perhaps it wouldn't have made a difference. She and the coaches believed the U.S. team needed Strug's final vault to win the gold. With the crowd screaming for victory and her teammates cheering her on, Strug did what any gritty athlete would have done: She took her place on the runway. She sprinted, leapt off the springboard and flipped in the air, knowing the searing pain that was waiting as her feet sailed toward the mat. She nailed the landing, tearing a second ligament. She quickly pulled her foot off the mat, hopping on one foot to salute the judges before collapsing in pain.

It became the defining moment of the Olympics.

Károlyi, ever the showman, carried Strug to the victory stand, her left ankle wrapped in a splint. The injury kept her from the individual all-around medal, but it made her the most famous athlete in Atlanta. She found herself at the center of conversations in offices and living rooms, on radio talk shows and nightly newscasts. Nobody could watch replays of her vault without being moved by her courage, and her anguished face left no doubt about how high a price athletes sometimes pay for a spot on the victory stand.

It was this issue, as much as her courage, that fueled much of the talk.

Should she have taken the vault? Was she pushed by her coach, the infamous Károlyi, to put her body at risk? How could a medallion be worth risking debilitating injury?

Having written this book, I was asked countless times in the days after Strug's injury what I thought of her decision to take the vault. Wasn't it, people asked, exactly what I wrote about: a gymnast driven beyond her limits by a sport often insensitive to the athlete's well-being?

The answer was no. There was almost no correlation between what I wrote about in this book and what happened that July night in Georgia. I believe completely that Strug did what almost every athlete in the Olympics would do in the same circumstances. Picture the scene: The U.S. seems to be cruising to the gold medal when suddenly Moceanu falls twice on the vault. Then Strug herself falls. The crowd and certainly the U.S. team senses the gold slipping away. So Strug hobbles back from her first vault in great pain, unsure of the severity of her injury. With the Olympic medal in the balance, she simply did what any dedicated athlete would do: She soldiered through—and became a hero.

Within hours of the vault, offers began pouring in. She signed on with superagent Leigh Steinberg, but the relationship wouldn't last. (Marketing a gymnast was very different from marketing football and baseball players, Steinberg discovered.) She showed up on *Saturday Night Live* and movie premieres. She turned down the offer to tour with the rest of the U.S. team in favor of a different tour that would be more flexible around her schedule at UCLA, where she enrolled as a student a month after the Olympics.

After two years at UCLA, where she helped for a while to coach the gymnastics team, she transferred to Stanford. She has taken up long-distance running, running her first marathon in 1999. She spends most weekends making paid appearances or donating time to charities—enjoying what most elite gymnasts never do: a long-term financial return on the investment of a childhood.

． ． ．

The success of the '96 team was no accident. It grew out of a painful, public transition that reached a head in the summer of 1995, when elite gymnastics seemed under siege. The sport already had

Olympic gold medalist Dominque Moceanu, right, and her father, Dumitru, listen as a judge reads the details of a one-year protective order hearing December 9, 1998, in Houston. (*Houston Chronicle*)

Dominique Moceanu in the floor exercise at the 1996 Summer Olympics. (*Houston Chronicle*)

Dominique Dawes performing on the balance beam during an exhibition at the Georgia Dome, Summer Olympics 1996. (José R. Lopez/ NYT Pictures)

Gymnast Kristie Phillips, 27, gets electric stimulation in her ankle to help reduce inflammation from U.S. Gymnastics national medical coordinator Larry Nassar at Arco Arena on August 25, 1999. (*Sacramento Bee* Staff Photo)

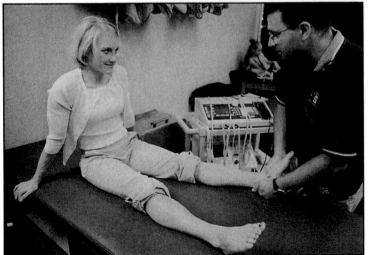

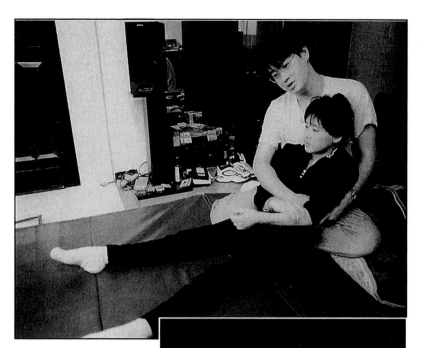

The Chinese gymnast Sang Lan and friend, Winston Sie, during rehabilitation after the gymnast's fateful accident at the 1998 Goodwill Games that left her paralyzed from the chest down. (Librado Romero/ NYT Pictures)

Kerri Strug's famous landing, which she nailed despite severe ankle injuries, leading the U.S. team to an overall victory. (Al Tielemans/ *Sports Illustrated*)

Kerri Strug being carried out prior to the awards ceremony by her personal coach, Béla Károlyi, as the U.S. women's team won the gold. (Walter Iooss, Jr./*Sports Illustrated*)

The U.S. Olympic champion team receiving their medals after a hard-earned victory in the 1996 Summer Olympics. (Barton Silverman/NYT Pictures)

Shannon Miller does her routine on the parallel bars at the 1996 Summer Olympics. (*Houston Chronicle*)

Tara Lipinski of the U.S. reacting to her landing a jump during her free skate program at the eighteenth Winter Olympics in Nagano, Japan. (Chang W. Lee/ NYT Pictures)

As bronze medalist Lu Chen of China looks on, Tara Lipinski leans down from her perch high atop the awards platform to congratulate silver medalist Michelle Kwan. Lipinski won the gold medal in ladies' figure skating in Nagano. (*Houston Chronicle*)

Tara Lipinski blows kisses to the crowd as she and Michelle Kwan do a victory lap after the awards ceremony in Nagano. (*Houston Chronicle*)

Michelle Kwan performing a perfect triple toe loop during the competition for ladies' free skate at CoreStates Center, PA. Kwan was a world champion at fifteen, slowed by doubt at sixteen, then favored to win the gold at seventeen. (Chang W. Lee/ NYTPictures)

Michelle Kwan and Tara Lipinski smiling as Nicole Bobek, right, gets her award for third place at the CoreStates Center after the ladies' free skate Championship for 1998. (Chang W. Lee/NYT Pictures)

Venessa Atler dismounts the balance beam at the U.S. Gymnastics Championships at Arco Arena, August 1999. (*Sacramento Bee* Staff Photo)

Vanessa Atler, left, gets a big hug from Kristen Maloney after Vanessa did well in the floor exercises at the U.S. Gymnastics Championships. (*Sacramento Bee* Staff Photo) taken its lumps from the public and the media for the thin, sullen American team it sent to the 1992 Olympics in Barcelona. Then Christy Henrich died from complications of anorexia, a national story that drew coverage from *People* magazine to the nightly news. *Little Girls in Pretty Boxes* was published soon after this tragedy, prompting examinations of gymnastics' darker side on such influential shows as *Oprah* and *60 Minutes*. Right on its heels came news from Romania that a coach there smashed an eleven-year-old gymnast's head against the balance beam and violently kicked her after she repeatedly fumbled her dismount. She died later that evening. (The coach was convicted in 1995 of manslaughter and sentenced to eight years.) A few months later in Australia, parents of several gymnasts accused the country's head coach of kicking, smacking and forcing the girls to run fully clothed in a sauna if they gained weight.

Reports of problems in elite gymnastics seemed to be flooding into newspapers and magazines every week. USA Gymnastics had already asked Nancy Thies Marshall, a 1972 Olympic gymnast, to head up a task force in the fall of 1994 to study the health risks in the sport. For two years, Marshall worked without pay, gathering research, talking to experts and conducting seminars at the annual Congress and national championships. Her task force produced an impressive, comprehensive report in 1995 that laid out the problems and called for reform.

A new USA Gymnastics began to emerge, one that, within four years, had become a model to other Olympic governing bodies looking to protect and improve the health of their female athletes.

USAG had been taking steps toward improvement even before the task force's report. It had hired nutritionist Dan Benardot to work with the national team. He stopped the practice of weighing the gymnasts at national training camps, and he banned talk of height and weight. He focused, instead, on a gymnast's strength relative to her size. Doctors at training camps began screening the gymnasts on their general health. If any showed symptoms of eating disorders, the issue was addressed directly with the girl, her parents and her coaches. The gymnast was put in touch with a nutritionist, a sports psychologist and a medical doctor. And she was told she would not be allowed to compete until she received a doctor's clearance.

"After Christy Henrich, we weren't going to hem and haw about this," Marshall said. "Coaches didn't complain. In fact, it was almost a sigh of relief."

The results of Benardot's and Marshall's work became clear at the 1996 Games in Atlanta.

"The United States was the biggest, tallest, heaviest team and also the fittest on the floor," Benardot said. "We proved that as long as you're strong and healthy, you don't have to try to stop growth in order to be a successful gymnast."

In 1992 most of the Olympic gymnasts had primary amenorrhea—they hadn't begun menstruating yet. By 1996, Benardot said, most of the 1996 team were menstruating normally. That alone pointed out the difference in just four years: In 1992, the United States had a team of children. In 1996, it had a winning group of women.

USA Gymnastics knew going into the Olympics that it was on the right track, but the group had yet to commit itself fully to the wellness program—which is to say, it had invested almost no money in it. During the 1996 Games in Atlanta, it got the shove it needed.

Even as its older, stronger gymnasts were working their way toward a gold medal, USAG once again found itself on the defensive against bad publicity. But it wasn't from newspaper reporters or disgruntled former gymnasts and parents. This time, the problems in elite gymnastics were being scrutinized by the august *New England Journal of Medicine*.

In its July 25, 1996 issue, the journal published a pointed, no-nonsense article on the often devastating physical and psychological problems in women's gymnastics. It cited forty-five sources, most of them medical researchers—a clear indication that the interest in and concern about elite gymnastics' harmful effects had widened far beyond the mainstream media. USAG could no longer brush away criticism of its sport as sensational and uninformed.

"Overtraining, injuries and psychological damage are common consequences (of elite gymnastics). Parents and coaches, in collusion with the young athlete, may seek to experience vicariously the success of the child, a behavior that could be called 'achievement by proxy,'" the article's four authors wrote. "...We suggest that in its extreme form 'achievement by proxy' may be a sort of child abuse."

By the end of the 1996, USAG had allocated $40,000 for its Athlete Wellness Program and hired Nancy Marshall as its paid director. By 1998, the budget had doubled to $80,000. Finally Marshall had the money and clout to put together the program that had been taking shape inside her head for years.

Almost single-handedly, she began to transform USA Gymnastics. Under her direction, USAG established a national advisory board of sport-science and health-care consultants to help guide USAG's administrators and coaches. It also put together a national referral network so that gymnasts training anywhere in the United States would have access to medical experts. It created a curriculum for seminars to be held at regional and national meetings. Its official magazine began carrying special "Sideline Support" inserts that discussed issues important to parents, and USAG began holding parents' meetings at the national championships to raise awareness on such topics as nutrition and sports psychology. USAG also created a mentoring program that matches current national team members with former members who act as advisors, sounding boards and supporters.

In the summer of 1999, Marshall pulled the many threads of the program together in a 118-page resource and information manual called "The Athlete Wellness Book." Marshall and USAG educational and medical consultants compiled the latest research and advice about motivation, mental-skills training, eating disorders, amenorrhea, osteoporosis, burnout, overtraining and child development as it relates to gymnastics.

But as Marshall well knows, there are still some stumbling blocks. The most frustrating one is convincing the coaches that the punishing Eastern Bloc style of coaching is not the only way to mold champions. If coaches such as Mary Lee Tracy continue to succeed with a more positive, caring style, other coaches are likely to follow suit.

"Coaches are searching," Marshall said. "They do feel they are held accountable for how they train these kids. They're saying, 'We want to do this the healthy way. How do we do it?'"

■ ■ ■

Yet just as USA Gymnastics was making the sport safer than it had been in years, the International Gymnastics Federation tossed them two curveballs that threaten to undermine the progress.

In a meeting before the 1996 Olympics, the International Gymnastics Federation (FIG) had taken the bold—and at first glance, positive—step of raising the minimum age for the 2000 Olympics from fifteen to sixteen. The intent was to keep parents and coaches from pushing young children into dangerous, pressure-packed competitions before their bodies and minds are mature enough to cope. Many agreed with the reasoning.

"I think that it can slow us down a little bit at the beginning so we can spend more time doing some of the basics that are necessary," coach Mary Lee Tracy told *International Gymnast* magazine. "And I think that in the long run it's going to pay off as far as injury prevention because we won't have to start pounding (the gymnasts') bodies quite so early. "

But others are more cynical. They felt if nothing else in the sport changed and gymnasts still needed freakishly thin and small bodies to succeed, then raising the age would simply exacerbate the eating problems. "Now," said one former coach, "you just have older anorexics."

Yet instead of figuring out how to fine-tune the judging criteria to reward an older, larger gymnast, the FIG did what seems almost unthinkable: It *increased* the difficulty level of required skills.

After each Olympics, the FIG issues a new Code of Points, the criteria used to judge routines. After the 1996 Olympics, it changed the Code of Points so that gymnasts have to perform greater, and more dangerous, acrobatic feats to attain the highest scores. In other words, while it was clearing the way for older gymnasts to compete, it was ratcheting up the skill requirements so that only the smallest, lightest and youngest bodies would excel.

Of all the developments in gymnastics since this book came out five years ago, the change in the Code of Points is by far the most distressing—not just to gymnastics' critics but to many of its most devoted supporters.

"The new road imposed by this Code is dangerous and will lead to more accidents if gymnasts feel pressured to attain the maximum 'start value,'" Nicolae Vieru, president of the Romanian

Gymnastics Federation, wrote in a guest editorial in *International Gymnast* magazine. "Raising the age limit is not consistent with increasing the difficulty requirements."

From 1993 to 1996, all routines started from a base score of 9.4. A gymnast would have to earn the remaining six-tenths of a perfect score by executing the most difficult tricks. Under the new code (in place through the 2000 Olympics), the base score is 9.0, meaning the gymnast has to have a routine filled with extraordinary tricks to earn a bonus of a full point. The requirements for difficulty have increased so dramatically that, under the new Code of Points, the start value of Kim Zmeskal's 1991 World Championship routine would be 7.9.

For all the talk of appreciating the artistry of the mature athlete in women's gymnastics, it is—now more than ever—the risky flips and twists that draw the highest scores.

"It's like the left hand doesn't know what the right hand is trying to do," elite coach John Geddert told one reporter. "They cranked the difficulty level up so you have to be almost suicidal to be competitive. We're already taking a beating from the media for being a sport that's very, very tough on bodies and on kids, and yet we go and do outrageous things with the difficulty."

Some coaches are afraid that young gymnasts will burn out faster than ever as they race to master ever more complex skills, leading to a drop in the number of elites overall.

"Many of the elements of the new Code are from pure imagination, released by some fanciful mind," Vieru wrote. "These skills—such as a Tsukahara with a double tucked somersault—require irrational risk and pose a threat to the health of the gymnasts.... The international symposiums of 1989 in Stuttgart and 1991 in Indianapolis brought to light the negative effects of high-risk training. Is everyone forgetting?"

. . .

In the summer of 1998, tragedy did, indeed, strike. But it had nothing to do with the riskier Code of Points. It resulted instead from a routine practice vault, pointing out again that even a slight mistake at the elite level can have dire consequences.

Seventeen-year-old Sang Lan was not well known when she arrived in New York for the Goodwill Games in the summer of 1998. She was tiny for seventeen—4 feet 8 inches tall and 77 pounds. A year earlier she had become the Chinese vault champion, but she had not yet attracted attention internationally. On July 21, a Tuesday night, Sang was warming up for the vault competition inside the Nassau Coliseum in New York. She was there with two teammates.

Sang's practice vault was one that many gymnasts use regularly as a warm-up. They simply sprint down the runway, pounce onto a springboard, place their hands on the horse then push off into a flip, landing on their feet. It sets their timing in preparation for the more complicated moves they'll use in competition.

Sang sprinted down the runway, hit the springboard and launched onto the horse. But she seemed to pitch too far forward in her handspring. She seemed caught between pushing herself through the trick and yanking herself back. She found herself in the air but unable to rotate. She landed on her head.

Several coaches standing nearby heard a sickening crack. Sang lay still on the mat as people rushed to help. "Her head was off her shoulders," one doctor told a magazine reporter later. Eyewitnesses say Sang didn't cry until she was moved onto a stretcher to be transferred to the hospital. "Can I still be a gymnast?" she asked the Chinese team's delegation leader. Then she said, "I wish I could stand up."

Kathy Johnson, covering the event for TBS television, had been taping her opening remarks for the broadcast as Sang warmed up. She saw the gymnast fall just as she launched into her remarks.

"My heart stopped but I kept speaking [on camera]," Johnson said. "In my head, I was saying, 'Get up, get up.' I have no idea what I said [in the opening]. When I finished, I jumped out of my seat in tears and ran off. I needed to move. I needed to go see my little boy, who was there with my husband and mother. My thought was, 'That's somebody's baby out there, and she's so far from home and nobody is there to hold her.'"

In a small house in China, Sang's parents had turned on the television to watch their only child compete. They lived a modest life in Ningbo, a city near Shanghai on China's east coast. Sang's father, Sang Shisheng, worked in a housing management office, and her mother, Chen Xiufeng, worked in a steel factory.

When their daughter was identified as a gymnastics prodigy, they agreed to send her at age eight to train at a sports school, though it meant they would see her only about once a month. At age eleven, Sang was chosen for the Chinese national team and moved to Beijing, more than 700 miles from Ningbo. Her parents saw her only three times in the next six years, but they talked by phone. Just a few days before Sang left for the Goodwill Games in New York, they had talked with her and wished her luck.

Now on TV, they were watching their daughter being carried away on a stretcher in an arena thousands of miles away.

"We were shocked," Sang Shisheng told the Associated Press later. "I never expected anything this terrible, not once."

The couple flew to New York three days later, their first trip abroad. (Goodwill Games officials paid their travel expenses.) Sang's mother cried most of the way, not just in grief and worry over her daughter's injuries, but over lost time. Sang's father shared her remorse. "How can we ever make it up to her?" he said to the AP. "She was separated from her mother and father at such a young age, with no parental love. Thinking back, I do have regrets."

He said his wife didn't want to go on living if their daughter's injuries were permanent.

Back in New York, doctors were not encouraging. The force of the fall had traveled down Sang's spine until it found the place of least strength, which for her were the C-6 and C-7 vertebrae. One of her two damaged vertebrae was shattered. A doctor, quoted in the *New York Times,* wondered if Sang had an existing stress fracture she hadn't known about, making the area more vulnerable. Or perhaps, the doctor speculated, she had an eating disorder that weakened her bones.

Those questions were, appropriately, pushed aside as doctors focused on Sang's recovery. Five days after the accident, Sang underwent four and a half hours of surgery to remove "a severe amount" of bone fragments from her spinal cord and to graft bone from her hip onto the spine so the broken bones would fuse into one solid piece. Doctors placed small plates and screws in the front and back of her neck, spanning the C5, C6 and C7 vertebrae.

Her chances of walking again were "very poor," said Dr. Kristjan T. Ragnarsson, a physician at Mount Sinai Medical Center in New York, where Sang was treated.

Her plight drew tremendous attention. Teen heartthrob Leonardo DiCaprio slipped into Mount Sinai about a week after Sang's accident and visited the gymnast for an hour. She received hundreds of cards, Beanie Babies and flowers. Singer Celine Dion showed up one day. She also received a visit from Dennis Byrd, the former New York Jets football player who recovered from a less serious spinal injury with the help of Sygen, the same experimental drug that Sang was given to try to regenerate damaged nerve cells.

Sang's psychological and emotional strength impressed everyone around her. When her parents arrived, carrying a sack of one thousand good-luck origami birds made by friends, Sang comforted them. "Mother, don't worry about me," she said. "You have to have courage to allow me to recover."

Meanwhile, the gymnastics community went on red alert with the media, and understandably so. The sport had taken heat the past few years, with books, articles and television programs examining the injuries, eating disorders, pushy parents and abusive coaches in the sport. And now, right in New York, the media capital of the world, a gymnast suffered a catastrophic injury in an international competition.

Accidents happen, gymnastics officials kept saying in press conferences and in interviews, and they were right. Every sport carries risk. There is no way to eliminate all injuries. "This was simply an accident that can occur in any kind of sport, very, very unfortunately," USA Gymnastics president Kathy Scanlan told the *New York Times* the day after Sang's accident. "But it is not the result of unsafe conditions."

Bart Conner agreed. "I don't think this is evidence of abuse in women's gymnastics. It's not like someone made her do this and she got hurt. It's a common routine that had a sad, unlucky result."

Sang Lan left the hospital in late October 1998 and moved into a 25th-floor duplex on 38th Street in New York, paid for by Sang's friend Winston Sie, a 25-year-old financial researcher at Paine Webber. She had some movement in her arms, but her hands and legs remained totally paralyzed. Still, she managed to learn how to comb her hair, brush her teeth and dress herself. She could go out in a wheelchair and gesture with her arms toward grocery items she wanted at the supermarket.

In the apartment, she slept on a bed that used air pressure to turn her over so she wouldn't develop bedsores. Rehabilitation specialists visited regularly to keep her muscles strong in hopes that one day doctors will find a cure for damaged spinal cords. Her father flew back to China after about three months in New York, and her mother stayed on to care for her, making up for the time lost to gymnastics.

In May 1999, Sang Lan returned home to China, where, in the fall, she watched from a wheelchair as the planet's best gymnasts, her former colleagues, competed in the World Championships.

■ ■ ■

The headlines about Sang's accident at the Goodwill Games in the summer of 1998 had barely faded when the gymnastics community found itself in the midst of another dark, controversial story.

Dominique Moceanu, the well-spoken, perky young Olympian who had captured America's attention in 1996, ran away from home on October 21 at age seventeen, claiming her parents stole both her childhood and her money. The news came as a shock. Until that October day, Moceanu's life story seemed to unfold like a fairy tale, inspiring the dreams of thousands of little girls across the world.

Dominique was born in Hollywood, California, on September 30, 1981, to parents who had been gymnasts in Romania. Her father, Dumitru, had been on the junior national team, but his Olympic aspirations were thwarted when his mother forced him to quit so he could focus on school. "From that point on," Dumitru said, "I made a commitment that my first-born, boy or girl, would be a gymnast. It was an unfinished dream."

By the time Dominique was ten, the family had moved to Houston so the little girl could train with Béla Károlyi. Dumitru commuted to a job in Florida for eighteen months before landing a position managing a car dealership in Houston. In two years, at the age of twelve, Dominique was the junior national champion. The following year, she was the senior national champion, the youngest in history. And at fourteen, she was the youngest member of the 1996 Olympic team.

At a time when gymnastics was under attack for its blank-faced, robotic athletes, Dominique seemed like a savior. "I think she is just what gymnastics needed," Bart Conner told *People* magazine, which did a feature on her. "She sparkles all over."

Moceanu was the newest darling, and her timing couldn't have been better. She would get to shine at an Olympics in her home country, as Mary Lou Retton did twelve years earlier. The media's appetite for cute superstars would be almost maniacal, and nobody was cuter than Moceanu. Annie Leibowitz photographed her for the cover of *Vanity Fair*. Every major news magazine wrote stories about her. Kodak featured her in an Olympic commercial. Thousands of letters from adoring fans poured in every month. She even wrote her autobiography, *Dominique Moceanu: An American Champion*, before the Games.

To keep up with all her obligations, Dominique dropped out of high school. She focused virtually full-time on training for the Olympics, spending about seven hours a day, six days a week, in the gym. She'd wake at 6:50 and arrive at Károlyi's gym by 7:30. She would practice until 10:30 then return home for lunch and several hours of home schooling with her mother. At 4:00, she'd return to the gym and stay until 7:30.

"I love this sport," she told reporters at the time. "And I'm doing what I have to do for me. But some people just don't get it. I'm not losing my childhood. I have the rest of my life to have a childhood."

She seemed unaware of the paradox of the statement. Only later would she understand that some losses can never be recovered.

Just weeks before the Olympics, Moceanu suffered an injury that would plague her through the Games. She arrived in Atlanta with a four-centimeter-long stress fracture in her right shin, which had kept her from competing in the Olympic Trials. (Like Shannon Miller, also injured, Moceanu made the Olympic team based on her scores in the national championships, where she finished third.) The fracture usually would take four months to heal, but Moceanu rested for only two weeks, receiving frequent ultrasound treatments to speed up the recovery.

During the individual competition in Atlanta, Moceanu caused a scare when she failed to get her hands down on a back handspring and crashed headfirst into the balance beam. Showing a stoicism and focus honed from early childhood, she didn't fall off and showed no reaction during the rest of the routine or afterward. Later, she performed her floor routine without noticeable effect from the fall, though not well enough to earn a medal. She finished fourth of eight competitors in the floor.

After the Olympics, Moceanu appeared on a Wheaties box with her six teammates, and then traveled with them—minus Strug—performing exhibitions around the country. But Moceanu's gymnastics had lost its edge. In the eighteen months after the Olympics, she grew 7 inches and gained 20 pounds, and her body strained to adjust. When Károlyi retired, she bounced from coach to coach until January 1998, when her father brought a twenty-six-year-old coach named Luminita Miscenco over from Romania.

It changed the Moceanu family forever.

Seven months after Miscenco arrived, Moceanu competed in the 1998 Goodwill Games in New York. The gymnast was only sixteen years old but seemed much older to the reporters covering the event, some of whom hadn't seen her since Atlanta two years earlier. Her pixie childishness had given way to a more womanly maturity. She talked about struggling with her growth spurt, how she suffered pain in her knees and back as her body grew. Some reporters figured she was on her way down that slope that claims so many gymnasts whose bodies begin to mature.

But Moceanu surprised them by winning the all-around title at the Goodwill Games. And a month later, she won gold medals in the vault and beam and finished third in both the all-around and floor exercise at the national championships in Indianapolis. Moceanu was a force in gymnastics again, and she gave Miscenco full credit.

But the coach's effect on Moceanu reached beyond the gym. Miscenco was encouraging the young gymnast to nurture her personal life. She would ask Moceanu if she knew what was happening with the money she was making. She asked why the gymnast was allowed no voice in decisions that affected her career.

Dumitru Moceanu, a loving but domineering father, didn't like the ideas Miscenco was putting in his daughter's head. She was muddying the clear hierarchy he had established from the start: He was the unquestioned leader, Dominique the acquiescent follower.

But on October 17, Dumitru pushed his daughter too far. He fired Miscenco, the woman who had helped Moceanu fall in love with gymnastics again, the ally who had cracked open the window to the world outside the gym. Moceanu argued with her father, but he wouldn't relent. So the gymnast secretly packed her bags and left home. With Miscenco by her side, she called a lawyer from a shopping mall and asked to meet with him. The following morning she shocked her parents—and the gymnastics community—by filing suit in Texas District Court to be declared independent of her parents and by securing a temporary restraining order that required them to stay away from her.

Then she told her story to the media, claiming that her parents squandered both her childhood and her fortune, pushing her relentlessly to succeed. The fairy tale, it turned out, wasn't what it seemed.

"I never had a childhood," Moceanu told a reporter for the *Houston Chronicle.* "When I went to compete when I was young, I always was in fear because I would get yelled at by my father, and I would say to myself, 'I'm thirteen years old, come on.' Instead of talking to me, they're always yelling with me, fighting with me."

"It always had to be about the gym," she said of her parents. "I would think, 'Don't you guys know anything besides gymnastics? Can't we go out for an ice cream? Can't you be my mom and dad instead of me being your business?' "

"Things have been getting rough for a while, a lot of people don't know. We've been trying to keep things hidden," she said.

"I kill myself training and going to school, and what is he doing with my money? They haven't been working since 1996. Where does their income come from? Me." She also told the *Chronicle* that she was taking a stand against her parents in part because she didn't want her nine-year-old sister to go through the same problems.

Dumitru hit the roof when he discovered his daughter had run away. He claimed Miscenco had poisoned Dominique's mind and simply wanted a piece of the gymnast's money. But Moceanu's court-appointed guardian disagreed.

"I've met with the coach, and I do not think she is a conspirator," said Ellen A. Yarrell. "Dominique has thought about this for a long time."

Indeed, Moceanu had contacted a lawyer, Roy W. Moore, several months earlier to explore her legal options. She couldn't find out what had happened to the $1 million to $2 million she had earned since turning professional at age ten. She knew much of it had been sunk into the $4 million, 72,000-square-foot gym her father built in Spring, Texas, in May of 1997, a monstrous building that *Sports Illustrated* called "a monument to inefficiency." Just the air-conditioning bill for such an enormous space was said to be between $5,000 and $7,000 a month. To pay his debts, Dumitru would need to sign up thousands of gymnasts in an area that already had three other large, well-respected gyms.

When Moceanu had asked her parents about the cost of the gym or for any other information about her earnings and investments, Dumitru got angry. He refused to allow her any say in decisions about her money, training and career. It made no sense to Moceanu that, on the one hand, she was supposed to conduct herself as an adult, competing in pressure-packed competitions, making personal appearances, working eight hours a day in the gym and soldiering through pain without tears. She was not supposed to complain as a child does, or spend an afternoon hanging out with friends or attending birthday parties and dances, as a child does. Yet when it came to decisions about her earnings, her career, her time and even her food, she was supposed to accept being treated like a child.

In other words, she had the responsibilities of adulthood but not the rights.

"Let me make this perfectly clear," Moceanu said in a statement released by her lawyer a few days after she left home. "No one is pushing me or pressuring me into this decision."

Moceanu also revealed that her father had hit her on several occasions—once when he found candy in her room and another time when he put her on the scale and saw she had gained weight. She also said her father forbade her from any activity that would take her away from training. She called her autobiography a "fable."

"I've never gone public with this and I never wanted to. This was something I kept private and I would have kept private. Some things you just keep for yourself and no one needs to know."

Moceanu's lawsuit made headlines across the country. A young gymnast—taught almost since birth to follow directions without question—was standing up for herself and telling the truth about her life. And this wasn't just any gymnast. This was the happy gymnast, the one who seemed so well adjusted, the one who praised her parents in her chipper autobiography. Now she, of all people, was revealing that her life was like the lives of other girls who compete in elite sports—with the kinds of problems that gymnastics apologists had been insisting were media fantasies and exaggerations: Lost childhoods. Fractured families. Parents so caught up in the dream and the money they begin to see the gymnast less as a daughter and more of a commodity.

In the weeks after Moceanu left home, friends, associates and observers weighed in on the front-page story. An agent who represented Moceanu during and after the 1996 Olympics remembered how unhappy the gymnast had been. He said he dropped her as a client in 1997 because, as he told the *New York Times*, he was "concerned about what was happening with her money and where it was being invested." The agent, Stan Feig of San Francisco, said Moceanu appeared to be supporting her entire family and claimed Dumitru Moceanu felt he could "build an empire off her and go into management." Dumitru "was a bad guy," he said in *Sports Illustrated*. "Dominique's truly a victim."

But others painted Moceanu's parents as supportive and caring.

"I can tell you who is right and who is wrong," Loretta Powell Dawes, the mother of Moceanu's Olympic teammate Dominique Dawes, told the *Washington Post*. "Her parents are right....I really can't explain [the Moceanu situation]. It's really, really hard to understand. Her mom and dad are fine people....I give the parents one hundred percent. A lot of people out there—agents, managers, coaches and even lawyers—try to do that with a child, twist them around and make them think things."

Dumitru Moceanu defended himself, saying the 70,000-square-foot gym had already doubled in value and thus was a prudent investment. He pointed out that he had bought Dominique a convertible Mustang and built her a 1200-square-foot bedroom complete with a hot tub, Chippendale four-poster bed and 53-inch television. He also built his daughter a 20,000-square-foot private gym so she could train without interruption for the 2000 Olympics.

On October 26, Moceanu met in private with her parents, who agreed not to fight her suit. Still, at the formal hearing two days later, State District Judge John Montgomery had to ask Dumitru three times whether he agreed with the settlement before the father would sign. Montgomery then declared Moceanu a legal adult. Dumitru remained trustee of his daughter's financial trust, which she cannot touch until she turns 35.

"This was the hardest thing I've ever done in my life," Moceanu said on the courthouse steps afterward. "It was something I felt I had to do. This is a great day, but a sad day. I want to get one thing straight: I'm not living at home. I'm not going back home."

But Moceanu's troubles didn't end with her legal emancipation from her parents.

The gymnast discovered her father had hired a private investigator to trail her and, she believed, to tap her phone. Sometimes, she'd see her father waiting nearby when she emerged from school, and other times he'd try to follow her. Moceanu became so rattled by her father's actions that she stopped going to school and briefly moved out of her apartment to a secret location.

By mid-November, she had become so frightened that she got another temporary restraining order against him. "I'm scared," Moceanu told the *New York Times*. "You just don't know what's possible....He's trying to control me and my life. He's been following me and knows my every move."

Then on November 13, Houston police detectives showed up at Moceanu's apartment with frightening news. They said they had three tapes in which Dumitru allegedly discussed hiring someone to kill Miscenco and Dominique's friend Brian Huggins. A source told *Sports Illustrated* that Dumitru was prepared to pay $10,000 for the two hits, which allegedly were to take place November 20 and be made to look like drug overdoses.

Huggins and Miscenco took off for the Cayman Islands while police investigated, but no arrests were ever made. Moceanu was told that her father broke off contact with the informant (who had made the tapes) before any money changed hands. So there wasn't enough evidence to charge him with conspiracy to commit murder.

"I had no problem believing in the plot," Moceanu told a reporter later. "He's capable of it. I don't know what happened to him. I don't know what makes him tick."

On December 10, the family was back in court. Moceanu wanted a stricter restraining order against her father. She testified for hours about her father's violent temper, the threats and occasional physical abuse he had inflicted on her throughout her life. She recalled him hitting her three or four times in the preceding year. Once, she said, he slapped her while she stood on a scale because she had gained weight.

When Dumitru was asked about trying to hire a hit man to

kill Miscenco and Huggins, he declined to answer, citing his Fifth Amendment right not to incriminate himself. He did admit, however, hiring a private detective to find out where his daughter was living.

Judge Montgomery, the same judge who had granted Moceanu adult status, decided that family violence had, indeed, occurred "and was likely to occur in the future." He ordered Dumitru to stay away from his daughter for one year, stipulating that he was prohibited from being within 500 feet of where Moceanu lives, works or goes to school.

Moceanu cried when the judge delivered his ruling. She knew her father was heart-broken and that he never meant it to come to this. Later, she told a reporter, "It kills me to do this to my father. I never meant to hurt him, but I had no choice.... The money's just money. Sure I could have been set for life, but I can start over. I wish we'd never had the money and still had a family."

She supported herself from the $10,000 check she received for winning the all-around title at the Goodwill Games. She also received $800 a month from USA Gymnastics for being on the national team, though she didn't train from October 17 until early January, when she began working out at former gymnastics coach Rita Brown's state-of-the-art gym in Katy, Texas.

A few weeks later, Moceanu transferred to another of Brown's gyms, in Altamonte Springs, Florida, so she could be reunited with Miscenco, who had taken a job there. Brown reportedly paid Moceanu's $15,000 moving costs and cosigned four-month leases on apartments for the gymnast and her coach. But Moceanu and Miscenco left after 2½ weeks to train in Colorado Springs at the Olympic Training Center. Brown said she found out Moceanu was moving when she heard it on TV. She told *Sports Illustrated* she felt "a little used" by the gymnast and called her "a lost little girl."

At the training center, she received free rent and food in a two-room dormitory unit she shared with Miscenco. She returned to training 6½ hours a day. She said in the early summer of 1999 that she planned to stay at the training center until September then try to qualify at the U.S. World Team Trials. The competition would help her gauge her progress toward the 2000 Olympics.

Meanwhile, Dumitru announced he was closing his gym, which had floundered once its star attraction left.

In April, Moceanu reached a financial settlement with her parents. The terms were not disclosed, but it included a provision lifting the restraining order against Dumitru. Moceanu didn't talk with the press. Instead, she released a statement through her new agents, Gold Medal Management in Boulder, Colorado. "I know that deep down my father loves me, and of course I love him, so I need to find a way in my heart to give him forgiveness. I hope there is a chance that someday things in my family can be normal again."

Knee and back injuries kept Moceanu from competing in the U.S. Championships in Sacramento in August 1999 and in the World Championships two months later in China. She hopes to be healthy enough for Olympic tryouts in August 2000 and the Olympics in September. To remind her of the Olympics in Australia, she named her Dalmatian puppy Sydney.

In the fall of 1999, the only other 1996 Olympic team member aiming for the 2000 Games was Amy Chow. Though majoring in biology at Stanford, she resumed training down the highway in San José, saying she missed the sport. But a broken ankle kept her out of the 1999 national championships and hampered her at the World Team Trials in September 1999—she finished eighth among fifteen competitors.

If Chow and Moceanu are healthy enough to make the 2000 Olympic team, they'll be valuable assets to an otherwise inexperienced team. The top U.S. gymnasts have not yet established themselves as contenders in international competition, which means the U.S. team isn't favored to fare well at the Olympics in either the team or individual competition.

At the World Championships in China in October 1999, the U.S. finished sixth in the team competition. The American gymnasts seemed rattled by the pressure and loud crowd. "It was the most nervous I've ever been," 1997 national champion Vanessa Atler told reporters.

Atler, a seventeen-year-old from California, might be America's best hope for a medal. She won golds in vault and floor at the 1996 Goodwill Games and has been considered the top U.S. gymnast for several years now. She has her own website, where she posts a diary, and has landed a television commercial. Some even predict her personality and smile will captivate America at the 2000 Olympics the way Mary Lou Retton's did in 1984.

But Atler has struggled in big meets. Two years in a row—1998 and 1999—she fell on the uneven bars to lose the national championship to eighteen-year-old Kristin Maloney. She also fell in the same event in 1997 but managed to finish in a tie for the championship with Kristy Powell.

"She's a dynamic, world-class gymnast," said one observer, "but she's missed the bar five times in major meets."

Just before the World Championships, Atler left her longtime coaches, Steve Rybacki and Beth Kline-Rybacki, a husband-and-wife team at Charter Oak Gymnastics in Covina, California. At Worlds, without her coaches and fighting an ankle injury, she finished thirty-first in the all-around individual finals and, though she qualified for the floor exercise in the individual event finals, she withdrew when her ankle problems became too painful.

Maloney, the two-time national champion, also withdrew from

the event finals at Worlds because of pain in her right knee, which she had injured earlier in the week. (She had qualified for floor and balance beam.) Maloney, from Pennsylvania, is not considered as precise a performer as Atler, but she is known for working hard and could emerge in 2000 as the premier U.S. gymnast if Atler falters.

Eighteen-year-old Elise Ray, from Columbia, Maryland, is another gymnast to watch in 2000. Training under Kelli Hill, Dominique Dawes's coach, Ray won the gold for floor exercise at the 1999 U.S. championship and earned the highest overall score at the World Team Trials. Even so, she wasn't expected to be the star of the U.S. team at the World Championships. But she excelled, finishing eighth in the individual all-around—by far the best among American gymnasts. And she was the only American to place in the event finals, finishing seventh on bars.

Other top American contenders for the Olympics include a familiar name: Jennie Thompson. Thompson, at age twelve, was described by her then coach Steve Nunno as "Shannon Miller and Kim Zmeskal wrapped up in one." But she didn't quite blossom as Nunno had predicted. She had trained with Béla Károlyi as a child and switched back to his gym when he came out of retirement before the 1996 Olympics. But after she missed the cut for the 1996 Olympic team, she moved to Cincinnati to train with Mary Lee Tracy. The change seemed to reenergize her. Thompson finished third at the 1999 national championships, her first medal in five trips to the competition. But she reinjured her left ankle during practice for the World Championship in China and couldn't compete.

Watching gymnastics in the five years since this book was published has given me cause for both hope and concern. USA Gymnastics has made a genuine commitment to making their sport healthier for its young athletes. But it's clear that gymnastics continues to struggle with the challenge of molding a child into a world-class athlete without endangering her health, breaking up her family or stunting her emotional and social development. The dream of Olympic glory is powerful, and our hunger for cute little stars is strong.

We know that our consumption and disposal of these young athletes are tantamount to child exploitation and, in too many cases, child abuse. But we still rarely ask what becomes of them when they disappear from view. We are reluctant to watch them parade past us with their broken bodies and spirits. We want our pink ballerinas inside the jewelry box, always perfectly positioned, perfectly coifed. They spin on demand without complaint. When one breaks, another pops up from the next box. To close the lid is to close that part of ourselves that still wants to believe in beautiful princesses and happy endings.

ACKNOWLEDGMENTS

My thanks to Glenn Schwarz, my editor at the *San Francisco Examiner,* who originally suggested the article on which this book is based; Jennifer McDonald, who pushed; and Betsy Lerner, whose pencil and patience never let me down. Thanks also to the coaches, parents, athletes and experts who shared their knowledge with me. And a personal thanks to Rose and Harry Tompkins and Alexandra Steiner for keeping Ryan happy; Steve Leiper for making sense of my tapes; and Bob and Peg Ryan, Ray and Kay Poggioli, Jan McAdoo, Ray Ratto, Dave Burgin, Donna and Doug Ruiz, Barbara Haynes, Bob Ryan, Gerard and Leslie Ryan, Andrea and Rob Menschel, Lainie Tompkins and Kathy Johnson for their help and support. Most of all, thanks to my husband, Barry.

ABOUT THE AUTHOR

JOAN RYAN is an award-winning journalist and the author of four books.

She was a pioneer in sports journalism as one of the first female sports columnists in the country. Ryan's wide-ranging newspaper work spanned twenty-five years, earning thirteen Associated Press Sports Editors Awards, the National Headliner Award, the Women's Sports Foundation's Journalism Award and the Edgar A. Poe Award from the White House Correspondents Association.

Little Girls in Pretty Boxes: The Making and Breaking of Elite Gymnasts and Figure Skaters was chosen by *Sports Illustrated* as one of the "Top 100 Sports Books of All Time" and by the *Guardian* in London as one of the "Top 50 Sports Books of All Time."

Molina: The Story of the Father Who Raised an Unlikely Baseball Dynasty, written with former Major League catcher Bengie Molina, was a finalist for the 2015 ESPN PEN Literary Award.

Ryan is a founding trustee of Coaching Corps in Oakland, California, and since 2008 has been the senior media advisor to the San Francisco Giants. Ryan lives in Sausalito, California, with her husband, sportscaster Barry Tompkins.